Sledgehammers for Tintacks

Bomber Command Combats the V-1 Menace 1943–1944

STEPHEN DARLOW

GRUB STREET · LONDON

Published by
Grub Street
The Basement
10 Chivalry Road
London SW11 1HT

British Library Cataloguing in Publication Data
Darlow, Steve
  Sledgehammers for tintacks: Bomber Command combats the
  V-1 menace, 1943-1944
  1. Great Britain. Royal Air Force. Bomber Command – History
  2. World War, 1939-1945 – Aerial operations, British.
  3. V-1 bomb
  I. Title
  940.5'449'41

ISBN 1 902304 96 9

Typeset by Pearl Graphics, Hemel Hempstead

Printed and bound in Great Britain by
Biddles Ltd, Guildford and King's Lynn

To Michael and Adam.
You are the reason your great-grandfather fought against tyranny.
Remember the men who put your future first.

CONTENTS

ACKNOWLEDGEMENTS

Firstly I must thank Maggie, my wife. Cheers, Marge.

Below are the people whose assistance made writing this book both possible and pleasurable. For the sake of space I have omitted the ranks of former RAF men, but I have included any decorations known to me.

Special mentions must go to Jim Sheffield, Bob Farrell, Jim Shortland and Martin Ford-Jones. Their support and guidance have been invaluable. I would also like to thank the following for their help through the research process; Lionel Lacey-Johnson, Wim Govaerts, Dr Alfred Price, David Fell, Steve Fraser, Bill Stevenson, Jason Holloway, Stan Brooks, Dave Sutherland, Pat McMonagle, T. Collins, James Buchanan, Rob Davis, H. Massy, Jill Skeet, Peter Hinchliffe, Martin Bowman, Rob Thornley, Albert Dean, Mark Briars, John Heathfield, Neil Hutchinson, Chris Bazalgette, Charles Bazalgette, Dave Birrell and the Nanton Lancaster Society.

Appreciation goes to the following for their assistance with regard to writing the photographic reconnaissance and interpretation story; David Oxlee OBE, Michael Mockford OBE, David Lain, Sir Alfred Ball, Jerry Fray, Bill Newby, Joe Townshend DFM, John Shelmerdine DFC, Gordon Hughes DSO, DFC, AEA, Gordon Puttick, Wing Commander T. Brignall MBE, David Mander TD.

The following institutions were helpful in supporting my research: Public Record Office Kew, Imperial War Museum and Stephen Walton, Mosquito Aircrew Association (Tony Wilson), The Spitfire Society and Group Captain David Green OBE, Stotfold Historical Activities Group, Middleton St George Memorial Association (A. Robson), Stotfold Library, the Medmenham Collection and the Medmenham Club, Barnet Museum, Bletchley Park (John Gallehawk), Churchill Archives Centre, Association de Sauvegarde du Site de V1 du Val-Ygot à Ardouval. I would also like to thank *FlyPast* and *Aeroplane Monthly* magazines for publishing requests for contacts. With regard to quotes from official histories, crown copyright is reproduced with the permission of the Controller of Her Majesty's Stationery Office.

In particular I would like to again thank Bob Farrell for giving up his time to guide and translate in France, and to Kathy Hewson, Marie Jeanne Cole, Jacques Nachez, L.D. Benson MA and Oliver Payne for their help in French and German translation.

The following people were helpful in providing material from France, and I extend my gratitude to; Raymonde Carbon, Paul Mercier, Huguette Rouillard, Claude Helias, M. Thuillier, Yves Thuillier, Norbert Greuet, Eric

Lepicard, Alix Leclerq, Bernard LeFrançois, Maurice Farcy, Eliane Gay, Roland Lacaisse, Pierre Carpentier, Jean Huré, Yves Franqueville Clavet, Georges Vergne, Louis Osmond, Tresel Jean Colette, André Fremont, Gerard Dubord, Rene Tabart, Robert Fortrie, Albert Bayard, Jacques Laloux, Jean de Witasse Thezy, Gérard Cadot and Norbert Dufour. I would also like to thank the town hall staff of Rilly-La-Montagne, St Leu d'Esserent and Nucourt, in particular Jean-Victor Risetto.

I would also like to make special mention of the following Bomber Command veterans and their squadron association secretaries and chairmen for providing material and support in the research. Their willingness to help never ceases to impress me and I hope this book does them and all the men of Bomber Command justice:

8 Group: Howard Lees, *7 Squadron*; Ronald Claridge DFC AEA, Jeff Lindsay, *9 Squadron*; George Maule, Bob Riches, Fred Whitfield DFM, Russell Gradwell, *15 Squadron*; Don Clark, *35 Squadron*; Kenneth Grantham DFM, *44 Squadron*; Ron Biggs, *49 Squadron*; Tom Gatfield, *50 Squadron*; Tony Harris, *57/630 Squadron*; Eric Blanchard DFC, Allen Hudson, Mervyn Davies, *61 Squadron*; Reg Dear DFC, Geoff Gilbert DFM, Don Street DFC, *75 Squadron*; Ronnie Hunt, *76 Squadron*; Bert Kirtland, Geoffrey Salisbury MBE, Dick Lee, *77 Squadron*; Thomas Fox, H. Laking, Ernie Drake DFM, Wally Braithwaite DFC, *78 Squadron*; John Erricker DFC, Alan Carter, George Parton DFM, *97 Squadron*; Harold Hitchcock DFC, *100 Squadron*; A. Webberburn, MBE *102 Squadron*; Tom Wingham DFC, *105 Squadron;* Tony Farrell DFC, AFC, *106 Squadron*; Syd Geater, *109 Squadron*; Ron Curtis DSO, DFC and bar, J.E. Tipton DFC and bar, *115 Squadron*; F.R. Leatherdale DFC, *149 Squadron*; Roy Abbot, Peter Rowland, *156 Squadron*; Jack Watson DFM, *158 Squadron*; Len Skipper DFC, *207 Squadron*; Len Barham, Norman Turton, Jack Fisher, Ron Winton, *218 Squadron*; Margery Griffiths, *300 Squadron*; J. Syratt, *419/420/428 Squadron*; A. Robson, *460 Squadron*; Gordon Stooke, *463 Squadron*; Fred Fossett, *578 Squadron*; Eric Bowden DFC, *617 Squadron*; Ken Brown, G.H. Hobbs, Ralph Briars DFM, *619 Squadron*; J. Whiteley, *622 Squadron*; C. Chandler, Keith Rea MBE, DFM, *627 Squadron*; Alan Webb, *54 Base*; John Dyer.

Addition to acknowledgements:

The following with thanks for their contributions and help with the photographs:
Jim Buchanan, Peter Rowland, Fred Whitfield, Ronnie Hunt, Ken Grantham, Fred Fossett, Ron Winton, Medmenham Collection, Rob Thornley, the Imperial War Museum and the Controller of HMSO (for the use of HU 88469, HU 88470, CH 14564 and HU 44870), Dr Alfred Price, Alix Leclerq, the Martyn Ford Jones Collection, Thomas Fox, Howard Lees, Don Street, Jim Shortland, R Kearns, Dave Birrell and Nanton Lancaster Society.Copyright for respective photographs remains with the contributor.

INTRODUCTION

Whilst in France conducting some of the research for this book I spent a few days touring the First World War battlefields of the Somme. A few miles north of Albert, the road to Bapaume passes between two small hills, the Tara and Usna. One afternoon, in a rather oppressive atmosphere of rumbling thunder in heavy air and flashes of lightning in the distance, I sat between the hills looking north along the road. This gave a perfect view of the Tara-Usna line, where on the morning of 1 July 1916 men of the British Army's 34th Division climbed out of their trenches and advanced in the direction of Bapaume toward the German front line. It was believed that the Germans would not have survived the artillery barrage that had been pounding their positions for the previous week. Their lines were thought to be smashed and all the advancing men had to do, they were told, was walk over and occupy their enemy's trenches.

How wrong they were. The Germans had dug deep, had survived and were now able to man the machine guns that would reap the advancing British youth. All along the front line that day the attacking troops faced fierce resistance and they made little if any gain. The British were to suffer nearly 60,000 casualties on that one day, of which approximately 20,000 men were killed. This one particular day in that appalling conflict gives a clear example of how the advances in weaponry, at that time the rifle and the machine gun, had begun to dominate the conduct of battles.

I realised that it was this, and the other appalling attrition battles of the First World War, that had resulted in future military air commanders and policy-makers looking favourably upon, and making plans for, the strategic use of air warfare in subsequent conflicts. No longer were warring nations, which had the technology, prepared to engage each other in the hell and stagnation of trench warfare. Technology would be developed to bring mobility back into the conduct of war. The latter stages of the First World War had demonstrated how the tank and the aircraft could provide this mobility and great advances were made in developing the necessary technologies. However the development of aircraft did not proceed at the rate required. It was hoped that precision bombing could be available at the start of the second world conflict of the century, but it soon became clear that the aircraft could not deliver and area bombing became the adopted strategy. Instead of risking a nation's own youth in trench warfare, civilians became the target with large forces of aircraft, attacking by night, populated areas associated with industrial production, particularly military industry. The civilians who manned the factories that were part of their nation's war economy were seen as worthy of attack. The Germans were even able to take this a stage further. They would develop a means of attacking their enemy's civilian population without risking their own airmen on the routes to the target and over the beleaguered cities and towns. In the summer of 1944 the civilians of southern England would be the first in world history to experience a new type of warfare. In June 1944 pilotless aircraft (the V1), to be called 'flying bombs', 'doodlebugs' or 'buzz bombs', would start to fly above them with engines droning. The people would soon learn that if the engine could still be heard as it passed over they could relax. If, however, the engine cut out, the flying bomb and its explosive warhead were coming down nearby and the warhead would explode causing death and destruction. Towards the end of the summer of 1944, armed rockets (the V2), fired from the continent, would bring further misery and suffering. These could not be heard approaching. There was no warning.

This book gives an account of how a strategic bombing force, the Royal Air Force's Bomber Command, was used in countering one particular menace, the flying bomb. The reader must note that this book does focus on the flying bomb. Reference is sometimes made to the other German secret weapons, in particular the V2 rocket and the V3 long-range multi-barrelled gun (which actually was never fired). This is necessary as the development of the V1, V2 and V3 was pretty much concurrent and Allied Intelligence, in the early stages, had difficulty identifying the separate programmes and distinguishing between them. As such the V2 and V3 programmes are referred to as they give context for the overall Allied counter-measure policy. The core time period covered by this book is December 1943 to the end of August 1944 at which point the main flying bomb offensive had ended. Flying bomb attacks did continue until the end of March 1945, (overlapping with V2 rocket attacks, which started in September 1944) but these flying bomb attacks were not on the same scale as those of the summer of 1944. However this book is about one particular aspect of the Allied response to the German secret weapon menace; Bomber Command's role in the flying bomb counter-offensive, which basically ended in the first week of September 1944.

The story tells of the circumstances leading to the decisions requiring Bomber Command's involvement in the flying bomb counter-offensive and how the airmen of Bomber Command, from their commander-in-chief right down to the aircrews and groundcrews acted upon the decisions. Decisions that would lead to many Allied airmen suffering serious injury, many losing their lives or being captured by the enemy. Decisions that would inflict further misery upon the oppressed population of the occupied countries. Decisions that were made in the belief that they would give some relief to the population of southern England, the main victims of the flying bomb menace.

The story is told using previously unpublished records, first hand accounts provided by Bomber Command veterans, Luftwaffe nightfighter veterans and accounts from French people who witnessed the whole German operation from the construction of the secret weapon installations to the launching of the flying bombs. These same people would also experience at first hand the full weight of the Allied bombing response. The story also gives brief details of the intelligence effort carried out by the Allies in order to understand the German secret weapon plans and hence make their own plans for effective defensive and offensive counter-measures.

It should be noted that the ranks of all the men quoted in the book are those at the time of the operations against the flying bomb targets. Many of these men would continue their operations and gain further promotion. It should also be noted that many of these men were decorated for their exploits on these and other operations and, where I have been notified, these decorations are given in the acknowledgements. The details of all the losses of aircraft on the operations in this book are mainly based upon W.R. Chorley's *RAF Bomber Command Losses 1944*. Usually only the pilots of the lost aircraft are named and can be assumed to be Royal Air Force (including the Volunteer Reserve) unless otherwise stated.

In the book I have detailed all the raids against flying bomb targets and mentioned raids against other German secret weapon targets. I felt the detail was necessary as no other published books give an operational reference work for Bomber Command operations against flying bomb targets. Martin Middlebrook and Chris Everitt's *The Bomber Command War Diaries* only gives daily summaries in the vast majority of cases. Interspersed between the operations are the experiences of the airmen involved in the operations. I have also focused on three particular nights when there were considerable air battles between Bomber Command and German nightfighters, and gone into further detail.

I am particularly conscious that the following pages record a lot of objective analysis of one particular aspect of the Second World War, i.e. the flying bomb attacks on England and the Allied counter-offensive. What must always be borne in mind is the extent of human suffering resulting from the German flying bomb offensive. Firstly, there were the aircrew casualties of both sides, men dying in horrific circumstances or dreadfully wounded. Secondly, there was the suffering of the civilians of the occupied countries, local to the flying bomb targets; many people would die as a result of stray flying bombs or Allied counter-offensive bombing. Thirdly, there was the population of southern England which daily ran the gauntlet of chance. Many lives would be wiped out, many people would spend the rest of their lives disabled owing to serious injury, and many people would always have the distressing memory of horrific sights and the loss of their homes, their friends, their loved ones. All this must be borne in mind when reading this book, which may go some way to answering the victims' question of 'Why?'

Bomber Command and the area bombing policy has had its critics over the years following the war. This book tells of how, in contrast, Bomber Command was used on a clearly defined military footing as a defensive force (by means of counter-offensive measures). In carrying out this policy, many of the airmen of Bomber Command would make the ultimate sacrifice.

Now may we lift our bruisèd visors up,
And take the flattering freshness of the air,
While the wide din of battle dies away
Into times past, yet to be echoed sure
In the silent pages of our chroniclers

– Gloucester, Act I scene 2 *King Stephen*, John Keats 1819

PROLOGUE

Early on the morning of 13 June 1944 those residents of Bethnal Green, London, who weren't asleep heard both a familiar and unfamiliar sound. The warning sirens were going. They had heard those before. But there was another sound, a strange roar like an aircraft engine. The second noise soon stopped. One witness recalled:

> When the warning went I saw my wife and family into the shelter and then stood at the entrance to watch events. I heard a plane, as if diving. There was an orange flash, followed by a terrific explosion. There were no sounds of bombs falling as in the blitz only that of a plane zooming.

A second witness saw 'a ball of fire in the sky and a terrific roar as though a plane was flying very low. The noise stopped and a second or so after came the explosion'.[1]

It was not a plane they had heard. It was a 'flying bomb', one of ten launched by the Germans that night, of which four had reached England. The flying bomb mentioned above impacted on the railway bridge over Grove Road, Bow. The bridge stood up well against the immediate explosion, but several nearby houses were not so sturdy. Six people lost their lives, with many others injured. These were the first casualties of the German reprisal weapon campaign, but the scale of attack fell way below that expected and for the next few days and nights no more flying bombs arrived.

On 15 June 1944, from the village of Varengeville, two miles west of Dieppe on the coast of northern France, Gérard Cadot set off with his mother to visit his grandmother in the nearby village of Longueil. In the lining of Gérard's jacket were certain items with which he was going to finish making the wireless he had promised his Uncle Jean. They climbed on their bicycles, left Varengeville and came to the crossroads where they would turn off to Longueil.

> We were very surprised to see an excited German soldier. After 15 minutes we heard this noise in the sky, resembling an aircraft engine, coming towards us in the direction of the sea. We decided to lie on the embankment as something noisily passed above us, out of sight owing to the low clouds. I said to my mother, 'It sounds like the noise of a huge plumber's

blowlamp.' We started out on the road again . . . and when we arrived in Longueil we heard a second machine, passing overhead in the same direction. Two excited German soldiers smiled at us as we huddled up against the embankment. When we got back on our bicycles a soldier cried out, 'Tommies *Kaputt – Krieg Fertig*' [the war's finished]. When we arrived at my grandmother's house we discussed the noises. The Germans were up to something. I told my uncle that I had his wireless and proposed that we connect it to the wire washing line, which would act as an aerial enabling us to listen to the BBC. At 1.30 we heard that General de Gaulle had, on 14 June, come ashore at Courseulles, but there was nothing about the machines we had heard. I listened again at 21.15 but again nothing.

On the morning of 16 June at 7.30 I listened to the BBC and before the personal messages was the following: 'Small pilotless aircraft, charged with explosives, fell on London.' In the afternoon I discovered that several fell in our region. In Auppegard one exploded causing several deaths. In the evening at about 9 o'clock I saw for the first time the machines with the long red flame coming out of the tube on their back. They all headed towards England.[2]

For the next two and a half months, thousands headed towards England and the population of London and the south-east would experience a destructive phenomenon unprecedented in the history of warfare. Thousands of casualties resulted. When the main weight of attack from this menace was seen off, Londoners would not only have to endure the further odd attack, but also fear a new separate kind of German reprisal weapon (the V2 rocket). The population of Southern England – the civilians workers, the military, the government, the medical services – would all be tested to the full by the opening of this new phase in international warfare.

CHAPTER 1

THE THREAT

The potential of conducting war using armed rockets as part of a country's arsenal was investigated by the Germans in the late 1920s and early 1930s. For the next few years the scientists and technicians, under Captain Walter Dornberger and Captain Ritter von Hostig, worked on the problems associated with rocket development, notably propellants and stability. In 1936, the Commander-in-Chief of the German Army General Baron Werner von Fritsch, visited Dornberger's research establishment and, realising the potential of the programme, requested development and design of an operational weapon. In partnership with the German Air Force, the German Army established a development station at Peenemünde, on the island of Usedom, in the Baltic. The rocket programme progressed slowly and it was not until the spring of 1942 that the first test launchings took place. The main difficulty encountered during testing was controlling the trajectory of the rockets, but the Germans had cause for great optimism when on 3 October one rocket did travel at least 120 miles, to a height of 50 miles, at 3,300 mph and with acceptable accuracy.

At the Peenemünde research station, the German Air Force had a team who had witnessed the testing of the rockets. At an armaments' conference in June 1942 two firms, Argus and Fieseler, already working on the development of some kind of pilotless aircraft/bomb, managed to persuade the Director-General of Equipment for the Luftwaffe, Field Marshal Erhard Milch, to give them high priority for production. Three companies, Argus (jet propulsion), Fieseler (design and manufacture of the airframes) and Askania (control mechanism) then proceeded to develop further the potential of the pilotless aircraft. In December 1942, following the launch of a prototype from a Focke-Wulf 200 earlier in that month, the first ground-launched pilotless bomb (flying bomb) was tested, and successfully catapulted 3,000 yards[3]. This news of the launching was greeted with enthusiasm and optimism by the German Air Force and the potential for conducting an attack across the sea on England was realised, with plans developing rapidly for the deployment of launch sites on the Channel coast. Debate ensued, however, on the means of conducting the offensive, centred on either using mobile launching ramps or building large concrete bunkers from which to launch the attacks.

On 18 June 1943, Commander in Chief of the Luftwaffe Air Marshal

Hermann Goering received an update on the progress of the flying bomb programme and he was informed that the testing had so far proved most promising. A provisional, ambitious, production programme followed, with mass production detailed for the Volkswagen factory at Fallersleben. Goering compromised with the launch site system, ordering the construction of 96 small launch sites and four large bunkers, with a possible start for the offensive of the end of the year. But whilst the higher echelons of the German Air Force made their plans for the conduct of the flying bomb offensive, the testing process began to falter. Co-ordinating the work of all the various parties involved in the manufacture and testing of the flying bombs was proving difficult. In particular the rocket production requirements were interfering with the flying bomb production. A German Air Ministry meeting of 29 July 1943 welcomed the positive news regarding test outcomes but was also informed of the shortfall in production plans. The manpower resources allocated to the flying bomb production plans were not as expected, since those required for rocket production provided competition. Priorities would need to be made.

Prior to the outbreak of war, British Intelligence had received and collated many reports on various secret weapon ideas. In November 1939 a certain Dr. R.V. Jones, head of the scientific section at the Air Ministry's Intelligence section, became aware of the Oslo Report, which, supported by information from other sources, passed on details of long-range rocket development at a place called Peenemünde. With suspicion arising that the information may have been planted by the Germans to mislead British Intelligence, and with no back-up information, the report was put to one side. Indeed it was not until 15 May 1942 that the Peenemünde research station was photographed from the air by Allied reconnaissance, following a routine sortie to Kiel after which the pilot, Flight Lieutenant D.W. Steventon, flew on eastwards in search of further game. Whilst revealing construction works and three large circular emplacements, the prints did not raise any alarm when scrutinised by the analysts in the Central Interpretation Unit at RAF Medmenham.

Throughout the next year, British intelligence kept receiving reports and information from agents and German prisoners concerning long-range rockets, developments at Peenemünde and launchings being planned from the French Channel coast. As the wealth of information accumulated it eventually became necessary to make positive moves. During April 1943 the Vice-Chief of the Imperial General Staff, Lieutenant-General A.E. Nye, was made aware of the developments regarding the German secret weapons. A memorandum concerning the suspected German rocket development was put to the Vice-Chiefs of Staff and Chiefs of Staff. On 12 April it was agreed, on the basis of the information so far received, to notify Prime Minister Winston Churchill of developments and the recommendation was also made to appoint someone specifically to establish the facts concerning the German rocket programme. They recommended Churchill's son-in-law, Mr Duncan Sandys, MP, who had been a Member of Parliament since before the war, and had been the commander of Britain's first experimental anti-aircraft rocket unit before leaving the Army as a result of an injury in a motor accident. In 1943 he took up responsibilities in government as Joint Parliamentary Secretary at the Ministry of Supply. On 20 April Sandys was indeed appointed to conduct the special investigation (code name Bodyline), part of which included further reconnaissance of the Peenemünde research station. On 17 May Sandys reported to the War Cabinet that there was tangible evidence suggesting the development of a long-range rocket. He also indicated that the rocket programme was probably proceeding alongside the development of jet propelled aircraft and airborne rocket torpedoes. The search for further intelligence intensified and the PRU (Photographic Reconnaissance Unit) took further photographs of the Peenemünde research station, which revealed numerous large, suspicious, but as yet unidentifiable, cylindrical objects. The Allies' evidence supporting rocket development continued to mount and when Sandys circulated a report on 28 June, considered by the Defence Committee (Operations) under the chairmanship of Winston Churchill, on 29 June, the decision to bomb the research station at Peenemünde was taken. The force to carry out such an attack would be from the RAF's Bomber Command.

During this period information also started coming in concerning an attack on England by another kind of German secret weapon. Sources from inside the weapons department of the German War Office provided one important piece of information to British Intelligence. A winged bomb was being developed, to strike against London, fired from catapults of which 30 already existed. Following considerations of the weapon's potential technical possibilities and range, a decision was made to photograph northern France within a radius 130 miles from London, and Peenemünde would again be the target for further PRU sorties.

Evidence continued to come in, becoming more specific; pilotless aircraft were now mentioned. On 22 August 1943 a pilotless aircraft crashed on the island of Bornholm in Denmark. Photographs and drawings reached London by 31 August. The flying bomb was now identified and on 10 September the Chiefs of Staff agreed that the Air Ministry, through Dr Jones, should take on the responsibility of processing information specifically with regard to the flying bomb threat.

Around this time new information started to come in from French sources. In particular a report supplied by a French agent reached Dr Jones, parts of which suggested how the pilotless aircraft attack would be conducted. At the time, however, the report did not distinguish between the flying bomb and the rocket. The report, containing information obtained from a captain attached to the experimental station at Peenemünde, began with a lot of technical detail, much of which was actually to do with the rocket. Importantly the report mentioned that trials were being conducted by *Lehr-und-Erprobungskommando Wachtel* and that a certain Colonel Wachtel was to form an anti-aircraft regiment, numbered 155W, consisting of 16 batteries of 220 men. This was to be deployed in France around Amiens, Abbeville and Dunkirk, about the end of October 1943, with 108 catapults made available to fire a bomb every twenty minutes. The report mentioned that a Major Sommerfeld, technical adviser to Colonel Wachtel, estimated that 50 to 100 bombs would destroy London and throughout the winter of 1943/44 the secret weapon offensive could destroy most of Britain's large cities. It was reported that reinforced concrete platforms were already being built in northern France and were expected to be available for operations in November.[4]

An Allied decrypt of a German signal sent on 7 September 1943 gave further weight to the fact that secret weapons were being deployed in the north of France.

> (I) Luftflotte 3 again requests the immediate introduction of Flak forces to protect ground organisation Flak Zielgerät 76. The urgency of this is emphasised by the following facts:
> According to report of C. in C. West, Abwehr Station France reports the capture of an enemy agent who had the task of establishing at all costs the position of new German rocket weapons. The English, it is stated, have information that the weapon is to be employed in the near future and they intend to attack the position before this occurs.[5]

By the end of October French agents had passed on the suspected location of 100 launch sites. The Allies were becoming aware that a major threat was building just across the Channel.

Following the success of the initial flying bomb trials, the German High Command set 15 December 1943 for the opening of the flying bomb assault on England. On 16 August the new Flakregiment 155(W) had been established under Colonel Max Wachtel, a first world war artillery officer (who spent the years between wars working in industry). Prior to his new appointment he had been in command of the Anti-Aircraft Artillery School. Wachtel's initial responsibility to his new command was to establish a firing drill for his units. Four *Abteilungen* (comparable with battalions) were set up to be responsible for firing the missiles and during August the regiment's commanding officers and their adjutants visited their operational areas in the north of France. There were numerous problems during further trials of the weapon, which, compounded by serious supply shortages, proved to slow down the preparation process. In particular construction of testing installations at Zempin, just south of Peenemünde, were slower than required, in the main due to manpower shortages, in terms of both the numbers of men and the standard of those allocated. Whilst this was going on, 40,000 workers in France were employed on the flying bomb programme and the construction of the launch sites. It was a massive operation and, as Wachtel informed General Major Prellberg, the senior commander of the Flak Artillery School, on 23 September, '178,000,000 bricks are required for the construction of sites and ancillary operations'.[6] Wachtel's regiment was in no doubt as to the importance of its orders. The regiment's diary recorded on 26 September:

In view of the recent political events (the beginning of the 5th year of war, Badoglio's treachery, the rescue of Mussolini, the 3rd anniversary of the Tripartite Pact between Germany, Italy and Japan) and military developments in the East and in southern Europe, it is understandable that the public is in a state of acute suspense, which is aggravated by the Anglo-American terror bombing of Germany. All the greater, therefore, is the hope of the entire German people not only that there will be reprisals against the terror bombing of Germany but that when the time is ripe, a counter-offensive will be launched. The call to the German people, which the Führer and Supreme Commander of the Wehrmacht made from his headquarters after the defeat of the Italian traitors, gave added force to the conviction that 'steps are being taken which will enable enemy terror bombing to be smashed and reprisal to be taken by other, more effective means'. Reich Minister Dr Goebbels expressed a similar view in his leading article in *Das Reich* at the end of August, in which he wrote: 'A new offensive weapon against the enemy air war is being developed. Countless industrious hands are engaged on this work day and night. They are putting a severe strain on our patience, it is true, but one of these days we shall have our reward.' Reich Minister Dr Speer, leading personality in the German arms drive, also drew attention to these developments in an address to senior officers of the Luftwaffe. At the conclusion of his speech Dr Speer said, 'One of these days you will see the results of our joint endeavours . . . If a citizen begins to lose heart, let him remember that we need put up with things as they are only for a little longer; then after our defences have steadily improved we shall again be able to go over to the offensive. Until then we must hold our tongues and keep working.'[7]

The Germans' initial organisational plan for the flying bomb offensive involved an 'arc' of launching sites from the Pas de Calais to the Cherbourg peninsula to be supplied with their weapons by eight of what the Allies called 'supply sites', chosen for their road and rail links. The majority of the launching sites were situated in the Calais to the river Seine area, clearly intended for an attack on London. The remaining sites were split between the Normandy area (to attack Southampton and Portsmouth) and the Cherbourg peninsula (to attack Plymouth and Bristol).

In August 1943 construction had started at the first three of the supply sites, located between Calais and the river Somme. These were at Renescure, Sautrecourt and Domleger. Construction would soon begin at further supply sites at Neuville-au-Bois (Oisemont), St Martin l'Hortier, Biennais, Beauvoir, and at the site at Valognes specifically for supplying the launch sites on the Cherbourg peninsula. Three sites were also chosen for bomb-proof bunkers for the use of flying bombs armed possibly with chemical warheads. These were planned for Siracourt, Lottinghem, and

Equeurdreville (the latter at first intended for the rocket programme).

On 14 October 1943 the first test 'shot' was fired from a launch site at Zempin by No.1 *Batterie* of *I Abteilung* (four *Batterien* to each of the four firing *Abteilungen*). On 16 October the first missile of a limited production series was readied for launching at Zempin.

> *Flakregiment 155(W) diary*; At No.1 ramp everybody waits tensely. The power unit roars, flare signals for the pursuing He111 rise into the sky [to monitor the flight], the launcher goes into action and with a long exhaust flame the missile takes off smoothly. Rising slowly, then quicker and quicker the FZG76 gains height and takes course. Very quickly it disappears from sight. In the meantime the He111 has set course albeit rather late. This shoot . . . carried out by No.1 *Batterie* is successful.[8]

Following the success of the test launch, No.1 *Batterie* of the *I Abteilung* left Zempin for France on 21 October 1943, and throughout the next few months, following training and test firing other *Batterien* would deploy. By the end of October 56 of the launch sites were anticipated to be ready in France. The Germans also worked on the construction of two of the large concrete bunkers at Siracourt and Lottinghem, but they would not be ready for some considerable time. Early in November it was estimated that 88 of the launch sites would be available for use in the middle of December. However the December opening began to look more and more unlikely. There were still specialist manpower problems, and technical problems were arising with the missiles themselves. As intelligence was indicating that the British were becoming aware of the programme, further security measures had to be implemented. Added to all these problems, Allied air attacks were disrupting the supply routes from the factories in Germany. At a meeting with the Army High Command on 12 November 1943 Wachtel envisaged that the earliest date for commencement of operations would be 1 March 1944. However the units of Flakregiment 155 (W) continued to deploy in France and on 7 December the regiment's HQ departed for France. After a week's difficult train journey the HQ personnel arrived at their temporary accommodation at Merlemont camp near Rochy-Condé, a few miles south-east of Beauvais. Construction work at the permanent accommodation at Doullens, approximately 20 miles north of Amiens, was still unfinished.

All this construction work on the flying bomb supply route, from the factory via the supply sites to the launch sites, required land to build on and a supply of labour and raw materials. On 15 August 1943, at La Croix au Guet, a hamlet very close to Saint Martin l'Hortier, about 20 miles south-east of Dieppe, Monsieur Paul Roinard returned with his wife and child from a family gathering, to their farm of 25 hectares. It was time to milk the cows. However when they arrived home they were met by a group of German soldiers, officers and technicians. In no uncertain terms they were told that their farm had been requisitioned and there was going to be a substantial amount of construction work carried out. They were told that they could stay on the farm if they wished and go about their 'normal' business.

In a short time two building sites had started up on their farm and hundreds of workers from numerous French and Belgian firms arrived. The work schedule was intense and conditions for the workers left a lot to be desired, with them having to sleep in camps set up at a nearby dairy farm. At night headlights were used so construction work could continue around the clock. A high level of effort was maintained with pressure applied by the Germans where necessary. One Sunday eight trucks arrived, which were full of scrap, and when the workers refused to unload them the German supervisor persuaded them to do otherwise with his pistol. One Saturday the German technicians found work at a standstill, and furiously they went to the market at nearby Neufchâtel. They forcibly took away 20 of the local tradesmen to the building site at La Croix au Guet and gave them shovels. Considerable construction work also took place on a rail line connecting La Croix au Guet to the rail station at Neufchâtel. This then brought in the raw materials necessary for the building work and sand, hardcore, cement bags and roof tiles all began to pile up. A road was also built in the shade of the apple trees to the rail station at Mesnières.

The local French people who lived in or near the town of Biennais, about 10 miles north of Rouen, witnessed similar construction work, the site being connected by rail to the station at Bosc-le-Hard. Numerous buildings went up at each of the sites, running water was installed and electricity and telephone systems connected. The Germans made every effort to give the new constructions the appearance of new farm buildings. At both sites well camouflaged large storage tanks were installed connected by special piping and pumping systems. It became clear to the workers what the tanks were to hold, the smell of the fuel that was pumped in by the delivery tankers was easily recognisable.

In the vicinity of the construction sites a number of anti-aircraft gun emplacements were built. Whenever a plane was heard a small siren went off resulting in considerable activity by the German soldiers. Ammunition also began to arrive at the rail stations and the Germans enlisted the farmers to transport it to the gun positions.

As Christmas 1943 drew near construction work on the launch sites and the supply sites in northern France had been in progress for approximately three months. In the area around the town of Tôtes, approximately 20 miles south of Dieppe, four launch sites were being constructed at Bosmelet, Belleville en Caux, Varneville-Bretteville and Bonnetot. Since September many of the young people from the area had been assigned to the building work. They were accommodated in the local schools, and clothed and housed by the Germans to avoid contact with the other French locals, and thereby prevent word getting out. Monsieur George Vergne was one of many of the local French civilians who became part of the labour supply:

> I was born in 1923 and at the age of 20 years I was recruited by
> an intermediary for the French Vichy government to work for
> the occupation forces. At the time I was living in Montville on

the Dieppe road about 13 kilometres from Rouen and I, together
with many others of my age group were recruited in the belief
we were to work on a temporary basis for the local council. For
my part I was sent to Bosc-Le-Hard where I worked in the
railway station yard making reinforced concrete blocks. We
learnt it was for some construction work at a site a few
kilometres away. It was some time later that we discovered it
was to protect the launching ramp at a V1 site.

At the farms selected for the flying bomb launch sites, large earthworks
appeared. Long strips of grass were lifted and stored, to be later used to
camouflage the buildings. Trucks delivered raw materials, night and day
concrete was mixed, roads laid and buildings erected. At Bosmelet the
work was overseen by a member of the German firm Badhauser, the
visible revolver in his belt going some way toward motivating the enforced
labour. Eventually the Germans told the farmers to evacuate their
properties, informing them that their farms were now required for the
defence of Europe. All access to the farms was now guarded and German
soldiers were billeted in the farmhouses. It was also noticeable to the
Germans and the local French people that every now and then British
reconnaissance aircraft flew low over the construction works. By the
Christmas of 1943 the flying bomb launch site at Bonnetot was ready, and
a few days before the local French people witnessed strange looking large
crates arriving by rail and being taken to a large 'hangar' at the local sugar
refinery.

Of course all this activity did not go unnoticed. Many of the local French
people took on the responsibility of making efforts towards informing the
Allies either directly or indirectly through the Resistance networks. One of
the direct methods employed was the use of pigeons. In the area around St
Martin l'Hortier, just before Christmas 1943, one local boy, Gaëtan Breton,
found attached to a parachute a small box which held a carrier pigeon. He
took it to his local school where one of the teachers, Madame Dumouchel,
took it with some doubt, fearing it could possibly have been a German
pigeon. Nevertheless Madame Dumouchel's husband decided to risk it and
cut from a road map the location of the Saint Martin l'Hortier construction.
He added a personal message *Pierrot a retrouvé Colombine pour
Christmas* (Pierrot to meet Colombine again for Christmas) and placed it
with the map in a tube attached to the pigeon. On Christmas Day 1943 the
apprehensive husband and wife released the pigeon praying that it would
not be shot down by one of the numerous German soldiers in the area. They
watched it nervously as it circled the church bell tower several times before
disappearing over the horizon. A week later English radio transmitted their
personal message.

In the town of Tôtes, which had several flying bomb launch sites under
construction in the nearby countryside, the local people had been told that
anyone finding pigeons that had been parachuted in were either to hand
them in to the Germans or to the Gendarmerie (French police). Many did
take them to the Gendarmerie where the gendarme Hilaire Gosse, who had

connections with the local Resistance, defied the occupying forces' orders and put them to their intended use. The locations of the local suspect constructions were copied, then slipped into the rings of the pigeons, which were then released.

All across the coastal areas of northern France the building work was making it clear to the local French people that something very important to the Germans was being constructed, evidenced by the numbers of anti-aircraft guns, the armed soldiers patrolling the sites, and the large fuel storage tanks. If the locals knew that something big was happening then so would the local Resistance. If the Resistance knew, then through their clandestine communication networks they would make sure Allied Intelligence agents also found out. Etienne Lepicard was just one of the many French patriots risking their lives gathering information. A veteran of the First World War he had continued in his country's service when the Germans again threatened his homeland. He became a prisoner but was released in 1942. In 1943 he, along with many others, began to work for Resistance groups trying to identify exactly what the Germans were up to with the recent construction activity in northern France. Etienne was given a bicycle and he set about gathering information on the building works. He found it rather easy. Firstly, in the army he had been trained to survey military bases. Also as a veteran with an officer card, when he was arrested or confronted by German soldiers he would show his ex-service card and immediately the well drilled German soldiers showed their respects, often springing to attention. Once he had gathered enough information he would return to Paris and pass the details over, which would be radioed to British Intelligence.

Throughout the second half of 1943 the numbers of reports from French agents to the Allies concerning the constructional works grew. Whenever intelligence was received from agents in the occupied territories regarding possible German secret weapon sites, the RAF's Photo Reconnaissance Unit (PRU) was called upon to check it out with aerial photography. This was a large task required of the PRU, and many sorties would have to be flown, but at least it didn't have the risks associated with the other requirements for the unit, such as photographing Berlin. Flying Officer Gordon Puttick flew high-level reconnaissance Spitfires:

> So far as the V1 sites are concerned, I was one of many in 541 and 542 Squadrons who covered the V1 site areas [late 1943 early 1944]. In those days we knew very little about them at squadron level; it was our job to cover certain areas in France and Belgium where V1 sites were thought to be sited . . . We photographed large areas . . . and we couldn't hang around too long. We simply called the areas Black or White, Dog or Cat, or some such name in order to let the interpreters know in which area we were operating.

Bill Newby, holding the rank of pilot officer at the time, flew as an observer W/T (wireless transmission) in Mosquitos with 544 Squadron:

Reconnaissance of the sites was purely routine and required little extra expertise. They were easily seen from 30,000 feet and given the map references they could be easily found/photographed. Being so close to the Channel there was little risk involved but we had to keep a sharp look out for FW190s; though there were often plenty of our fighters in the area doing low-level 'bashes' which kept them occupied . . . Ops over and around the sites were much less stressful than long trips over enemy territory to inner Germany, France, Italy, Balkans et al. In the first case, we could see our target areas before we left the English coast (in daylight). Usually after dark we could make out the French coast by the fluorescent strip along the shore-line.

Squadron Leader John Shelmerdine DFC flew a Spitfire in 541 Squadron.

The photographing of V1 sites was pretty simple and in no way compared to the business of covering damage assessment photos of places like Hamburg, Berlin, etc. It should be noted that . . . complete coverage of all the Channel coastline at high, medium and low water [had been carried out] for the D-day landings. All the V1 sites were of necessity close-by, so detailed further coverage and no doubt the subsequent interpretations were not too complicated.

At the end of October 1943 an agent in France reported the building of a construction, believed to be associated with secret weapons, at Bois Carré ten miles to the north-east of Abbeville. Reconnaissance of this site (and others reported in the area) revealed a 30 foot long and 12 foot wide concrete platform aligned on London and one square building with a wide opening, on the same alignment as the platform, which suggested to Allied Intelligence that it might be where a pilotless aircraft's guidance gyroscope was set before being taken to the launch ramp. There were two further rectangular buildings and three long buildings, which were curved at the end. These buildings were to give these sites an identifying name when Wing Commander Douglas Kendall, the senior interpreter of the Central Interpretation Unit, commented that they looked like skis turned sideways. These buildings were to be used for the storage of the flying bombs and the curved end was there to limit blast damage from bombing attacks. From then on the sites were called 'ski' sites. Further examination of all photographs of northern France, both new and old, revealed many more of these ski sites and by 22 November, 95 had been identified.

On 13 November 1943 Section Officer Constance Babington Smith of the Central Interpretation Unit identified a small aircraft on photographs of Peenemünde taken on 23 June. Unclear at that time what the small aircraft was, she named it Peenemünde 20, as the wing span was measured at 20 feet. This discovery led to the further inference that the French ski sites might be launching sites for pilotless aircraft. Babington Smith examined previous photographic coverage of Peenemünde and her search was rewarded when she found an inclined ramp, very close to the shoreline, facing the sea. Allied Intelligence also had reason to believe, owing to information about a German signals unit, that the flight paths of pilotless aircraft launched from Peenemünde and nearby Zempin were being monitored. New photographs of Peenemünde, taken by Squadron Leader John Merifield on 28 November, arrived and the small aircraft Babington Smith had named Peenemünde 20 was actually seen on the ramp. On Merifield's coverage of Zempin, ramps were identified with foundations that matched those at the French ski sites. The link was established and it was now clear that a flying bomb offensive from northern France against England was imminent. With the Allies estimating that there was enough storage for 20 missiles at each of the 95 sites identified, the potential scale of attack of nearly 2,000 missiles a day, was certainly a matter of great concern. On 4 December photographic reconnaissance of the whole of northern France within 140 miles of London or Portsmouth (the anticipated range of the flying bomb) was called for to ensure all sites would be identified. Plans were also made to start counter-offensive bombing operations.

CHAPTER 2

SLEDGEHAMMERS – THE RAF'S HEAVIES

By mid 1943 Bomber Command was fully engaged in the strategic air offensive against Germany. During the course of the war it had grown into a force that could send over 1,000 aircraft to a German city, with the potential of creating utter devastation. The early days of dead reckoning, 1,000 lb bomb loads, daylight operations, twin-engined aircraft, Blenheims, Hampdens, Wellingtons, Whitleys and solitary sorties had been replaced with electronic navigation and target marking aids such as Oboe and H2S, cookies (4,000 lb bombs), four-engine Lancasters, Halifaxes and Stirlings, twin-engined, high flying Mosquitos, the marking of targets for the main force by Pathfinder aircraft, concentration over the target, area bombing and bomber streams. The men who implemented the offensive strategy now had a leader who was prepared to take the fight to the German nation, as per Air Ministry policy, and shrug off the immorality of total war. Sir Arthur Harris was appointed Commander-in-Chief Bomber Command in February 1942. He had total belief in the potential of a bomber force to win the war outright. Here was someone prepared to attack the German war machine in its totality, from the Army's high command down to the machine worker, their factories, indeed their homes. Directives to Bomber Command, taking into account the limitations of a bombing assault with the weaponry available, allowed such total war application. The Casablanca directive of 21 January 1943, to Bomber Command, opened with the statement: 'Your primary object will be the progressive destruction and dislocation of the German military, industrial and economic system, and the undermining of the morale of the German people to a point where their capacity for armed resistance is fatally weakened.'[9]

The directive went on to be more specific and prioritise target areas. Harris was able, within the directive priorities, to carry out an area bombing policy. On the night of 30/31 May 1942 he put the bomber offensive at the forefront of Allied war policy. By sending over 1,000 bombers to reek havoc on Cologne he attempted to demonstrate the potential of his force. In the spring and early summer of 1943 he engaged his force in an attempt to destroy Germany's Ruhr industrial centre. On the night of 27/28 July 1943 his command razed Hamburg to the ground with a firestorm. But this accession of strength had not been without cost for attrition rates were high. The German High Command had responded to the bombing threat, channelling increasing resources towards the defence of their homeland. The flak, searchlights and nightfighter aircraft would exact their toll on the Allied bomber forces. The intelligence and scientific battle between the opposing air forces developed rapidly, each air force vying for that important edge.

On 10 June 1943 the Pointblank directive was issued to Bomber Command, which still fell in line with the Casablanca directive but required a change of priority. With the United States Eighth Air Force entering the bombing offensive against Germany, efforts were made to ensure that the targeting of both forces was complementary. It soon became clear that the German day and nightfighter force would need to be defeated to ensure a successful bombing campaign. Air superiority would also be essential when considering a land invasion in Western Europe, the main priority for the Allies and seen by most as the only means of achieving a German defeat in this sphere of the war. The Pointblank directive was intended to address the situation.

> *10th June 1943. Air Vice-Marshal N.H. Bottomley, Assistant Chief of the Air Staff (Operations) to Air Chief Marshal Sir Arthur Harris* [the Pointblank directive]:
>
> 3. The increasing scale of destruction which is being inflicted by our night bomber forces and the development of the day bombing offensive by the Eighth Air Force have forced the enemy to deploy day and nightfighters in increasing numbers on the Western Front. Unless this increase in fighter strength is checked we may find our bomber forces unable to fulfil the tasks allotted to them by the Combined Chiefs of Staff.
>
> 4. In these circumstances it has become essential to check the growth and to reduce the strength of the day and nightfighter forces which the enemy can concentrate against us in this theatre. To this end the Combined Chiefs of Staff have decided that first priority in the operation of British and American bombers based in the United Kingdom shall be accorded to the attack of German fighter forces and the industry upon which they depend.

Priority objectives were allocated to the United States Eighth Air Force. The directive went on further with regard to Bomber Command: 'While the forces of the British Bomber Command will be employed in accordance with their main aim in the general disorganisation of German industry their action will be designed as far as practicable to be complementary to the operations of the Eighth Air Force.'[10] Sir Arthur Harris still found scope within the directive to maintain his attacks on German cities. He firmly believed that a bomber offensive alone could bring Germany to her knees. Indeed he felt it was time to focus on assaulting the capital of the Reich, Berlin. In a minute to Churchill on 3 November 1943 Harris stated: 'We can wreck Berlin from end to end if the USAAF will come in on it. It will cost between us 400 – 500 aircraft. It will cost Germany the war.'[11]

However, the aircraft of Bomber Command were also, now and then, called upon to carry out special raids. One such raid was on 20/21 June 1943. The Friedrichshafen Zeppelin airship factory had been associated with the manufacture of the Würzburg radar, which was used as part of the German fighter defence against bombing raids. This raid would see the use of Pathfinder aircraft. On 5 July 1942 Wing Commander D.C.T. Bennett was appointed to command a new Pathfinder force. Bennett worked on developing ways for his force, initially comprising five squadrons, to identify and mark targets for Bomber Command attacks. In January 1943 the Path Finder Force (the designation of the force having changed) became a separate group and the now Air Commodore Bennett became the first Air Officer Commanding No. 8 (PFF) group. The raid to Friedrichshafen on 20/21 June involved 60 Lancasters, four from 8 Group and the rest of the force from 5 Group.

The attack was conducted in two phases, with a Master Bomber instructing bombers over the target and controlling the raid. The first phases involved Pathfinder marking of the target and the second phase a 'time and distance' bomb run from a point on the shores of Lake Constance to the aiming point (this last method would see further development by 5 Group). Despite having to climb to avoid flak and strong winds, leading to bombing difficulties, the Zeppelin works received heavy damage and plans for the output of 300 V2 rockets a month were scrapped.[12] This raid was Bomber Command's first serious blow at the German secret weapons programme, albeit unintentional as the attack was meant to disrupt radar manufacture, and it was at no cost as the bombing force continued on to North Africa after the attack, thus avoiding the German nightfighters prowling on what they expected would be the return route.

The next counter-measures attack on the German secret weapons programme was certainly planned. As the intelligence concerning rocket development at Peenemünde grew it had been decided, following the recommendations made by Sandys at the Defence Committee (Operations) meeting on 29 June 1943, that the research station should be bombed. Bomber Command was the force chosen to carry out the attack.

On the night of 17/18 August 1943 therefore, Harris's force launched a major attack on the research establishment at Peenemünde. Through the daylight hours prior to the attack, ground crews at the RAF stations prepared the aircraft and the aircrews attended briefings. The airmen knew something big was on as security was unusually tight. The pre-operation briefing revealed the target to the expectant crews, and, as was repeatedly emphasised, this operation required a maximum commitment from all those involved. It was made clear that if the target was not sufficiently damaged, the crews could expect to be sent again and again until satisfactory results were achieved. Again and again on the long route across the North Sea to Denmark, over the Baltic and back, with a flying time of seven to eight hours.

Eventually 596 aircraft commenced the long run to the target, with a Mosquito diversion to Berlin despatched to draw the German nightfighter force away from the bomber stream and its concentration over the target area. Fighter Command supported the night's activity, operating Intruder sorties, searching for combat with the Reich's night defenders. The Bomber Command plan involved bombing on three aiming points in three phases, the experimental works, two large production workshops and the housing for the scientists. The bomber's attentions were to be directed over the target by a Master Bomber, Group Captain J.H. Searby, the commanding officer of 83 Squadron. Marking of the targets was to be conducted by 8 Group and the last wave of the attack involved a further use of 5 Group's time and distance runs to the target, using Ruden Island, three miles north of Peenemünde.

The Mosquito diversion had its desired effect early in the night's activities, drawing the majority of the German airborne defences, initially to Berlin. As the Peenemünde raid opened, some of the German pilots flying above the Reich capital, amidst the turmoil created by the flak, searchlights and aircraft, were able to see the Peenemünde raid markers and bombs going down north of their position. A number of pilots took the initiative and left the skies above Berlin, to investigate what appeared to be the start of a major raid elsewhere.

At Peenemünde the first two waves of bombers managed to avoid almost completely the attention of the German nightfighters. Ground defence had minimal effect, with the small force of flak guns only accounting for three Halifaxes. The smoke screen used did have a small impact upon the bombing accuracy. The third bomber wave encountered the German nightfighter aircraft arriving from Berlin and suffered considerably as a result. On leaving the target area the bomber stream was pursued, suffering further loss. By the end of the night 40 bombers had been lost on the raid. In addition two Mosquitos were lost on the Berlin diversion and one Mosquito on the Intruder ops. Bomber Command lost 290 men, 245 of them killed.[13]

The raid was fairly successful, despite some initial marking difficulties, with considerable damage and numerous casualties amongst German personnel. It also had the effect of making the Germans change the production plans for the rocket, in particular the assembly locations, and launching trials were now to take place at Blizna in Poland. This was too far for the bombers to attack, but it gave opportunity for the Polish underground to supply information to the Allies. The raid had very little effect on the flying bomb programme but it was Bomber Command's first intentional attack as part of the German secret weapon counter-offensive campaign and it gave the Germans the clear indication that the Allies were aware, to some extent, of their reprisal weapon plans.

The next Allied bombing operations conducted as part of the German secret weapon counter-offensive campaign took place on 27 August 1943 when American bombers were sent to attack a suspicious construction at Watten, about 16 miles to the south of Dunkirk in northern France. A force of 185 Boeing B-17 Flying Fortresses conducted the attack, and it was followed up by a smaller raid on 7 September. Whilst Watten had not been identified for certain as a secret weapon site by Allied Intelligence, it was believed to be very important to the Germans and worthy of attack. In fact the site was intended solely for storing, servicing, fuelling and launching rockets. The American raids were very accurate and seriously damaged the construction. In considering the damage the Germans decided that they could no longer use the site for its intended purpose and made plans to find an alternative site.

Less than a week after the Peenemünde raid Sir Arthur Harris opened up his large-scale offensive against Berlin, sending 727 aircraft to the German capital. For the next seven months he would deploy his bombing force in trying to destroy Berlin. In the period 41 major raids against German cities would take place, involving 24,858 sorties. Nineteen of these were against Berlin, involving 10,813 sorties. Bomber Command lost 1,303 aircraft on the 41 raids, 625 of which were lost on operations to Berlin.[14] Other minor operations would be conducted, such as minelaying, small Mosquito raids, leaflet raids. Sir Arthur Harris would also be called upon to allocate some of his force against further German secret weapon operations.

During October 1943 Bomber Command conducted two operations that can be called classic area bombing attacks, and they also had an important unintentional effect on the progress of the Germans' flying bomb programme. The first of these raids took place on the night of 3/4 October when Bomber Command sent a large force of 223 Halifaxes, 204 Lancasters, 113 Stirlings and 7 Mosquitos to Kassel. Even though the bombers experienced some opposition, initial raid assessments suggested promising results. Flight Sergeant Arthur Darlow[15] was piloting a 427 Squadron Halifax and recorded the 7 hour 40 minute raid in his flying log book: 'Op successful. Port inner and m.u. [mid upper] turret hit by flak. 3-engined trip back. Concentrated attack. Very good.' However despite the optimism of the returning crews, problems in marking led to the majority of the bombs falling on the western suburbs and nearby towns and villages. Some success could be claimed as there were fires at both the Henschel aircraft factory and the Fieseler works, heavily involved in the flying bomb production process. The cost to Bomber Command was 24 aircraft and crews.

On the night of 22/23 October 1943, Bomber Command carried out another large attack on the city of Kassel with 322 Lancasters and 247 Halifaxes. Flight Sergeant Darlow again piloting a 427 Squadron Halifax, recorded the slightly shorter raid than previously (6 hours 50 minutes): 'Op successful. Red markers bombed. Fires well concentrated. Very good trip.'

This time the returning crews' optimism was well founded. Following initial inaccurate blind marking (from marker aircraft using electronic equipment and signals to locate the target and place the markers), visual markers were more successful in their task. The main force (apart from a few that were misled by German decoys) then carried out a concentrated and accurate attack, resulting in a massive firestorm that devastated the city. The wooden-beamed old town suffered greatly from the attacks with properties burnt down to about two feet above the ground and the newer part of the town virtually gutted. Following the raids, well over half the population evacuated the town, moving into the villages and farms surrounding the stricken city. The local police chief of Kassel sent a memorandum to Berlin which was copied to other German cities detailing how to deal with burnt bodies and recommending that rescue teams should carry bolt cutters with which to remove any rings to help identification.

Research by Martin Middlebrook and Chris Everitt for *The Bomber Command War Diaries* uncovered that all three Henschel aircraft factories were seriously damaged. In addition:

> Kassel records give dead recovered up to the end of November as 5,599 of which 1,817 bodies were unidentifiable . . . . Missing department was still trying to trace 3,300 people. 459 survivors' however, had been recovered from ruined houses 'after many days of heavy work'. 3,587 people were injured – 800 seriously – and a further 8,084 people were treated for smoke and heat injury to their eyes.[16]

Early in October, because of the air raids, the Fieseler works at Kassel had moved to nearby Rothwesten. The company's flying bomb production problems were compounded by an inadequate supply of compressed air and power. Owing to the Bomber Command attack of the 22/23 October many of the factory's workers stayed away, only 60 per cent arriving at the new location. It was not until the start of November that power was supplied, but the telephone and transport networks were still seriously disrupted. On 3 November, at one of Field Marshal Erhard Milch's conferences, Air Staff Engineer Bree informed his superiors of flying bomb production problems:

> Because Kassel has been lost, Rothwesten is to all intents and purposes lost as well. The men live in Kassel and their homes and transport are wrecked. In consequence, the final trials of the weapons power unit, control-gear, diving mechanism, compass and air log were held up.[17]

At this stage of the war the attack on German industry and the area bombing of German industrial towns was, where relevant, clearly adversely impacting the German flying bomb programme.

On the same night as the Kassel raid, 28 Lancasters and 8 Mosquitos carried out a diversionary raid on Frankfurt (1 Lancaster lost). However the German nightfighter controllers were not fooled and identified the main target area for their airmen. As such all the damage and human suffering was not just restricted to the population of Kassel. Bomber Command had 48 aircraft lost or written off (28 Halifaxes and 20 Lancasters) resulting in the deaths of 245, the capture of 78 and injury to 7 of their airmen.

CHAPTER 3

THE CALL TO ARMS

In November 1943 the Allies adopted the codename Crossbow for the German secret weapons investigation. As part of the planning for the Overlord campaign (the planned Allied invasion of Normandy) the Allied Expeditionary Air Force (AEAF) came into being, under the leadership of Air Chief Marshal Sir Trafford Leigh Mallory. With the impending threat of flying bomb attacks from northern France, he received orders to involve the Allied heavy bomber force in attacks on the suspected launch sites, drawing upon the United States Eighth Air Force and RAF Bomber Command. Five sites were initially allocated to Bomber Command but, initially, after protests from Harris, Leigh Mallory had to find other ways to attack the sites.

A letter from the Air Ministry to Bomber Command on 2 December indicated that it was anticipated that the whole of the AEAF bomber forces would be needed against these sites for a considerable time. Whilst it was hoped that no substantial use of heavy bombers would be required, an immediate test of the heavy bombers was called for.

> In order that operational data for precision attacks with 'Oboe' marking [an electronic aid detailed later] may be obtained, arrangements have now been made to screen three virgin sites and to reserve them for attacks by No. 617 Squadron with 'Oboe' marking. The sites in question are as follows . . .
> Cherbourg area   –   Bristillerie (or La Glacerie)
> Abbeville area   –   Ailly-le-Haut-Clocher
>   –   Domart-en-Ponthieu (or Flixecourt)[18]

Experimentation with types of bombs was also requested, suggesting that for the 617 Squadron attacks 'it would be of great value if separate attacks could be made with 12,000 and 4,000 lb bombs; both types should not be employed in the same attack if this can be avoided'. It should be noted that the raids would have a secondary value. The attacks on flying bomb ski sites would give the air commanders important information that could be applied when planning the bombing prior to the Allied invasion of northern France, the nature of which required some level of precision.

Before Bomber Command could effect these experimental operations, other Allied air forces started to attack the flying bomb targets. On

18

5 December 1943 the 2nd Tactical Air Force and US Ninth Air Force, utilising their fighters and light bombers, attacked three out of the 64 sites known to Allied Intelligence. Results of the raids were poor, however, in terms of damage done to effort required. When the winter weather limitations of the fighter and light bomber operations were also taken into account it became clear to the counter-offensive planners that should they wish to take out the ski sites in sufficient numbers as to seriously disrupt the expected scale of the German attack, then the Allies would have to deploy their medium and heavy bomber force.

Whilst these raids took place there was further high level discussion on the deployment of Bomber Command's aircraft. An Air Ministry letter of 8 December, from Air Vice-Marshal W.A. Coryton, Assistant Chief of the Air Staff (Operations) to Air Vice-Marshal R.D. Oxland CB, CBE (HQ Bomber Command), asked for Bomber Command's commander-in-chief, Sir Arthur Harris's, reaction concerning an economical method of dealing with Crossbow targets: '. . . As Stirlings are of little use in the bomber offensive, and since we do not wish to find ourselves later in a position of having to call in heavies to this purpose, I think there is every advantage in fitting Stirling squadrons with G-H and using them against Crossbow targets.'[19]

The Air Ministry letter went on further to request the fitting out with G-H of three Stirling squadrons at a rate of one per fortnight (G-H was a blind electronic bombing device and will be detailed shortly). Air Vice-Marshal Oxland basically agreed but only, initially, to using one G-H Stirling squadron, with further consideration needed for the use of any more.

The Stirling, at this stage of the bomber offensive, was being withdrawn from attacks on German targets. It did not have the altitude performance of the Lancaster and Halifax and its bomb load similarly fell short of the carrying capacity of the other four-engine heavies. From August to the third week in November, 109 Stirlings were lost on raids to Germany, a high loss rate of 6.4 per cent.[20] All these factors led to a reappraisal of the role of the Stirling. Whilst still seen to be of use in the continuation of minelaying duties, attacks on the nearby targets in northern France would also provide an opportunity for the employment of Stirling squadrons.

On 8 December Bomber Command informed all Group Headquarters of sites then under preparation in the Pas de Calais and Cherbourg area. The letter indicated that Bomber Command would be called upon to act from time to time, with attacks directed against markers dropped by Oboe aircraft. It did also mention that aircraft fitted with the navigational aid G-H would be called upon. No. 3 Group, in particular 218 Squadron, would continue to develop the G-H technique but in February 1944 a conservation policy was adopted, training ceased and the equipment was withdrawn.

The results from the bombing attacks on the ski sites in the first week and a half of the counter-offensive had been poor. Considering the rates of construction of the ski sites, Allied Intelligence suspected an attack by the flying bombs in the not too distant future and it was felt that it was high time to call in the heavy bombers. A cypher telegram to Washington on 15 December 1943, from the Air Ministry, summed up the situation:

A large number of sites in North France have become suspect in connection with possibility of pilotless aircraft attack on UK. All evidence tends to show that most immediate threat is from this form of attack. 69 sites for discharge of pilotless aircraft have been confirmed and number will probably eventually total 100. 35 sites are already 50% or more completed. 20 sites may be ready early January and remainder by February. Launching points appear to be oriented [sic] on London and Bristol, possibly others on channel ports.

2. Disregarding consequences of bombing counter-measures enemy might launch full-scale attack in February or smaller scale January. J.I.C. [Joint Intelligence Committee] have estimated possible scale of attack from 100 sites equivalent to 2,000 ton bomb raid in under 24 hours.

3. In order to avoid any undue diversion of our offensive over Germany, the task of destroying or neutralising these sites has been given to Tactical Air Forces. It was considered that this task might incidentally produce air battles under tactical conditions favourable to ourselves. Owing to prolonged unfavourable weather this month, no success has yet been achieved in these attacks.

4. We now consider that we can no longer refrain from employing the heavy bomber forces on this task and with the concurrence of General [Ira] Eaker, [commander of the US Eighth Army Air Force] we are arranging as a first step for Eighth Air Force to plan for a large scale operation with all available heavy bombers with the object of destroying or neutralising on the first favourable day the maximum number of the sites 50% or more completed. The Air-Commander-in-Chief A.E.A.F [Allied Expeditionary Air Force] will co-ordinate his operations in order to give maximum support and in order to take advantage of any air battles which this operation may provoke.

5. Our reasons for this course of action are:

a) If we depend on the less effective medium and light bombers, we may not find enough days of favourable weather available for operations during the period before pilotless aircraft attacks commence. The menace is a grave one.

b) We are anxious to achieve surprise and particularly to obtain maximum results before flak defences are strengthened.

c) It is unlikely that favourable weather conditions over the North of France will coincide with those which are suitable enough for precision bombing over Germany. Our offensive over Germany therefore would not necessarily be seriously affected.[21]

It was clearly time for Bomber Command to start its 'experiment'. Harris had a substantial force of heavy bombers to draw on. For example, on the night of 22/23 November 1943 he had sent 753 heavies, accompanied by 11 Mosquitos, to attack Berlin. He would, however, limit the use of his resources in conducting the experiment against the German secret weapon targets in northern France.

The first attack by Bomber Command aircraft and crew on a flying bomb installation took place on the night of 16/17 December 1943 on one of the targets near Abbeville. The plan for the raid involved Pathfinder Mosquitos marking the site using the 'blind' ground-controlled electronic bombing device Oboe. The use of Oboe was now a regular feature of Bomber Command raids. It had had a major impact on the target-finding abilities of the bombing forces. Two ground stations in England sent signals to the Oboe-carrying aircraft. Ron Curtis DSO, DFC and Bar, a navigator, flew on Oboe-equipped Mosquitos with 8 Group's 109 Squadron. In January 1944 (holding the rank of Flying Officer at the time) and the summer of the same year he would be involved in the marking of flying bomb targets. He would end the war having completed 104 sorties using the Oboe technique.

The system required two ground stations situated on the English coast about 100 miles apart. One station, called the 'Cat', sent signals to the pilot, which enabled him to maintain a constant track over the target, and the second, called the 'Mouse', sent position signals to the navigator followed by the release signal. In the aircraft there was a receiver and a transmitter. Thus signals could be received, and transmitted back, to the ground stations thereby allowing the exact position to be calculated.

Our flight plan was based on Met forecast of wind speed and direction given at briefing. To the time calculated to reach point A, 10% was added as a safety factor against any adverse conditions, which might be encountered. Being at operational height on leaving the English Coast I could obtain the actual wind speed and direction and revise the ETA (estimated time of arrival) at point A. Invariably it was necessary to lose part of the extra 10%. A rate 1 orbit would lose 3 minutes and a 60% dogleg 1 minute. Timing was of paramount importance to avoid 400 or 500 main force bombers being in the target area waiting for the target markers.

The receiver was switched on well before arrival at Point A. Each crew had its own call sign. Ours was TK. This was sent to us when it was our turn to be called in. On receipt of this I switched on the transmitter so that the ground stations could see our exact position and send the control signals. To obtain the accuracy of release and timing, each aircraft required 10 minutes to settle on the run. As more ground stations became operational, more aircraft could be controlled at the same time. One also had to fly straight and level at a constant speed so that the Mouse could calculate the ground speed and send the release signal.

When the aircraft was exactly on the arc of the circle with its centre the Cat station, my pilot would hear a steady note in his headphones. If nearer the Cat station, dots were received and if outside the range dashes were received. The width of the beam (steady note) did not vary with the distance from the Cat. I received A's (morse code) at 10 minutes flying time from time on target, B's at 8 minutes, C's at 6 minutes and D's at 3 minutes. At approximately $2\frac{1}{4}$ minutes after D's the release signal was sent. This was 5 high speed ($\frac{1}{2}$ second) dots followed by a $2\frac{1}{2}$ second dash, then silence. At this point I pressed the bomb release button and switched off the transmitter. Thus the exact time of release was recorded and the next aircraft could be called.

When attacking some of the flying bomb targets in northern France, some of the Oboe runs would actually start over the Thames estuary. The method was limited in that the ground stations could only control six aircraft per hour. Three was the maximum number of stations that could be used, hence 18 aircraft per hour was the maximum number of aircraft that could use Oboe. The signals were also limited by the curvature of the earth. The further the target area from the ground station, the higher the altitude required for the Oboe aircraft in order to receive and send signals. As all the flying bomb targets were situated in northern France this did not become much of a limiting factor on these raids. The Mosquito proved the most well suited aircraft to carry the equipment, particularly owing to its ability to reach high altitude and extending the range if necessary. Later on in the anti-flying bomb campaign Lancasters would also be equipped with the device to use as a marking and bombing aid. Tony Farrell DFC, AFC began piloting Mosquitos, and using Oboe, with 105 Squadron (8 Group) in the summer of 1944:

> We had heard a lot about the Mosquito. Aircraft get reputations from crew-room gossip, but I have never heard anything but praise for the 'Mossie'. It lived up to its reputation and was a superb aircraft for all the different (and difficult) operation roles in which it was used. It was of necessity cramped, but that had advantages for co-operation with one's navigator. It was not easy to get in and out (I was glad I was thin!) but it handled like a dream. I have never heard a bad word spoken about it.

Tony Farrell gives a pilot's perspective of using Oboe:

> When the aircraft's call sign was received the Oboe was switched on and the navigator got down on the floor to receive the signals giving the positions along the line of the 'beam' and to operate the bomb release if and when this was given. When using target indicators this would not be given unless the final few minutes of the run-in achieved the required degree of accuracy. The pilot concentrated hard on making a steady run along the beam, which was very narrow indeed and . . . was curved – the longer the range the slower the rate of change of heading and the higher one had to go to receive it. About three minutes before release the pilot opened the bomb doors and

then had almost to open up to full power to overcome the extra drag. Probably all windows except the clear vision panels ahead were iced up, so it was concentration on instruments.

After the markers were released a further short period of flying steadily and accurately was required whilst cameras recorded the results. We were generally too high to be bothered much by flak (anti-aircraft fire), though occasional minor damage was sustained. One did not consider the threat of nightfighters, you probably would not have seen one attacking you. Fortunately the war was over before the German jet fighters were numerous enough to threaten us. On the return to base we parked our aircraft in its dispersal and were taken back to the operations room for debriefing, and they already had our results phoned through from the ground stations. It was impressive to be told what our bombing and marking errors were. Anything over 100 yards was considered third-rate and if we were badly inaccurate we would not be given a release signal if markers were being carried.[22]

The target-marking aircraft's bombload would include markers, such as TI (Target Indicators), to identify the target to the main force on a raid. TI had undergone considerable development up until late 1943. By this stage of the bombing campaign there were various types of TI available. The first TI were 250-pound bomb casings filled with coloured pyrotechnic candles, which were then released by a barometric fuse at a set height above the ground. These cascaded to the ground to burn brightly and assist in identifying targets to the bomber force. The basic TI was then developed to obtain longer ground burns, delayed burns, to overcome German decoys and provide daylight marking using coloured smoke. In addition Spot Fire TI were developed, a 250-pound casing filled with chemically soaked cotton wool, to give a bright burn on the ground. If a target was to be cloud-covered skymarkers were developed; in the main these were flares but candle TI with parachutes were also available. This array of various types of TI gave those planning the marking of targets, plenty of options when considering weather conditions, size of targets, size of attacking force and the countering of German decoys.

It would be worthwhile at this point to mention other navigational and target-finding aids available to Bomber Command. In August 1941 Gee was first used over Germany. Gee involved three ground stations transmitting signals to be received by an aircraft. One station was called the Master, the other two stations, Slaves. Each of the transmissions from the Slave stations was locked into a Master transmission. On the receiving aircraft a cathode ray tube would display the difference in time, for each of the signals to reach the aircraft. This would then result in the production of Gee co-ordinates, from which a ground position could be obtained using grids on Gee charts. Gee was never really developed as a blind bombing aid, its accuracy could vary between from less than half a mile to five miles.

Its maximum range was about 400 miles and accuracy diminished as the range increased. Not long after its introduction the Germans were able to implement jamming countermeasures. However, as for Oboe, the relatively close proximity of the flying bomb targets to England and the ground stations, meant that raids would be conducted within Gee's range and it could be used as a blind bombing aid. It still also retained fundamental value as a navigation and homing device as aircraft neared England.

A navigational aid and blind bombing device called H2S was introduced operationally in January 1943. A circular cathode ray tube in an aircraft displayed radar echoes, returned by ground features, which were initially transmitted from a rotating radar transmitter. The distinction between land and water features was particularly clear. Built-up areas also provided good responses. Comparison of the H2S display with maps of areas provided a position fix for the navigator. If the target area had discernible features, H2S could be used as a blind bombing device. The main advantage of H2S was the range, which, of course, was limited by the range of the aircraft carrying the device. Disadvantages included recognition of built-up areas, as the cathode display image did not often correspond with the actual shape of a town or city. It had little use in blind bombing on raids against the flying bomb launch sites owing to the small size of the targets, but it could be used in terms of time and distance runs from discernible land features such as coastlines.

One spin-off from H2S was a device called Fishpond, which used H2S transmissions and any resulting echoes from aircraft below the bomber to produce a display on a screen in front of the wireless operator. Whilst not distinguishing whether the blips on the screen were from hostile aircraft or not, if the blip was approaching on a convergent course then the wireless operator could bring his crewmates to readiness for a possible attack. The crews also had another device, called Monica, which could indicate another aircraft approaching. Radio pulses transmitted from the Monica-carrying aircraft would be reflected by other nearby aircraft and the pilot would hear a series of clicks in his headphones. If the frequency of the clicking increased then the reflecting aircraft was approaching and the pilot could bring his crew to readiness. Unfortunately for the Bomber Command crews, once a few of both the devices had got into German hands from bombers lost over German territory, the Germans were able to produce devices for their nightfighters that could home in on the bombers' transmissions.

G-H was a navigational and blind bombing aid that was similar to Oboe, incorporating Gee. The G-H aircraft, carrying both a transmitter and a receiver, was able to plot its position from the intersection of two lines respective to two ground stations. Its range was limited respective to range from the ground stations but it was more accurate than Gee, particularly as the range increased. The main advantage over Oboe was that substantially more aircraft could use the device, about 100. Although unlike Gee and H2S, if the raid were large then obviously not all the aircraft would have the use of G-H. A disadvantage was that the device was worked by the aircrews. One member of the bomber crew would have to work a fairly complicated device over a target, ignoring the searchlights, the flak bursts, the nightfighters and flares. On 3 November 1943 the first G-H heavy bomber attack was made by 38 G-H Lancasters on Düsseldorf. However as Bomber Command had begun to prosecute the Battle of Berlin, out of the range of G-H, use of G-H was limited. The possibility of using G-H as a navigational and target finding aid on the raids to northern France and the flying bomb sites was not overlooked, however, and as we have seen Stirling squadrons were being considered.

On 21 March 1943, 617 Squadron had been formed as part of 5 Group with specially selected crews with a specific operation in mind. On the night of 16/17 May 1943, 19 of the squadron's Lancasters were sent to conduct the famous Dam Busters raid. The force was successful in breaching the Möhne and Eder dams at a cost of eight Lancasters and crews. Following the raid it was decided that the squadron should remain together to carry out attacks on special targets. Throughout July 1943 attacks were made against targets in Italy and in September attacks were conducted against the Dortmund-Ems Canal and Anthéor Viaduct. On 10 November 1943 Geoffrey Leonard Cheshire took command of the squadron, then based at Coningsby. Wing Commander Cheshire[23] had already completed tours with 102 Squadron and 35 Squadron, receiving a DFC, DSO and bar. Following a period instructing he returned to operations commanding 76 Squadron and achieved a second bar to his DSO. He then went on to command the RAF station at Marston Moor before returning once more to operations, this time with 617 Squadron.

The 617 Squadron bombers attacked the Anthéor viaduct on 11 November but Cheshire did not arrive at the squadron until a few days later. On 16 December the squadron received orders to attack a constructional works at Flixecourt/Domart-en-Ponthieu. These constructional works were in fact a flying bomb ski site. It had been a frustrating time for the airmen of the squadron prior to this raid. Numerous briefings had taken place for attacks on a variety of targets but bad weather had stepped in to curtail operations. However as evening drew in on the night of 16 December the crews climbed into their Lancasters, began their pre-flight checks and started taxying to the runway.

Target and aircraft despatched

Abbeville (Flixecourt)
6 Mosquitos, 9 Lancasters
Bombload – 9 x 12,000 lbs

Plan of attack

Zero hour – 1900 hours
3 Mosquitos to place yellow markers 10 miles east of the target then to mark the aiming point with green TI. There would also be primary marking from 2 other Mosquitos at zero – 2 and zero + 8 (a reserve Mosquito was also sent, should it be required). The Mosquitos were to run in every three minutes starting at zero – 2, only releasing on a satisfactory run i.e. clear Oboe signals. 9 Lancasters each with one 12,000 lb H.C. (high capacity) bomb were to attack the markers

No. 617 Squadron's Flight Lieutenant R.S.D. Kearns flying Lancaster III ED912, lifted his aircraft from the runway at RAF Coningsby into the night air at 1653 hours, the first Bomber Command heavy bomber to take off in a raid against a flying bomb site. It took thirteen minutes for all nine of the squadron's Lancasters, laden with their 12,000 lb bombs to take off.

Squadron Leader P. J. Channer DFC from 105 Squadron took off from RAF Marham at 1717 hours in Mosquito LR508-G, the first Bomber Command Mosquito to take off in operations against flying bomb sites. He was accompanied by two other Mosquitos from the squadron, all three detailed to act as secondary markers. The three primary markers for the raid were supplied by 109 Squadron, also based at RAF Marham.

Once over the target only one yellow was seen by seven of the Lancasters in approximately the right position. Both other route markers failed and none of the Mosquitos from 105 Squadron went on to mark the target. Further problems arose when the first primary marker from 109 Squadron returned early, but the other two Mosquitos, piloted by Flying Officer Wolland and Squadron Leader Cox, continued to the target. The first Mosquito, which was actually the reserve, came in and unfortunately marked the target at z-5, its TI having gone out by the time the main force arrived at z+1. The main force then had to wait until the second TI was dropped at z+8, which the ground station in England described as a very good run. The main force then accurately bombed the TI. The night was cloudless, but very dark and the bombers encountered negligible enemy resistance to their efforts.

On return from the target the 617 Squadron crews reported their unhappiness with the marking. The Squadron ORB (Operations Record Book) recorded that owing to the fact that the markers broke up once on the ground, and that they burned for only about a minute and a half, they were 'entirely inadequate'. However the accuracy of the bombing was considered excellent, each crew bringing back bombing photographs with the aiming point at the centre. Two of the bombs were later plotted as 30 yards from the aiming point. The squadron also claimed that the bombing was 'undoubtedly the highest concentration of night bombing that has yet been done in this war'. So the bombing of the markers was accurate but it depended on the accuracy of the marking for its success. Unfortunately the markers fell 350 yards from the centre of the target area. Subsequent analysis of photographs did show four craters in the target area, the other five within 500 feet. Further detail of the bombing results will be dealt with later.

The second target for the night's operations was also in the Abbeville area. Bomber Command called on the Stirling squadrons for the raid. Flight Sergeant Ronnie Hunt was a Stirling pilot with 75 (New Zealand) Squadron and was detailed to take part in the raid:

> The Stirling was a beautiful aeroplane. They looked very odd on
> the ground with the high undercarriage, but the handling was
> very light. They really were a joy to fly. It was pretty dangerous

taking off and landing and there were an awful lot of accidents. The big snag with them was that they could not get the height. The Lancasters and Halifaxes were up at 20,000 to 23,000 feet and we were lucky on a warm night to get to 14,000 feet, which made us easier for all the German fighters. They didn't need to bother going up if they could get someone at 14,000 feet.

On the night of 16/17 December 1943, 75 Squadron prepared some of their Stirlings and crews for minelaying operations. Eight aircraft were also detailed to join Stirlings from other squadrons for the attack on the flying bomb launch site at Ailly-le-Haut-Clocher. Ronnie Hunt was one of their pilots:

> The briefing, well it was very brief. They were frightened to say anything about what we were really bombing. We had an idea. We were told that it was important because it could have an effect on the civilian population in the south of England. We thought they were perhaps rockets, but we didn't know for sure.
>
> At the time . . . it was known to the Air Force and Government people that the flying bomb attacks were going to start, but it wasn't known to the general public. The bombing raids were therefore regarded as secret operations. So nothing much was said to us except that we must not mention the target in our logbooks. We had to put down 'Special Operation'. These raids were mixed up with a lot of Gardening [minelaying operations]. Some of these were very easy down on the Bay of Biscay coast. Some of them were up in the Baltic, the Skagerrak, the Kattegat and Kiel Bay, and they were a bit difficult because of the heavy defences. The flying bomb sites were mostly fairly easy operations. Fortunately the raids were fairly quick, we were never more than about 3 hours there and back.

The plan for the raid was as follows (see also Appendix 4):

Target and aircraft despatched
Abbeville (Ailly-le-Haut-Clocher)
6 Mosquitos, 26 Stirlings
Bombload – 106 tons,
using 500lb bombs
(10% long-delay fused)

Plan of attack
Zero hour – 1930 hours
3 Mosquitos to mark the aiming point with red TI and 3 other Mosquitos to place green TI as secondary markers. As these secondary markers were dropped on a different Oboe channel they were deemed to be probably less accurate, hence the main force were instructed to bomb the reds if visible. The Mosquitos running in at zero – 2, zero and then every 3 minutes were only to release their TI on satisfactory runs. The main force was to make a timed run from a point 20 miles south west of the target, arriving over the target between zero and zero + 4.

Things did not start too well for the 75 Squadron Stirlings. One aircraft failed to take off and another crashed, fortunately without any injury to the crew.

> *Flight Sergeant Ronnie Hunt, pilot, 75 Squadron:* They usually tried to organise it that you could bomb run down wind, because your ground speed was faster. If it was a windy night, say a 50 mph wind blowing behind you, and you were doing about 220 mph airspeed coming up to the target, that put you up to 270 mph over the ground. This was really taking into account the target where there was a lot of flak. You got out of the target area as quickly as possible. Nearly always they were marked by the time we got there and you would just go round. Usually your route took you so that you were able to turn straight onto a bombing heading when you saw the markers. If you didn't meet much opposition at that point then it was a fairly simple bombing operation. If you met opposition on the way then you could be into all sorts of activities.

Only two of the 109 Squadron primary markers, piloted by Flight Lieutenant Stephens and Flight Lieutenant Watton, attacked at Ailly-le-Haut-Clocher with red markers, one, on a good run, at z+1 and the other at z+14. The third, a reserve, was not required. Two of the 105 Squadron secondary markers, piloted by Squadron Leader Blessing DSO DFC and Wing Commander Green DFC, attacked with green markers, one, on a medium run, at z+2 and one on a poor run at the same time. The other Mosquito experienced a technical failure. Twenty-one of the Stirlings bombed, and between z and z+12 at least 17 of them attacked the first salvo of reds, 3 attacked the greens.

Post-raid analysis showed that the first salvo of reds fell 450 yards from the aiming point, the greens fell two miles to the east. The main force provided 15 bombing photographs, 10 of which were grouped around the TI, average distance 370 yards. All of the aircraft on the night's raids against the flying bomb targets returned. There were some minor incidents. In addition to the two aircraft (from 75 Squadron) damaged during take-off, one aircraft hit a tree while coming in to land and another collided with one of the Berlin force. Another aircraft crash landed. No injuries resulted from enemy action.

On 18 December 1943 an Air Ministry cypher added five further flying bomb sites to Bomber Command's list of targets, bringing their allocation up to eight. These were Bois des Huit Rues, Bois de la Justice, Herbouville, Bonnetot and Freval. In the Public Records Office file AIR 14 743 there are some notes at the front referring to this cypher, which demonstrate the Bomber Command leaders' reluctance to be part of the flying bomb counter-offensive. The first is from Air Vice-Marshal Sir Robert Saundby, Deputy Commander-in-Chief of Bomber Command, 'The wedge is being driven in quite fast', with Harris's reply: 'Only when we have nothing better to do – and then only Stirlings & 617 sq'n.'

On the night of 22/23 December Bomber Command aircraft attacked the ski sites at Freval and Ailly-le-Haut-Clocher. A force of three Mosquitos and ten Lancasters from 617 Squadron was sent to attack Freval but the main force was unable to see the TI owing to the cloud cover. The heavy bombers circled the target area for 15 minutes after the attack was supposed to have ended, but they still could not see any of the markers. The raid was abandoned. Ailly-le-Haut-Clocher was attacked by 30 Stirlings, 3 Halifaxes (the first time Halifaxes were used against flying bomb targets) and 3 Mosquitos, with accurate ground marking and bombing reported by the returning crews.

Bomber Command's Operational Research carried out a detailed analysis of the raid of 16/17 December to Flixecourt, and the raids of 16/17 and 22/23 December to Ailly-le-Haut-Clocher, with damage to both targets found to be negligible. It was surmised that this was to be expected with the systematic error of the primary marking techniques used, being of the order of 400 yards. Apart from the marking they reached the conclusion that the bombing was good, the Stirlings with an average error of about 500 yards and the Lancasters, fitted with special bombing sights, with an average of 80 yards. They also made a recommendation concerning the bombloads used: '. . . if the 5 Group aircraft had carried 14 x 1,000 lb bombs instead of 1 x 12,000 lb bomb, there would have been some 28 hits in the target area instead of 4 on the extreme edge.'[24]

The initial experiment had given poor returns in terms of damage caused. Nevertheless the ski sites remained as targets for Bomber Command. Early in December the Allied Chiefs of Staff, fearing an imminent German attack, decided to conduct, when the conditions were right, an all-out attack by the United States Air Force heavy bombers against as many flying bomb launch sites as possible. The relevant orders were issued on 15 December but it was not until 24 December that conditions were suitable, when 672 Fortresses dropped 1,472 tons on 24 sites.

Further raids on the ski sites allocated to Bomber Command were also conducted and analysis on these raids revealed the following:

30/31 December raid to Flixecourt/Domart-en-Ponthieu, 10 Lancasters from 617 Squadron carrying 12,000 lb bombs, and 4 Mosquitos.

The Pathfinder Mosquitos utilised cascading markers on the raid in an attempt to improve marking accuracy. The use of this method, against using impact markers, was not popular with 617 Squadron, the Operations Record Book (ORB) clearly indicating their dissatisfaction: 'They could not hope to lead to such accurate bombing as the latter type [impact markers] because of the wide area of the sky which they covered.'[25] The ORB went on to claim a high bombing concentration around the two TI dropped, but the TI were too far from the target to achieve success. The marking problems were further compounded when three of the bombs fell inside the TI and temporarily blew them out. Analysis revealed no craters in the target area and the target remained undamaged.

29 December to 5 January, 16 Mosquitos sent to Bristillerie of which only 13 attacked: 500lb G.P. (General Purpose) bombs used.

Photographs on 5 January showed 45 craters within 1,500 yards of the aiming point. 14 craters (representing 27% of the bombs) in the target area. None appeared to have scored damaging hits.

Once more the results of the Bomber Command raids demonstrated a poor return for its airmen's efforts. Up to the new year 52 sites had received the direct attention of the Allied bomber force with Bomber Command attacking just five of these. Over 3,000 tons of bombs had been dropped, of which Bomber Command contributed 344. Allied intelligence now started to classify the state of ski sites following attack as:

> Category A – Concentrated groups of hits in the target area with one or more direct hits on essential buildings.
> Category B – Hits within the target area near enough to cause probable damage to essential buildings i.e. 'ski' stores.
> Category C – Some hits in the target area but none near essential buildings.
> Category D – No hits in the target area.[26]

Of the 52 sites attacked up to the new year Allied Intelligence classified 12 as category A, 9 as category B, 15 as category C; 6 had been completely missed with the assessment of the 10 other sites so far not possible. The results of the raids recorded in the diary of Flakregiment 155(W) suggested that the Allies had been somewhat optimistic in their analysis. The diary did record that the regiment was having serious problems as a result of the bombing raids but that only seven had been destroyed, three of which had been completely obliterated.[27]

On the night of 4/5 January 1944, in addition to the small Mosquito force sent to Bristillerie, three other bombing raids were initiated. Ailly-le-Haut-Clocher received the attentions of 29 Stirlings and 3 Mosquitos, which dropped a total of 664 bombs (each 500 lb) on red TIs attempting to swamp the target area and increase the probability of damaging the installations. The theory worked, with severe damage to two of the skis. Bois des Huit Rues was attacked by 28 Stirlings and 3 Mosquitos, but poor marking led to scattered bombing. However subsequent reconnaissance revealed numerous craters in the target area with one direct hit and a near miss on a ski. Freval was targeted by 11 Lancasters (from 617 Squadron) and 3 Mosquitos, but the results were poor owing to poor marking. One Mosquito failed for technical reasons. The other two Mosquitos did manage to release their TI but not on the target. The controlling ground stations had trouble in giving the release signal at the right time, blaming an unforeseen high tail wind. The last Mosquito was estimated to have overshot the target by three to four miles. The Lancasters came in, and between them, as expected, bombed the TI. When the Bomber Command analysts were able to plot the TI, one was plotted ¾ mile from the target and another 3¼ miles away. Follow-up reconnaissance, unsurprisingly showed no fresh damage in the target area.

On the nights of 5/6 and 6/7 January small forces of two and three Mosquitos, respectively, attacked Bristillerie. This brought the total number of sorties by Bomber Command, since the opening of their campaign on 16/17 December, to 210. Flixecourt had been attacked twice by Lancasters and Mosquitos with minimal, if any, damage caused. Freval had been attacked twice by Lancasters and Mosquitos, one raid abandoned and the other raid 'missed'. Ailly-le-Haut-Clocher had been attacked three times by forces of Stirlings and there had been substantial damage to the target. Bois des Huit Rues was attacked once by Stirlings with some damage to the target. Bristillerie received the attention of seven small Mosquito raids.

This could really be viewed as the end of the experimental stage. Sir Arthur Harris wrote to the Air Ministry on 11 January 1944:

> I have the honour to refer to a telephone conversation with D.C.A.S [Deputy Chief of the Air Staff, Air Marshal Bottomley] on the subject of attacks on 'Crossbow' targets by Bomber Command.
>
> When the original three 'Crossbow' targets were allotted to this Command for night bombing they were so allotted as an experiment. They were accepted by this Command with grave doubts as to the feasibility of hitting such targets at all at night. Subsequently five more targets were added to the original three in the terms of Air Ministry signal . . . dated 18 December 1943, upon receipt of which I represented by telephone that while I had grave doubts as to our ability to knock out the three already allotted to us at night, I was certain that we could not profitably take on any more.
>
> In the interim the Stirlings have been used against these targets as a matter of first priority and in addition some bombing has been carried out by 617 Squadron with 12,000 lb bombs. The results, as anticipated, have been ineffective.
>
> The error . . . with Oboe when it is functioning at its best at that range is in the neighbourhood of 400 yards. The subsequent error of bombing by the main force on the Oboe markers with 617 Squadron would be at least 100 yards, and with ordinary Stirling squadrons considerably more. In addition Oboe has of late been proving very unreliable, partly due to apparent enemy interference and partly to the unreliability of the sets themselves.
>
> In these circumstances, while I am prepared to continue experimenting with three of the targets with 617 Squadron, and to give the Stirlings – for which I have little other use except mining – first priority on these targets as well, I still do not anticipate that results will accrue pointing to the feasibility of

this type of operation.

I do not, in fact, regard bombing of a pin point-target at night by heavy bombers as a reasonable operation of war.

617 Squadron are now awaiting a weather opportunity in which to try out a scheme of marking the vicinity of the target with 'Oboe' and then putting in an individual aircraft low down to mark the exact target by visual search. This method, however, even if it is successful, which I much doubt, will lead to the enemy protecting these targets with light flak and searchlights, thus putting a speedy term to such methods of attack.[28]

Bottomley, at the Air Ministry, replied to Harris on 14 January, partly agreeing with Harris's reservations but suggesting that these were not insurmountable:

I am to inform you that the Chiefs of Staff have now decided that the effort to be devoted to the destruction of these sites [Crossbow sites] is to be intensified. The destruction of the eight sites allocated to your Command . . . should therefore be accomplished as expeditiously as possible, and I am accordingly to request that this may be made a first charge upon the operations of your Stirling squadrons when these are not being directed onto targets in Germany.

The results so far obtained by your Command in attacks on 'Crossbow' targets suggest that the difficulty in destroying them may be due not so much to lack of precision in the bombing as to the fact that the inherent accuracy of 'Oboe' is insufficient to ensure exact marking of the target. I am to suggest in this regard that attacks might be directed onto the more readily definable targets, such as Domart-en-Ponthieu, in moonlight by means of visual identification using 'Oboe' markers to indicate to bomb aimers the approximate location of the target.

It is appreciated that a limiting factor in the effort which you can devote to the attack of these targets may at times be the provision of a sufficient number of 'Oboe' Mosquito sorties; the employment of 'Oboe' aircraft in this role is not, however, to take priority over their employment in the attack of targets in Germany, or in support of the main force operations.[29]

So despite Harris's reservations he had to continue to target his allocation of flying bomb sites. Following on from what should really be classed as the limited success of the Stirling forces, unrecognised in the above letter by their Commander-in-Chief, the Stirling squadrons would be used. On the night of 14/15 January three forces were despatched to attack flying bomb sites. Four Mosquitos and 13 Halifaxes attacked the site at Bonnetot. Only two Mosquitos were able to drop their markers, one doing so after the main force had attacked; the TI plotted 300 and 440 yards from the aiming point. None of the main force took photographs when bombing but they all made a second run to do so. Eight were plotted, one 550 yards from the aiming point, the rest 880 to 2,000 yards away. Thirty Stirlings and 3 Mosquitos paid their respects to Ailly-le-Haut-Clocher, 17 of the 24 night photographs taken by the bombers grouped round the markers, all within a half mile of the target area. Twenty-nine Stirlings and 3 Mosquitos raided Bristillerie in a scattered attack. Reconnaissance of Bristillerie and Ailly-le-Haut-Clocher was not obtained until there had been further attacks on these targets, and will be detailed later.

Two aircraft on the raid to Bristillerie were hit by flak. The attacking forces had to date experienced very little opposition from either German ground defences or nightfighters. If there was any flak defence over a target, however, it basically had to be ignored. Nightfighters were a different matter:

> *Flight Sergeant Ronnie Hunt, pilot, 75 Squadron:* You had to ignore the flak really. Sometimes if there were bursts coming fairly near you it would get a bit bumpy and jerky because we were at a fairly lowish level. So you could get jerked off course. I know of one occasion when I was being attacked by a fighter on the bombing run and our normal way of avoiding it was a manoeuvre called a corkscrew which threw you miles off course. So you had to go round again, do a bit of an orbit and come in again to drop your bombs. The only alternative if you had been badly hit was that you may have to unload your bombs and get to the coast as quickly as possible.

The Crossbow Counter-measures Progress Report[30] to 15 January recorded that since the start of the bombing counter-offensive, over 6,500 tons had been dropped by the Allied heavy and medium bomber forces, and 76 sites had been attacked; 17 of which were classified as category A, 32 as category B (with 3 possibly category A), 13 category C (one of which was possibly category A), 9 category D, with no evidence available for the state of the other five sites.

This gave the Allies optimism and during January the Allied bombing raids continued with a believed improvement in results achieved. The Allied powers still felt, however, that to maintain the initiative further bombing was necessary.

On the night of 21/22 January 1944 Bomber Command despatched its largest force to date to four sites, again using 617 Squadron and 3 Group Stirlings.

Target and aircraft despatched

Domart-en-Ponthieu
3 Mosquitos, 12 Lancasters
(617 Squadron)
Bombload – 36.6 tons high
explosive (1,000 lb and
500 lb bombs)

Plan of attack

Zero hour – 1900 hours
3 Oboe Mosquitos, using green TI to mark the aiming point every 10 minutes starting at zero hour. The leader of the 617 Squadron Lancaster force, Wing Commander Cheshire, was to mark the aiming point visually, from a height of not more than 8,000 feet, with red spot fires, assisted by flares dropped from

other Lancasters, between zero and zero + 10. Cheshire was then to estimate the accuracy of the marking and issue instructions to the bomber force. If no instruction was issued at all the aircraft were to aim at the second TI dropped by the Mosquitos or, failing that the third TI.

Bristillerie
3 Mosquitos, 29 Stirlings
Bombload – 114.9 tons high explosive, 500 lb bombs.

Zero hour – 2115 hours
3 Mosquitos to run in at the aiming point at zero, zero + 10 and zero + 20, marking with 2 red spot fires. The main force were to aim their loads at the centre of all visible red spot fires. If no markers were visible then the main force were to orbit and come in again.

Ailly-le-Haut-Clocher
3 Mosquitos, 30 Stirlings
Bombload – 143.3 tons high explosive, 500 lb bombs.

Zero hour – 2030 hours
(Same as Bristillerie)

Bois des Huit Rues
3 Mosquitos, 30 Stirlings
Bombload – 156.7 tons high explosive, 500 lb bombs.

Zero hour – 1945 hours
(Same as Bristillerie)

The method of marking the target on the Domart-en-Ponthieu raid clearly takes into account the suggestion made by Air Marshal Bottomley in his letter to Harris (previously quoted). One of the Mosquitos on the raid to Domart-en-Ponthieu experienced an Oboe failure and was unable to mark the target. The other two, experiencing good visibility over the target with no cloud, managed to release their green TI and Wing Commander Cheshire then looked to place his red spot fires. On the bomb run some flares burst in front of the nose of his aircraft. The bomb aimer then had to drop the markers in a salvo as opposed to a stick in order to prevent an overshoot. Cheshire then circled, reporting to the main force that the markers were in the north-east corner of the woods in the target area. Whilst over the target Cheshire became aware of prowling hostile fighters attempting to reach the bomber force; only one got within five miles, however, and the bombers avoided combat. All the main force aircraft bombed between z+25 and z+40. Day reconnaissance of the target area would later indicate to the interpreters that a successful attack had occurred with the target area well cratered and two of the skis, one building and the launch point damaged.

At Bristillerie only two of the three Mosquitos marked the target, one having returned early. The Stirlings bombed the first markers down, amidst fairly intense flak and an estimated 15 to 20 searchlights. Every one of the Stirlings managed to avoid any serious damage and returned safely to England. However one Stirling was badly damaged soon after take-off in a collision with another aircraft. A plot of the night photographs of 13 aircraft suggested that the bombing was scattered; 10 of them grouped 300 to 1,500 yards to the east and south-east of the aiming point.

All three Mosquitos on the raid to Ailly-le-Haut-Clocher dropped their markers (at z-1, z+8 and z+19½), but the second Mosquito experienced problems with interference and received the Oboe release signal one second late. Such a small amount of time would be relatively inconsequential if this were an area bombing attack. This attack however, required accuracy and one second could place a marker hundreds of yards from the aiming point. The target was attacked by 28 of the Stirlings, with 24 of them bombing on the first set of markers. A plot of night photographs from 19 aircraft suggested scattered bombing, with 15 in a group 500 to 1,600 yards north-east of the aiming point. The attacking force experienced no opposition, and all returned although one was damaged by a bomb from another aircraft and another collided with a Stirling that was on the Bristillerie raid.

The three Mosquitos on the raid to Bois des Huit Rues dropped markers at z-½, z+12 and z+26, with 27 of the 30 Stirlings aiming at the first set. In the follow-up analysis of the raid it was possible to plot 8 of the sticks of bombs; one ran across the middle of the target, three were near the edges of the target area and the other four were each a mile away. There was no opposition over the target and all the aircraft returned to base, five of them having some flak damage sustained on the routes in and out of the target. Day reconnaissance on the raid to Bois des Huit Rues, as with Bristillerie and Ailly-le-Haut-Clocher was not obtained until further raids had been carried out. It would seem from initial raid analysis, however, that using visual identification to mark the target with prior Oboe marking to identify the approximate location, had been successful.

On the night of 25/26 January a total of 76 aircraft were despatched in four forces to attack ski sites. Bristillerie, Ailly-le-Haut-Clocher and Bois des Huit Rues once more received the attentions of Bomber Command as all three were attacked by forces of Stirlings and Mosquitos. At Bristillerie and Ailly-le-Haut-Clocher the Stirling forces of 17 and 20 aircraft respectively bombed the Mosquito markers. At Bois des Huit Rues, seven of the 19 Stirlings abandoned their task after failing to see any TI but the other 12 did manage to release their bomb loads. The other target for the night, attacked by 3 Mosquitos and 12 Lancasters (from 617 Squadron, carrying a load of 500 lb and 1,000 lb bombs), was Freval where the deputy leader, following up the initial Mosquito marking, accurately placed his red spot fires, two within 50 yards of the aiming point and another within 100 yards. These were then bombed on by the main Lancaster force. In an effort to cause additional disruption to any repair attempts at Freval, three of the bombers carried six delayed-action bombs (6-hour) each.

Reconnaissance of all four targets covered a number of raids. At Bristillerie (covering raids between 21 January and 3 February) there was no fresh damage although there were craters in the target area. At Ailly-le-Haut-Clocher the target was photographed on 3 and 5 February (covering all raids on that target to date). One ski had a direct hit and two near misses, another was surrounded by craters and had its roof stripped. There was a near miss on the launching point and some of the roads in the area were also hit. Photographic cover on 30 January at Bois des Huit Rues (covering raids from 14 January) revealed many craters in the target area with one direct hit on a ski. At Freval photographs (covering raids from 14 January to 4 February) revealed seven craters in the target area and four others blocking approach roads.

The raids on 25/26 January completed Bomber Command's initial phase of using heavy bombers to attack the flying bomb targets. Since the opening of the flying bomb counter-offensive, Bomber Command had attacked six sites, conducting 479 sorties (65 by 617 Squadron Lancasters, 16 by Halifaxes, 82 by Mosquitos and 316 by Stirlings) dropping approximately 1,850 tons of explosives. The results of the raids, in terms of damage to the sites, had been varied, no damage at Flixecourt, Bristillerie and Bonnetot, some damage at Freval, one ski damaged at Bois des Huits Rues and one ski destroyed and one damaged at Ailly-le-Haut-Clocher[31]. With regard to the testing of new styles of bombing the experiment was giving some reward in terms of operational data. It was also highlighting the limitations of the precision bombing of small targets with Oboe and providing opportunity for 617 Squadron to develop its low level marking technique.

The attacks on the flying bomb sites had resulted in a partial success. The French civilians living near the ski sites observed this partial success first hand. One example of the experiences for the local French civilians came at Bonnetot, attacked by a small force of Halifaxes and Mosquitos on the night of 14/15 January. It had been a clear evening and families had just finished their dinner when they heard the hum of aircraft approaching. This was something to which they were becoming accustomed. For many months now they had heard, on numerous nights at around the same time, the Allied bombers heading east, then in the early hours of the next morning returning towards England. This night appeared no different, the hum of the bombers also indicating that they were at a considerable altitude. Suddenly the sky above Bonnetot was lit by the Pathfinder markers and then the whole area around Bonnetot shook with the following explosions. As we have already noted, the plot of night photographs from those bombers who were able to take them showed quite a spread of bombing. The farm at Bonnetot was hit, and in one of the cattle sheds a number of cows were killed. Produce stored in one of the barns was burnt. One of the farm's larger buildings was flattened. A line of beech trees bordering the farm became uprooted. All across the area windows broke. However no bombs fell on the flying bomb construction works. Miraculously there were no civilian casualties.

As we have seen, the poor accuracy of the bomber weaponry relevant to the small target areas was a feature of most of the bombing raids conducted against flying bomb targets thus far. The harrowing experience of the local people living near the ski site at Bonnetot had been mirrored by French civilians all over areas where ski sites were being constructed. Many French people still had these terrors to come.

On 17 February 1944 Bomber Command received a new Air Ministry directive, backed by the Combined Chiefs of Staff. Part of this directive stated that 'Operations under all means available will be taken to neutralise threats developing under Crossbow.'[32]

With operation Overlord, the Allied Invasion of Normandy, nearing, a further directive was issued to Bomber Command in April 1944, giving very general requirements. Basically it provided for a continuation of the Pointblank directive and a focus on the disruption of the enemy rail transportation and communication system. Included was a paragraph relative to Crossbow placing responsibility for countering the threat with the Air Commander-in-Chief, AEAF, Air Marshal Sir Trafford Leigh-Mallory, who could when required call on the strategic air forces through the Deputy Supreme Allied Commander, Marshal of the Royal Air Force, Sir Arthur Tedder.[33]

However, for the next few months, Bomber Command conducted only small attacks against German secret weapon sites and the only aircraft used were Mosquitos. The large site at Sottevast (a rocket site) was detailed for attack seven times with 14 Mosquito sorties conducted. La Glacerie was detailed for attack twice with four Mosquito sorties flown and Wissant (a rocket site) was attacked once by two Mosquitos. Four raids were carried out by Bomber Command Mosquitos on the flying bomb site at Herbouville. The first raid took place on the night of 27/28 January. Of the nine Mosquitos sent on the raid, all to use Oboe, only seven made successfully controlled runs, the other two aircraft aborted their attacks. Whilst reconnaissance did show a number of craters near the aiming point there was no damage deemed important. Two nights later another ten Oboe Mosquitos were sent, all making successfully controlled runs. Herbouville was next attacked by a Bomber Command Mosquito on the night of 19/20 February but an Oboe failure resulted in the crew having to use dead reckoning. Two nights later two more Mosquitos were sent but again there was Oboe failure resulting in one having to bomb on dead reckoning, the other by using a Gee fix.

Following the attacks against ski sites on the night of 25/26 January 1944, the heavy bombers of Bomber Command were not used in continuing the attack on flying bomb targets in northern France until after the Allies had initiated the invasion of Normandy in June 1944. The American heavies and the 2nd Tactical Air Force would conduct the vast majority of Crossbow operations between February and the middle of June. Initially Sir Arthur Harris was able to maintain his focus, deploying his bomber force in the Battle of Berlin. As D-Day approached however his force would be called on to support the invasion preparations, benefiting from the lessons learnt from the attacks on the ski sites in December 1943 and January 1944.

CHAPTER 4

A NEW THREAT

On 1 December 1943 Hitler had authorised that the LXV Armee Korps, under Lieutenant-General Erich Heinemann, was to command all secret weapons formations in the planned attack on England. Soon after Heinemann took up his position he toured the flying bomb launching sites in the north of France. He quickly found out that local French labour had been used in the construction of sites, security at sites had been minimal and locals were talking freely about the sites themselves. The fact that Wachtel's Regiment had been sent to northern France months before there was any prospect of actually launching the flying bomb offensive, had made security problematic. Measures to tighten security were put in place and severe punishment was handed out to anyone failing to meet the required standards. In February 1943 a Leutnant Busse from No.1 *Batterie* of *I Abteilung*, living with a French family, had made the mistake of leaving some classified drawings lying around in his room. He received a court martial for the security breach and the court passed the death sentence. On 7 January 1944 No.5 *Batterie* of *II Abteilung* recovered a carrier pigeon that had been dropped from an Allied aircraft. The pigeon was carrying propaganda literature requesting help from the local French civilians (included in the small package was a pencil and a bag of corn).

Heinemann also felt that the sites were far too elaborate and could easily be seen from reconnaissance aircraft and hence become bombing targets. He concluded that there would need to be a major change and that the ski sites should be replaced by much simpler versions, later to be called modified sites by Allied Intelligence. During January *Abteilungen* of Flakregiment 155(W) were asked, as a result of the heavy air attacks, to look for new sites which would accommodate a simpler construction than at the ski sites. Heinemann also did not have much faith in the large bunkers that were under construction (Siracourt and Lottinghem) but decided to persevere with them. Without doubt the bombing conducted by the Allies against the ski sites in December 1943 had been the major factor in Heinemann deciding to make major changes to the flying bombs' launching organisation. He did also have the flexibility to make this change owing to the fact that the flying bomb offensive was unlikely to take place as early as had at first been anticipated. German industry was falling way behind on flying bomb production, partly owing to technical problems and skilled labour shortages and partly because of Allied bombing raids on German industry, such as the Kassel raids of the previous October.

Whilst the bombing of the sites in northern France had in fact caused little damage with regard to the massive weight of bombs used against the sites, it had resulted in one indirect yet very significant problem for the German construction plans. On 7 January 1944 *Abteilungen* detailed for firing responsibilities reported on the bombing attacks:

> *I Abteilung:* Progress in construction work is being impeded by the behaviour of the foreign workers. At present only 2% of the original labour force is working on the sites, as at the slightest suspicion of the sound of an aircraft they throw up work and leave the site. Productive work is impossible in such circumstances.
>
> *III Abteilung:* With the exception of site No.51, where there were no workmen during the night raid [4/5 January], all the sites attacked have been deserted by the workmen. They did not return later. The workers are very nervous and even in the sites not attacked leave their work at the sound of an engine and often do not return for hours. There is scarcely any work going on. If the enemy is not prevented from carrying out these large scale raids against the remaining 50% of the sites within 14 days all sites will have been attacked and at least heavily damaged, as well as deserted by workers. This will mean complete stoppage of work.[34]

The *II Abteilung* made recommendations that defences be improved, temporary accommodation be arranged away from the sites and a new labour force be called in with German foremen to 'control foreign workers and not take flight with them at the sound of aircraft engines'. To further compound the problem of keeping workers on site, the Allies had also been using a proportion of delayed-action bombs on some raids.

Heinemann's change to the launch site plan was made. New sites were constructed, with buildings kept to the bare minimum. There were no curved buildings (skis), and at most sites only the foundations of the square building and launch platform were laid (at a few the square building was completed but heavily camouflaged). The final completion of constructing the launch sites would take place with pre-fabricated parts closer to the start of operations. Work was still carried out on the original ski sites to act as a bluff to any Allied reconnaissance. Indeed on a number of ski sites the Germans brought in foreign labour, many of them Russian prisoners, to carry on the construction work of the flying bomb launch sites. George Vergne, a local French civilian, had been working on the sites:

> I worked with a number of Belgian volunteers and 'recruits' under the TODT organisation [German controlled labour force] and we were guarded/protected by German soldiers. We had to endure attacks by low flying British aircraft, but fortunately there was little damage. However a neighbouring site . . . was

bombed many times during the day by American aircraft. We could see the bombs being dropped and the ground would shake with the explosions. I remember that after one of the raids on a neighbouring site, German soldiers arrived . . . and distributed cigarettes and alcohol, I believe to boost the morale among the workers. Our site was eventually abandoned in February/March 1944 and our identity papers, which had been taken from us in 1943, were returned. Once back in civilian life I went to work at Quincampoix, which was about 1.5 kilometres from a V1 site called La Mare-aux-Loup. I remember it was impossible to approach the site during working hours. However I learnt that construction work on the site was completed by Russian prisoners. I remember seeing them in their striped uniforms being driven back to Rouen in trucks.

By the end of 1943 the LXV Armee Korps expected a planned production programme for factories in Germany of 1,400 flying bombs for January 1944, 1,200 for February, 1,240 for March, 3,200 for April, 4,000 for May and an increase to 8,000 per month from June to September. Wachtel believed that his units would be in a state of readiness from 1 March 1944, fully expectant that the manufacture of the catapults would progress well.

As a result of the change over to modified sites it was felt that the storage and supply organisation should be adapted. Further storage facilities were developed. Two of these were in existing caves, one at Nucourt, north-east of Paris, the other at St Leu d'Esserent, north of Paris in the valley formed by the river Oise. A third storage facility was the railway tunnel at Rilly-la-Montagne, just south of Reims. These storage facilities were clearly chosen with an Allied bombing counter-offensive in mind, the flying bombs being placed well underground.

During February 1944 the Allied bombers continued to rain down bombs on the ski sites. The diary of Flakregiment 155(W) recorded 392 attacks against sites, involving about 7,000 aircraft dropping about 19,000 bombs. The regiment did also feel that the amount of damage caused by the bombing was in no way commensurate with the weight of the attack. The diary recorded that by 24 February 9 sites were damaged beyond repair, 29 were seriously damaged, 20 fairly seriously, 20 slightly and 25 sites that had been attacked had been completely undamaged. In addition to the site damage the diary also recorded personnel casualties. The regiment had lost six men killed and 9 men wounded; from the Guard regiment, TODT Organisation and German and foreign workers, 155 people had been killed and 121 injured (the majority being foreign workers). By this time the local civilian population was beginning to evacuate the areas around the construction sites. They blamed Wachtel's troops for the air attacks in their areas around their villages and hostility against the German units steadily increased as the air raids continued.

During March 1944 the Allied Tactical Air Forces and the American heavy bombers continued to target the launch sites, with, they felt, some success; the Crossbow Counter-measures Progress Report covered raids up to the 1 April, recording 65 sites as category A damaged, 20 category B and 11 category C. The diary of Flakregiment 155(W), whilst certainly not recording similar damage levels, does indicate that there had been considerable damage: 9 sites completely destroyed, 35 seriously damaged, 29 with medium damage, 20 slightly damaged, 10 undamaged and 4 not attacked. However at this stage of the campaign it was not the Allied bombing that was delaying the start of the German flying bomb offensive; that owed more to German industry's technical and manpower problems. Earlier German hopes for a mid February/early March start had faded. Wachtel's troops had been ready, once more, to launch attacks in March subject to the production and construction of the modified sites. Milch was keen to start at the end of April but the supply of flying bombs fell way below any previous expectations. The offensive was, once more, put back. The German High Command was now anticipating that the Allies would soon be launching an invasion from England, across the Channel, but there was doubt as to exactly where. It was now hoped that the flying bomb offensive could be initiated on the day of the Allied invasion. But the Allies were able to start the greatest military invasion of all time without the disruption from any pilotless aircraft.

The approach of the Allied invasion and the demands it was to place on the resources of Bomber Command proved most timely with regard to the attrition of the RAF's heavy bombers. The German nightfighter force was proving a considerable adversary. The nightfighter tactics of 'Wild Boar' (engaging bombers over targets) and 'Tame Boar' (where the fighters sought out the bomber streams with the aid of radar and broadcasted radio control) could, on certain occasions, inflict considerable loss rates on Bomber Command. Indeed since the beginning of 1944, the bomber forces sent to Germany had on many raids, suffered massive losses. On the night of 19/20 February 1944, 78 bombers and crew did not return from the attack on Leipzig. On the Berlin raid of 24/25 March 1944, 72 bombers and crews were lost. The night of 30/31 March 1944 is recognised as the high point for the German nightfighter action when 96 Bomber Command crews and their aircraft failed to return from the raid to Nuremberg.

Now, however, the bombing priorities were to change. The Allied commanders had a more pressing need for the RAF's heavy bombers, the 'Transportation Plan'. The French and Belgian transportation system, the railways and railyards were targeted. The plan was to seriously disrupt the system, isolate the planned Allied invasion area and seriously hinder any German troop movements and reinforcements. These railyards were small targets for a force that had spent the last two years conducting an area offensive where degrees of accuracy were often measured in miles. They were of course larger than the flying bomb launch sites and the data obtained from Bomber Command attacks on the flying bomb targets assisted the operational planners of these new raids. The French and Belgian rail targets were also politically sensitive, often situated within civilian population areas. Attack accuracy was of paramount importance and there was lengthy political discussion. However it was eventually decided that French and

Belgian casualties, deemed inevitable, would be an unfortunate necessity in achieving invasion objectives, but the politicians maintained that the casualties from friendly fire had to be minimised.

On the night of 5 April 1944, 144 Lancasters and 1 Mosquito from 5 Group, commanded by Air Vice-Marshal The Hon. R.A. Cochrane CB, CBE, AFC, attacked the aircraft factory at Toulouse, France. This particular raid is worthy of note in relation to our story as it had a significant impact on the methodology that Bomber Command would use in subsequent attacks on flying bomb and pre-invasion targets. The raid to Toulouse involved low level marking by a Mosquito piloted by Wing Commander Cheshire, backed up by two Lancasters and then bombed by the main force. The whole operation was under the guidance of radio telephone communication from the Mosquito. The raid was very successful, as virtually complete destruction was achieved in the target area. The following day Bomber Command effectively made 5 Group an independent force. Two squadrons, 83 and 97, were transferred from Air Vice-Marshal Bennett's 8 Group to 5 Group to assist in the marking of targets. Mosquito squadron 627 was similarly re-assigned from 8 Group to support the expected low level marking requirement.

This was not at all popular with Bennett. Following the Peenemünde raid in August 1943, Cochrane had been critical of the Pathfinder marking and the two group commanders argued about the relative merits of time/distance running (Cochrane) and direct marking (Bennett). By February 1944 Cheshire had convinced Cochrane of the value of his experiments with low level marking, who in turn promoted this methodology with Harris. Bennett was not in agreement but Harris decided to side with Cochrane, ordering the transfer of the squadrons. Throughout the preparations for the Normandy Invasion antagonism between 5 Group and 8 Group over their target-marking methods remained. However as the demands of not only marking invasion targets but Crossbow targets as well, increased, both groups' methods were used.

During the pre-invasion period 5 Group would develop its technique. Offset marking was developed whereby main force crews aimed at spot fire markers deliberately placed away from the real aiming point. The main force crews took aim using 'false' distance, direction and wind speed measures broadcast to them once the markers' relation to the aiming point had been measured. In this way the marking would not become obscured as the air filled with smoke and dust while the raid progressed. Early raids using these techniques gave excellent results. But there was one notable defect in the method, which involved the time that would be required over a target if there were difficulties in marking. It was a difficulty that would soon be exposed.

One raid during the period prior to operation Overlord did have an impact on the German secret weapon programme, mainly on rocket development. Prompted by the Air Ministry, Bomber Command attacked Friedrichshafen on the night of 27/28 April. The town was noted as having factories making tank components, and the Zeppelin and the Maybach works had been reported as being concerned with the manufacture of components for secret weapons. In addition just less than four miles to the north-west of Friedrichshafen lay Ober Raderach, where hydrogen peroxide was believed to be manufactured. Photographic reconnaissance of Ober Raderach had identified three installations resembling in plan an installation at Peenemünde. A force of 322 Lancasters and 1 Mosquito was despatched on this risky raid. The town was deep in southern Germany and the disaster of the Nuremberg raid would still be fresh in the minds of the Bomber Command planners. However various diversionary ruses appeared to work and it was not until the force had reached the town that the major engagement with the defending nightfighters occurred. The raid proved a major success in terms of damage caused, but at a cost of 18 Lancasters and crews. Reconnaissance photographs would later show severe damage to the factories associated with German secret weapons. In addition Bomber Command would later assess two thirds of the town's built-up area as devastated, with major damage to factories.

Between February and May 1944 the Bomber Command heavies had not been called upon to attack the Crossbow sites in northern France. Whilst raids were still being conducted by the Tactical Air Forces and the United States heavy bombers, the Allies were satisfied with the observed rates of destruction. However there was another ominous development, although it was deemed to be of little immediate risk. In February 1944 Allied agents in France passed on information concerning new types of launching sites, though it was not until April that photographic reconnaissance identified one at Belhamelin in the Cherbourg peninsula. The Crossbow Counter-measures Progress Report for the end of April noted:

A structure similar to the 'ski' site launching points, has been photographed . . . It is orientated on Bristol. Near it is a heavily camouflaged building oriented on the same line as the first structure, in the same manner as the square non-magnetic buildings at ski sites. Other buildings in the vicinity are so heavily camouflaged that accurate measurements are impossible. No 'ski's' are visible.[35]

Further examination and reconnaissance led to Allied Intelligence making the following statement about these new launch sites in the Crossbow Counter-measures Progress Report to 13 May:

Possibly realising that the rate of construction of 'ski' sites was not keeping pace with the destruction caused by our bombing, the Germans have embarked on a new building programme of pilotless aircraft sites. So far 20 have been photographed; 11 in the Cherbourg peninsula and 9 in the Pas de Calais.

The characteristics of these sites, most of which are in an early stage of construction appear to be:

They consist essentially of a launching point and a 'square' building. There are signs of other buildings at some sites but it is too early to establish any standard form.

They are all near existing roads.

Careful attention is paid to camouflage.

There are no signs yet of water or power supply.

Individual flak protection has not yet been provided.

By comparison with earlier photographs it appears that the enemy began the new programme in early April. The final form of the new site is not yet certain and it is therefore difficult to estimate the rate of construction. Assuming however that the launching point and the square building take longer to construct than any other building that may appear, it seems that the shortest possible time for completion of a site would be about 6 weeks.[36]

This report also detailed that since the start of the bombing operations 22,564 tons had been dropped on 96 ski sites: 76 were classed as category A damaged, 14 as category B (with 2 of these possibly category A) and 3 category C (with 1 of these possibly category A). This assessment of damage made the Allies most optimistic toward the success of their bombing efforts to date. The Bomber Command Intelligence digest dated 15 May 1944 gives a clear example of this optimism:

The most immediate part of the problem was to discover what kind of bombing could produce the most effective counter measure. Every kind of aircraft in the Anglo-American Commands was tried, with an even wider variety of bombs. The results were photographed, the tonnages and sorties measured against both the evidence of destructive result and the time required for the reconstruction which the Germans so feverishly continued.

The fact of reconstruction itself, which progressed with remarkable tenacity, was evident proof of the Germans' determination, even in the face of an overwhelming scale of bombing, to continue their development of the weapon . . . Although nine months have passed since the first site was identified, the Germans have not yet launched a single one of these weapons against us. That, in fact, is exactly the purpose for which the bombing was begun.[37]

Now there was a new set of potential targets for the Allied planners to worry about, the modified sites. However Allied Intelligence anticipated a month or more would be needed by the Germans to 'finish' them. Also, because of the difficulty of bombing these small targets – one raid was carried out on 27 May by 24 single-engined Hawker Typhoon bombers without success – and the optimism generated by the believed progress against the ski sites, resulted in these new sites not being deemed a bombing priority. Flakregiment 155(W) thus continued to prepare for the launch of attacks against England and was even appreciative of the fact that they now had a better launching system than previously planned, owing to the limitations of the original launch structure as highlighted by the Allied bombing. An entry in the diary of Flakregiment 155(W) on 2 June stated:

> One would even be justified in saying that these attacks on the regiment's sites have furnished valuable experience for future operations. Although today numerous sites in site system No.1 [ski sites] are destroyed, they served a two fold purpose:
> By making it clear that a modified site construction plan was necessary and that technical equipping of the A-sites had to be put on a mobile basis, to take into account a swift change of site.
> By providing a very good camouflage for the new site system, which in contrast to system No.1 has not been discovered by the enemy, and at any rate up to 26 May has not been attacked.[38]

The appearance of the modified sites also gave Allied Intelligence problems with regard the purpose of eight supposed supply sites. The Allies had been following construction at the sites at Valognes, Domleger, Neuville-aux-Bois/Oisemont, St Martin l'Hortier, Beauvoir, Renescure, Sautrecourt and Biennais, but they were clearly not to be used for launching; the nature of the building suggested they were part of the flying bomb supply line from factory to launch site. A decision was made to conduct experimental attacks on the supply site at Beauvoir, partly to see what the German reaction would be. American bombers obliged on 29 May when 67 Marauders dropped 112.7 tons and on 2 June when 65 Liberators dropped 167 tons, but the experiment failed to produce any conclusive results. The Crossbow Counter-measures Progress Report to 10 June[39] concluded that the exact purpose of the supply sites remained obscure, with the American attacks not causing sufficient damage to indicate what the buildings were there for and what they contained. Reconnaissance did show that the railway spur leading to Beauvoir had been cut in eight places in the attack on 29 May but there had been no repairs by 4 June. Neither were there any repairs to three slightly damaged buildings.

Further analysis by Allied Intelligence showed that there were considerable flak defences for the supply sites. As at 23 May the following flak defences had been identified as follows:[40]

Supply Site	Heavy Guns	Light Guns
Valognes	28	7
Domleger	16 and 4 under construction	34
Neuville-aux-Bois/Oisemont	19	17
St Martin l'Hortier	18 and 12 under construction	18
Beauvoir	17 and 4 under construction	38
Renescure	11	11
Sautrecourt	26 and 10 under construction	16
Biennais	26 and 6 under construction	20

This was a considerable defensive commitment by the Germans and one that influenced Allied Intelligence's future counter-attack targeting decisions.

CHAPTER 5

VERGELTUNG, REPRISAL

On 16 April 1944, Josef Goebbels, the German Reich's propaganda minister, wrote an article in *Das Reich*, entitled *Das Leben geht weiter* (Life Goes On). With Allied air attacks devastating areas of German cities, he assured his countrymen that Germany could take the pounding and still maintain its war effort. He also hinted that the Allies would soon have their own defence to worry about.

> They are using air terror solely to terrorise. They cannot understand that they will never reach their goal. They do not see that they are driving our people together, not apart. It will take drastic measures to persuade them that in the long run the air war is neither materially nor morally productive. The discussion is only beginning, but it will not be long before we are forced to give the enemy far more persuasive proof. The British people above all will be forced to prove whether they in the fifth year of the war possess the same steadfastness as the German people. The worst of this phase of the war is behind us. England is facing it. We did not break. The British must still endure the trial.[41]

On 16 May 1944 and with the Allied invasion considered as imminent, Hitler issued his orders for the start of the flying bomb attack on England. Wachtel's troops were certainly ready and the attack was to be coordinated with a bomber operation and an artillery bombardment across the Channel. All was scheduled for mid June, with the exact timing of the launch to be decided by Field Marshal Gerd von Rundstedt, Commander-in-Chief West. Subsequent to the first launchings a continual night bombardment was also to be made. In preparation for the start, Wachtel ordered his troops to abandon the ski sites and take up position at the modified sites. Now it was a matter of waiting for the final launch order.

> *Flakregiment 155(W) diary:* . . . the past few months have seen a bitter unremitting struggle with an enemy who enjoys the advantage of air supremacy and believes even today that he can stop the 'rocket guns' coming into operation. In the brief interval between now and X-day the battle will enter its decisive phase. The question is SHALL WE GET IN FIRST or WILL

THE ENEMY BE ACROSS THE CHANNEL BEFOREHAND. Every man in the regiment is firmly convinced that *Maikäfer* [the new codename for the flying bomb] will be on the other side before Sammy and Tommy are over here.[42]

On the morning of 6 June 1944 Sammy and Tommy arrived on the Normandy beaches. The Allied Armies' fortunes varied on each of the five invasion beaches, but by the end of the first day beachheads had been established, although not to the extent hoped for. On the evening of the first day of the Allied invasion of Normandy, Wachtel received a signal from LXV Armee Korps containing the word *Rumpelkammer* (translated as lumber room), which was the codename for Wachtel's troops to start the process of transporting the launching catapults (ramps) to the modified launch sites. The regiment was given six days to complete the moves, with the assembly of the launch sites completed by the evening of 12 June.

Over the next few days there was feverish activity as equipment was brought up and sites prepared. The operation was, however, coming up against a major obstacle. The French transport system was still being subjected to the attentions of Allied air attacks, as it had been in the months prior to the invasion. Anything that moved was being shot at. Trains and rail lines were particular targets for attack. On 8 June an Allied attack by six Thunderbolts had a serious impact on the Germans' preparations. Near Beauvais, a train pulling 22 trucks containing low octane fuel for the flying bombs was attacked. There was a massive explosion as 15 of the trucks went up and 270,000 litres of the fuel burned. On the same day a train carrying some flying bombs was attacked and a number destroyed. The transporting of the equipment, missiles and fuel to the modified sites was being seriously disrupted.

On 11 June none of the launching sites was ready, but Wachtel was still ordered to launch the weapons on the set date. The regiment was required to launch the flying bomb offensive against London, in co-operation with an attack from aircraft of *Fliegerkorps IX*, with two salvoes at 2340 hours and 0040 hours with harassing fire continuing up to 0445 hours. This order did not go down too well with the regiment, which was becoming concerned that the launch sites would not be ready in time. The regiment's diary recorded that 'in spite of everything it is not easy to dismiss the impression that the Korps order for operations looks very much like an armchair directive'. However Wachtel's troops applied themselves in the hope of being ready for the 12 June deadline. On 12 June the commanding officers of each *Abteilung* attended a regimental conference and Colonel Wachtel addressed his subordinates:

> After a long period of waiting, the day has at last arrived for our weapon to be employed on operations! I know that the months between your training and the beginning of assembly have been a hard testing time for you. Duties have been extremely heavy because of the variety of work to be done, and there has been no

sense of satisfaction because operations have been so long delayed.

Hence the order to begin assembling has been a great relief to us all! I myself have seen, at the unloading stations and in the sites, the endurance and devotion to duty with which you have set about bringing up and assembling your launchers and equipment, uninterrupted by day and night. I wish to express my gratitude and recognition to all officers, NCOs and men.

Now at last your patience and labour will have their just reward. The order for operations had been given.

We approach these operations with complete confidence in our weapon. This will undoubtedly be arduous, at a time when our enemies in the West are making every effort to get a foothold on the continent. Our operations are therefore all the more important, and when we fire our missiles today and in the future we shall be thinking of the misery and damage which the enemy has caused us with his terror bombing.

Men! The Führer and our homeland are watching us in the expectation that our operations will be rewarded with complete success. We shall do our duty with unyielding determination but in a joyful spirit of self-sacrifice. But at the beginning of our operations our thoughts go out in love and loyalty to our German homeland. Long live our German people. Long live our German Fatherland. Long live our Führer.[43]

The preparation activity and air of anticipation was clear to French civilians in the areas around the launch sites. On 12 June Gerard Dubord, a student, was returning to his home village of St Hellier in the La Varenne valley, approximately 15 miles south-east of Dieppe, after completing his end of year exams in Paris:

The journey home was a little difficult because there were no buses, trains or cars as Allied aircraft monitored everything on the roads and it was impossible to distinguish between civilian and military traffic. However I arrived home late that night as the curfew was in force. I discovered that a number of German military transports assisted by Russian prisoners were stationed in the village . . . they were loaded with supplies (food and ammunition). The vehicles were hidden under the trees and I remember thinking there was an atmosphere of war about the place. Allied aircraft circled over the area both singly and in groups.

Despite the German enthusiasm for the long awaited start of the flying bomb offensive, problems continued. An Allied air attack on the Beauvais-Tille airfield damaged 60% of the He111 bombers detailed to bomb in support of the flying bomb attacks. Reports continued to come in detailing problems at the launch sites. From the 64 launch sites supposed to be ready to launch the attack, only 18 had fired trial shots, and safety equipment was absent from most sites. Eventually the large-scale attack, originally planned, was considerably downsized, and despite 55 launchers being ready for firing only ten flying bombs were eventually launched: four crashed on take-off, three of these exploding and one a dud. The regiment also lost two of its personnel at one launch site; both men were asphyxiated when they used an emergency power unit. For the next few days various high-ranking officials inquired into the failure of the opening offensive and the regiment continually laid blame on LXV Armee Korps. Heinemann had been present at the regiment's headquarters during the first night debacle and could back up the problems experienced by the launch units. Eventually it was agreed that the main problem had been the disruption to the supply routes caused by Allied air action.

Across the Channel, early on the morning of 13 June, 33 German artillery shells reached the area around Maidstone and Folkestone. At 4 a.m. the artillery bombardment ceased. At 4.18 a.m. the first flying bomb crashed near Gravesend, the second at Cuckfield, Sussex, the third at Bethnal Green, killing six people, seriously injuring 30 and rendering 200 people homeless. The fourth came to earth at Platt near Sevenoaks. The two remaining launched flying bombs did not reach the English coast. The German secret weapon programme was no longer just a threat. It had arrived, it had claimed civilian casualties and extensive defensive counter-measures were initiated.

Some of these counter-measures also posed a threat to Allied airmen. Sergeant Fred Fossett, a bomb aimer with 463 (RAAF) Squadron, took part in a raid to France on the night of 12/13 June:

> It was not long after D-Day, and our troops were consolidating their hold on the narrow stretch of land in Normandy. To reduce the risk of enemy troops and munitions being sent up from southern France, a force of bombers had been dispatched to attack the marshalling yards in these areas, also bombing in close support of our own troops. For the return trip, we had been routed over Portsmouth, and at briefing the wisdom of this had been queried, for the RAF aircrew were of the opinion that the Royal Navy shoot first, then identify the aircraft from the wreckage. We were assured that the Navy had been informed of the time and route of our return, therefore we should have no difficulty.
>
> Having successfully left our bombs safely behind in France, we were relieved to be able to make out the outline of the English coast on our return, knowing that any searchlights would be trying to assist us, and that the risks of fighter attacks would be minimal. Our elation was soon dispelled when we were met with a barrage of anti-aircraft fire. Soon every aircraft was firing off the colours of the day, just adding to the general fireworks display, but it seemed to have little effect, so cursing the Royal Navy, we continued on our way, complaining bitterly when we were interrogated back at base. Later on the radio, we

heard that the Germans had sent a number of unmanned aircraft over the south coast of England; again we thought 'What idiots! That was us returning!', but we soon learned that there were indeed unmanned aircraft. The difference is that they would probably be flying at a thousand feet or so, whilst we would be at five to eight thousand feet, and a damned sight slower.

By 15 June Wachtel's launching problems had been dealt with and his regiment was ready to start the attack on England in earnest. Across northern France Wachtel's firing *Abteilungen* initiated the launching process. The parts of the flying bomb had arrived at the launch sites by lorry and following assembly, checks and the setting of the compasses in the square building, the flying bombs were taken to the launch ramps and lowered on to the launching cradles on the 156-foot ramps. When all was ready and personnel safely positioned, calcium permanganate and hydrogen peroxide were mixed in the combustion chamber at the base of the ramps, producing pressurised steam and oxygen. Simultaneously the Argus pulse-jets on the flying bombs were started up. The force from the expanding steam and oxygen combined with the pulse-jet's power until a restraining bolt sheered. The high pressured steam and gas drove dumb-bell shaped firing pistons up tubes in the centre of the ramps. The surface of the ramp had a small gap in the middle running its full length through which the firing piston connected to the flying bomb. As the piston accelerated up the ramp it drove along the flying bomb. At the end of the ramp the piston, the launching cradle and the flying bomb parted company, and the piston and cradle fell to earth, gouging the ground in front of the ramp. (This scarring would be visible to Allied reconnaissance and show them which launch sites had fired.) The flying bombs, their pulse-jets firing, flew off at about 250 mph carrying their 1,870 lb of high explosive.

At 1855 hours on 15 June all the firing *Abteilungen* were given the order that all launchers were to fire at London, in a salvo, at 23.18 hours (to hit London at 23.40 hours) and then to maintain continuous fire until 04.50 hours. In fact it was 23.16 hours when the first flying bomb was fired, part of the initial salvo of 27 missiles. The last missile of this second opening of the offensive was fired at 15.41 hours the next day. In total, up to noon on 16 June Wachtel's troops were able to launch 244 flying bombs, from 55 modified sites, of which 45 bombs crashed just after launching. Up until midnight on 16 June 155 of the flying bombs were seen by the English defences, 144 crossed the coast, and 73 reached Greater London.[44] Flakregiment 155(W) was proud of its achievement although things had not gone completely smoothly. One flying bomb crashed at Auppegate and killed ten French civilians and nine launch sites were wiped out by flying bombs exploding on ramps. However at that time the regiment's firing capacity, with regard to manpower, was from 64 launch sites so there was the capacity to make use of the reserve sites.

Some Bomber Command crews, although they did not know it at the time, witnessed the opening of the Germans' main flying bomb offensive.

Sergeant Jack Watson, a flight engineer in 156 Squadron, took part in the bombing raid to the Lens railway yards on the night of 15/16 June:

> The first sightings of the V1s we saw were some strange-looking lights coming in the opposite direction to us when we were flying over the south coast to take part in a raid, although we were unaware of what they were at the time.
> *Flying Officer John Dyer, navigator 54 Base:* They were aimed at the London area and a number of our aircraft [returning from France] were damaged by the flak from the London barrage. We ourselves took evasive action by turning east and got almost over the sea before turning north-west again to return to Coningsby.

Nor was it only RAF airmen who would now start witnessing the strange spectacle of the flying bombs. German nightfighter radio operator Walter Heidenreich, with the 6th *Staffel* of NJG2[45], recalls:

> We were on a mission between Paris and the Channel coast, when we had a strange experience. We were flying very low, perhaps only a hundred metres high, in a northerly direction. Only a few kilometres in front of us an exhaust light suddenly rose. Immediately, somewhat to the right, probably only a few hundred metres away, came a second light and hardly a minute later a third light came. They all had the same course, it may have been 330 degrees. We were surprised and accelerated. We came even nearer, but after a short time the three lights flew straight off. In the mess we discussed our encounter with those of other crews. As far as I can remember no one else had seen anything similar. Two days later the Wehrmacht reported that unmanned planes had been shot down. That was the mystery solved.

On 10 June 1944 the Air Ministry in London received information from a reliable source giving details of a goods train of 33 wagons, each 60 feet long, travelling through Ghent in Belgium towards France. Objects described as rockets were seen on the trains. The next day nine of the modified sites were photographed, with activity apparent at six of these. A link between the transportation of what were probably flying bombs and the making ready of the launch sites was made. On 12 June Air Vice-Marshal Frank Inglis, Assistant Chief of the Air Staff (Intelligence), brought these disclosures to the attention of the decision-makers and possible attacks on the supply sites became a focus. Following Wachtel's limited opening of the flying bomb offensive, and with the assumption that to take out the modified sites would require thousands of sorties, the recommendation was made to General Eisenhower, backed by the War Cabinet, to attack four of the supply sites and completed modified sites when the heavy bombers were not acting in support of Overlord. The United States Eighth Air Force began the attack on two of these sites between 13 and 15 June. Beauvoir was attacked twice; 112 tons were dropped by 50 Liberators on 14 June and 157 tons dropped by 59 Fortresses on 15 June. Domleger was attacked by 44 Liberators on 14 June, dropping 112 tons.

Following the main opening of the flying bomb attack, the Bomber Command counter-offensive began in earnest. Harris was asked to attack the four supply sites. On 16 June 1944, RAF bomber stations and ground crews in England prepared their aircraft and airmen. Whilst this was happening American Liberator forces attacked some of the supply sites; 43 Liberators attacked Domleger (112 tons), 44 attacked Sautrecourt (104 tons), 21 attacked Beauvoir (56 tons) and 48 attacked Renescure (108 tons). That night 405 Bomber Command aircraft were eventually despatched, with the purpose of knocking out, seriously damaging and disrupting the German flying bomb supply organisation.

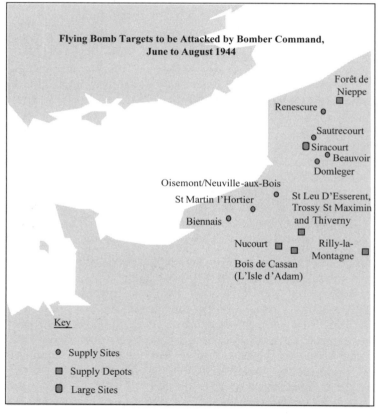

Flying Bomb Targets to be Attacked by Bomber Command, June to August 1944

Forêt de Nieppe

Renescure

Sautrecourt

Siracourt

Beauvoir

Domleger

Oisemont/Neuville-aux-Bois

St Martin l'Hortier

St Leu D'Esserent, Trossy St Maximin and Thiverny

Biennais

Nucourt

Rilly-la-Montagne

Bois de Cassan (L'Isle d'Adam)

Key

⊙ Supply Sites

▢ Supply Depots

◨ Large Sites

Supply Depot co-ords
Forêt de Nieppe 5040N 0230E
Bois de Cassan 4907N 0214E
St Leu d'Esserent 4914N 0226E
Nucourt 4910N 0151E
Rilly-la-Montagne 4908N 0401E

Large Site co-ords
Siracourt 5022N 0216E

Supply Site co-ords
Beauvoir 5014N 0217E
Renescure 5044N 0222E
Domleger 5007N 0205E
Sautrecourt 5025N 0217E
St Martin l'Hortier 4945N 0123E
Oisemont/Neuville-aux-Bois 4958N 0148E
Biennais 4938N 0110E

left: Flight Lieutenant Malcolm Buchanan DFC, RAAF. 18/19 July 1944 Buchanan piloted his 78 Squadron Halifax, damaged in a nightfighter attack, back to England. His skill was recognised with the DFC. Tragically he lost his life on 21 November 1944 when, returning from a raid on Sterkrade, his Halifax crashed beyond the runway at RAF Breighton with a total loss of life.

right: Flight Lieutenant Malcolm Buchanan DFC, RAAF (first left) and crew in front of their 78 Squadron Halifax.

Bottom left: The crew of Pilot Officer Ken Grantham DFM, wireless operator 35 Squadron. From left to right: Lieutenant Dawson Kornegay DFC, DFC (USA); Flight Sergeant Alan Wooller DFM; Flight Sergeant Bert Chapman DFM; Flight Sergeant Bill Wilcox DFM; Pilot Officer Ken Grantham DFM; Flight Lieutenant Chuck Prosser DFC and Flight Lieutenant George Williams DFC.

Bottom right: Flying Officer Ken Grantham DFM.

Top: The crew of Sergeant Peter Rowland.
From left to right: Flight Sergeant Alex Crisp; Sergeant
Jack Chamberlain; Flight Sergeant Felix Martin RAAF;
Flying Officer Gerry Tenduis; Sergeant Peter Rowland;
Sergeant Bob Graves and Pilot Officer Ted Lukey RNZAF.

Middle left: Damage to the Stirling of Sergeant Peter
Rowland, sustained on 17 July 1944.

Bottom right: Sergeant Peter Rowland, flight engineer,
149 Squadron.

p: Rear gunner Sergeant Fred Whitfield DFM, (middle)
th fellow 9 Squadron crew members.

Bottom: Rear gunner Sergeant Fred Whitfield DFM (left),
and crew mate Sergeant Frank Stebbings DFM (centre)
with their friend Sergeant Bobby Younger who was killed
on the raid to the railyards at Revigny on 18 July 1944.

Top left: Sergeant Fred Fossett, bomb aimer 463 (RAAF) Squadron.

Top right: Sergeant Bill Anderson, mid upper gunner 463 (RAAF) Squadron (crew mate of Fred Fossett), performing routine checks in JO-K PB290.

Middle left: Fred Fossett's pilot, Flying Officer Denholm DFC, RAAF, 463 (RAAF) Squadron, in JO-K PB290.

Middle right: 35 Squadron A-Apple taking off at Graveley for the attack on the flying bomb launch site at St Philibert Ferme.

Bottom right: Lieutenant Dawson Kornegay at Graveley, receiving his DFC, awarded for his skill on 2 July 1944, from Air Vice-Marshal Don Bennett.

op: 463 (RAAF) Squadron Lancaster JO-K PB290,
eing bombed up. Bombloads from this Lancaster were
leased by Fred Fossett on Bois de Cassan 2 August
944 and Trossy St Maximin 3 August 1944.

Bottom: 'A' Flight 75 (New Zealand) Squadron aircrew.
One of the first Bomber Command squadrons to attack a
flying bomb launch site on 16/17 December 1943. (Flight
Sergeant Ronnie Hunt, back row ninth from left.)

Top left: Damage caused by a flying bomb to the Guards Chapel, 18 June 1944. 121 people lost their lives and 68 were seriously injured. (Imperial War Museum HU 88469)

Top right: St Leu d'Esserent memorial to the victims of the Allied bombing during 1944.

Bottom left: A stretcher case being carried away from a building struck by a flying bomb, July 1944. (Imperial War Museum HU 88470)

Bottom right: Memorial in Nucourt to the civilians killed in 1944 by the Allied bombing.

Top left: Reconnaissance photograph of the St Leu
d'Esserent flying bomb storage caves.

Top right: Aerial photograph of the entrances (bottom
left) at the underground flying bomb storage depot at
St Leu d'Esserent taken after the Bomber Command raid
of 7/8 July 1944. (© Crown copyright 1944/MOD reproduced with
the permission of the Controller of HMSO)

Bottom left: Low level reconnaissance photograph (15
August 1944) showing the bombing devastation at one of
the entrances to the caves at the St Leu d'Esserent flying
bomb storage depot. (© Crown copyright 1944/MOD reproduced
with the permission of the Controller of HMSO)

Bottom right: Aerial photograph of one of the entrances
(bottom left) at the underground flying bomb storage
depot at St Leu d'Esserent taken after the Bomber
Command raid of 4/5 July 1944.

Top: Modern photograph showing a bomb damaged building at the preserved flying bomb 'ski' site at Val Ygot, Forêt d'Eawy, France.

Bottom: Flying bomb on the launch ramp aligned on London, at the preserved flying bomb ski site at Val Ygot.

Top: Flying bomb on the launch ramp at the preserved flying bomb ski site at Val Ygot. To the right is the concrete command post from where the launch sequence was initiated. In the background is the non-magnetic 'square' building where the flying bomb's directional compass was set.

Middle left: Oberst [Colonel] Max Wachtel. Commander of Flakregiment 155(W).

Middle right: Remains of the non-magnetic square building, where the flying bomb's directional compass was set at Val Ygot. Through the arch can be seen the launch command post and the launch ramp.

Bottom right: Pilot Officer Don Street DFC, 61 Squadron.

Top left: Flying bomb being loaded onto the base of a launch ramp.

Top right: Flying bomb in flight shortly after launching.

Middle right: Flying bomb at the base of the launch ramp.

Bottom right: Wreckage of the 635 Squadron Lancaster of Squadron Leader Ian Bazalgette VC, DFC, lost on 4 August 1944 whilst on a raid to the flying bomb storage depot at Trossy St Maximin. After damage from flak, Bazalgette attempted to crash-land the partially abandoned Lancaster and thereby save two of his crew who were still on board. This he managed but almost immediately after touching down the Lancaster exploded. It was for this display of courage that Bazalgette received his VC. The people in the background are attending a memorial service to the killed airmen.

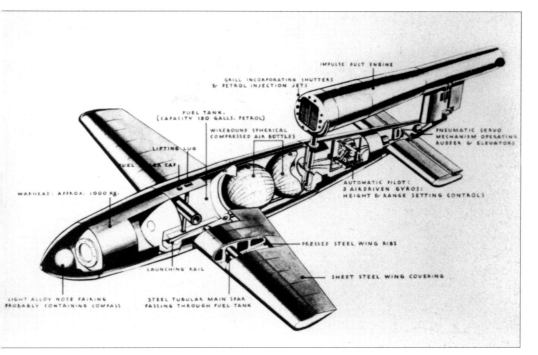

IMPULSE DUCT ENGINE

GRILL INCORPORATING SHUTTERS
& PETROL INJECTION JETS

FUEL TANK.
(CAPACITY 130 GALLS, PETROL)

PNEUMATIC SERVO
MECHANISM OPERATING
RUDDER & ELEVATORS

LIFTING LUG

WIREBOUND SPHERICAL
COMPRESSED AIR BOTTLES

FUEL TANK CAP

WARHEAD: APPROX. 1000 Kg.

AUTOMATIC PILOT:
3 AIRDRIVEN GYROS:
HEIGHT & RANGE SETTING CONTROLS

PRESSED STEEL WING RIBS

LAUNCHING RAIL

SHEET STEEL WING COVERING

LIGHT ALLOY NOSE FAIRING
PROBABLY CONTAINING COMPASS

STEEL TUBULAR MAIN SPAR
PASSING THROUGH FUEL TANK

Top: The inside workings of a flying
bomb.

Bottom left: Squadron Leader Ian
Bazalgette VC, DFC.

Bottom right: Air Vice-Marshal Hon.
Ralph Cochrane, Air Officer
Commanding 5 Group, 1943-1945.
(Imperial War Museum CH 14564)

They paid the ultimate sacrifice…

Top left: Commonwealth war grave of Sergeants Norgate, Trayhorn and Picton, the last three Bomber Command airmen killed on operations to flying bomb installations in northern France, 28 August 1944.

Top right: Harrogate (Stonefall) Cemetery. The burial site of 10 Squadron pilot Pilot Officer Norman Colin Campbell Leitch. He was killed on the night of 16/17 June 1944, the night Bomber Command began its main counter-offensive against flying bomb targets in France. Pilot Officer Leitch's crew were detailed to attack the supply site at Domleger, but his Halifax crashed just after take-off with only one survivor from the crew of seven.

Bottom: Terlincthun British Cemetery. The collective grave of six airmen who were killed on the raid to Siracourt on 22 June 1944. Warrant Officer Herbert William Sedgwick RAAF, Pilot Officer Meredith Burford Parker RAAF, Squadron Leader John Francis McMullan RAAF, Warrant Officer Clarence Archibald Jones RAAF, Warrant Officer Thomas Harrison and Flying Officer Nelson Ellis Bowman. These men were in the first Bomber Command aircraft to be lost over enemy territory on raids to flying bomb targets in France.

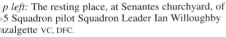

Top left: The resting place, at Senantes churchyard, of 635 Squadron pilot Squadron Leader Ian Willoughby Bazalgette VC, DFC.

Top right: Omerville Communal Cemetery, Val d'Oise, France. The centre two headstones display the name of 630 Squadron pilot Wing Commander William Inglis Deas DSO, DFC, & Bar and the names of five of his crew, killed on the raid to St Leu d'Esserent on the night of 7/8 July 1944.

Middle right: Communal grave in St Hellier churchyard of Flight Lieutenant J A Platten and crew shot down on 20/21 July 1944.

Bottom right: Abbeville Communal Cemetery Extension. The burial site of Flying Officer James Alexander Flint-Smith DFC, DFM and Flying Officer Geoffrey Ernest Heath DFC, DFM. Both men died on the raid to Beauvoir on 29 June 1944 when their 627 Squadron Mosquito was believed to have been destroyed by a flying bomb exploding whilst in flight.

VENLO AIRFIELD
GSGS 4081/82a/148927

Screened a/c shelters

grid ref
1593

Screened 'square
buildings'

LONDON LINE

VENLO AIRFIELD

A HE111 base associated with the air launching of V1s.

This annotated print illustrates the findings which were

confirmed by a subsequent APIS ground check when the

airfield fell into Allied hands

Top: A typical scene at the Photographic Interpretation
Section room at Medmenham, whilst gathering
intelligence information concerning German secret
weapons.

Bottom left: Aerial reconnaissance of Venlo airfield
identifying 'square buildings' and associating the airfield
with the air launching of flying bombs from He111s.

Bottom right: Flying bomb modified launch site in
northern France. The square building is to the right of the
road T-junction, centre of picture. The ramp is to the left.
In the field, bottom left corner can be seen scars resulting
from the firing pistons falling to ground after launching.
The photograph has been set up by the Medmenham
interpreters so that when viewed through a stereoscope
the image appears three dimensional.

op: Flying bomb modified launch site. The launch ramp
'A' is hidden in an orchard. The square building 'B',
'here the magnetic directional compass was set, is on the
'ame alignment as the launch ramp.

Bottom left: Flying bomb launch ramp in Holland
being inspected by Canadian soldiers following
liberation of the area.

Bottom right: Leonard Cheshire who earned his
Victoria Cross whilst with 617 Squadron, in
recognition of his skill and bravery developing and
executing low-level marking techniques. Many of the
raids on flying bomb targets involved marking at low
level by an aircraft piloted by Cheshire.

Top: The ski site at Bois Carré near Yvrench, the first flying bomb launch site in France to be analysed with photographs. The site is still under construction. The long building in the foreground clearly shows the distinctive shape of the 'ski'.

Bottom: The flying bomb launch ramp at Belloy et Vignacourt, just after the Germans had retreated.

p: RAF Bomber Command's Air Officer Commander-
-Chief, Air Chief Marshal Sir Arthur Harris (second
om right), studying bomb damage photographs, 27
ebruary 1944. First and second left are Senior Air Staff
fficers Air Vice-Marshal H.S.P. Walmsley and
ir Vice-Marshal R.D. Oxland. On the right is the Deputy
ir Officer Commander-in-Chief, Air Vice-Marshal
r Robert Saundby. (Imperial War Museum HU 44870)

Bottom left: Modern photograph showing the entrance to
the flying bomb storage depot at Nucourt.

Bottom right: Pilot Officer Thomas Fox, flight engineer,
77 Squadron (second from right) with crew, September
1944. Behind is a Halifax III, KN-U MZ812.

This page: Low level reconnaissance photograph (7 July 1944) showing the large site at Siracourt, to be used for the protected launching of flying bombs, and the devastation of the area around resulting from the Allied bombing.

Top: Modern photograph of the ski site at
Tilly-le-Haut-Clocher.

Middle: Modern photograph of the flying
bomb ski site at Gorenflos, showing the
square building and an intact ski.

Bottom right: 500lb bombs dropped from
582 Squadron Wing Commander Walbourn's
Lancaster on the cloud-covered flying
bomb launch site at St Philibert Ferme on
6 July 1944.

Top left: A 12,000lb Tallboy bomb earthbound. This type of bomb was used on a number of raids against flying bomb targets, notably against the large site at Siracourt and the caves in which flying bombs were stored at St Leu d'Esserent.

Top right: Air Commodore Don Bennett (later Air Vice-Marshal), Air Officer Commanding 8 Group (Pathfinder Force) accompanies HM Queen Elizabeth during a royal visit to RAF Wyton on May 26, 1943.

Bottom: Flight Lieutenant R.S.D. Kearns (third from left) and crew, 617 Squadron. The first crew to take off in an RAF heavy bomber to attack a flying bomb launch site.

Top: Mosquito Mark IX LR503 used by both 105 and 109 Squadrons, to mark the target on numerous raids to flying bomb targets. These include, whilst with 109 Squadron, the first attacks by Bomber Command on flying bomb ski sites on the night of 16/17 December 1943, and, whilst with 105 Squadron, the attack on the flying bomb supply depot at St Leu d'Esserent on the night of 4/5 July 1944.

Bottom: Morning conference at 8 Group Headquarters, with operational planning in process (1944). From left around table, Wing Commander Finn (Oboe Controller), Mr Jukes (Operational Research Section), Wing Commander Thomas (Met. Officer), Air Vice-Marshal Don Bennett (Air Officer Commanding 8 Group), Air Commodore Boyce (SASO), Wing Commander Rathbone (Armament Officer) and Wing Commander Deacon. By the map is Squadron Leader Hastings (Navigation Officer).

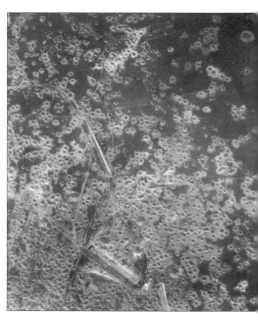

Flixecourt/Domart-en-Ponthieu flying bomb 'ski' site.

Plot of markers and bombs dropped on Bomber Command attack of 16/17 December 1943.

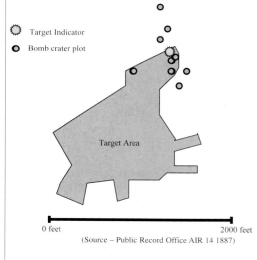

⊙ Target Indicator

◉ Bomb crater plot

Target Area

0 feet   2000 feet

(Source – Public Record Office AIR 14 1887)

Top left: A Halifax bomber over the flying bomb large site at Siracourt.

Top right: The cratered landscape around the flying bomb large site at Siracourt.

Bottom left: Modern photograph of the flying bomb launch bunker at Siracourt. The launch ramp extended from the entrance in the foreground in the direction of London. In the left background can be seen bomb damage.

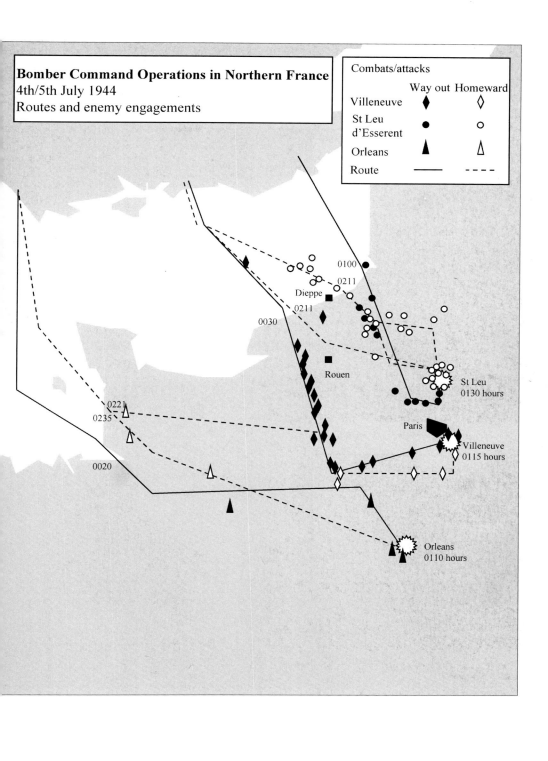

Bomber Command Operations in Northern France
4th/5th July 1944
Routes and enemy engagements

Combats/attacks

	Way out	Homeward
Villeneuve	◆	◇
St Leu d'Esserent	●	○
Orleans	▲	△
Route	——	- - - -

0100
0211
Dieppe
0211
0030
Rouen
St Leu
0130 hours
0221
0235
Paris
Villeneuve
0115 hours
0020
Orleans
0110 hours

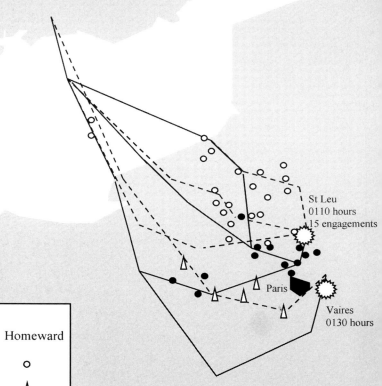

Bomber Command Operations in Northern France
7th/8th July 1944
Routes and enemy engagements

St Leu
0110 hours
15 engagements

Paris

Vaires
0130 hours

Combats/attacks

	Way out	Homeward
St Leu d'Esserent	●	○
Vaires	▲	△
Route	——	- - - -

CHAPTER 6

COUNTER-ATTACK

Sergeant Fred Fossett took part in five Bomber Command raids against flying bomb targets, and details a typical day on an operational squadron before a night operation in the summer of 1944:

The time of rising would depend upon the circumstances, such as whether the individual had been flying the previous night, and the time of his return, but in most instances it would be before 10.00 hours, and breakfast seemed to be provided up to that time. After breakfast, a quick search of the noticeboards for 'daily routine orders', which would carry general information on normal happenings of the day, such as who was duty orderly officer, orderly sergeant, and so forth. These did not affect the flying crews directly, as they were exempt from such duties whilst operational. Operational orders known as 'Battle Order' would appear on these boards at any time, therefore it was a quick check on an early take-off.

Having checked that there was nothing urgent, if we had been operating the previous twenty-four hours, some of the crew would take a stroll to the intelligence section of the operations building to have a look at the previous night's photographic results. These would be displayed on a large noticeboard, with a post operation PRU photograph, or the previous night's target map or photo in the centre. Each photo would then be arranged around this, with a piece of ribbon from the photo taken from a particular aircraft to the equivalent position on the target map, or photograph. Certain photos would then be marked A/P, signifying that the photograph is of the actual proposed aiming point for that target. When bombing above clouds at 'Wanganui' flares [8 Group codename], no ground detail would be visible, therefore there could be no *credit* for having an aiming point photo.

Somehow, wherever a person was on the station, the bush telegraph would flash around the message 'OPS ON', and everyone would make their way to the noticeboards to see who was flying that night, and in which aircraft. Even though a crew had an allocated aircraft, they would sometimes find themselves flying a different aircraft, as their own had been reported as unserviceable. The 'Battle Orders' carried quite a bit of information about the aircraft such as its Mark, boost rate, or special equipment.

If time was available, the three gunners would dash out to the aircraft, remove the guns, return to the armoury, strip the guns, re-assemble them and return them to the aircraft. This could be incorporated with the rest of the crew proceeding to the aircraft for an initial check of the equipment whilst the engines were running, as the normal check before take-off could be too late to correct any faults. It was essential to check the equipment with all four engines running, as different engines provided the sources of energy for different services. Hydraulics were supplied by the starboard outer for the mid upper turret; the starboard inner for the front turret; the port inner to the mid under turret where fitted; and the port outer for the tail turret. The starboard inner operated a compressor for the pneumatics of wheel brakes; radiator shutters; supercharger rams. Each inboard engine had a vacuum pump for operating the flying instruments, and bomb sight gyro. A compressor was fitted on the port inner for the Mk XIV bomb sight. Electrical generators were also on the inboard engines, in parallel for all of the host of electrical services.

Aircrews would then start preparing themselves for the operation ahead:

Fred Fossett: As air bomber, I would make sure I have sufficient pencils, sharpened at both ends, for if the lead breaks it is quicker to just turn the pencil over than find another one, and time can be important during briefing, or during the operation. I would then sort out my flying maps, which normally covered the whole of Europe, for we never knew where the target lay. I made sure that my protractor and ruler were in my map case, a supply of note-paper, and that nothing in there carried any clues as to my base station, should it fall into enemy hands.

The operational meal was sometimes provided before the briefing, sometimes after. Briefing would take place in the operations briefing room, some four hours before proposed take-off. This could be a lengthy procedure, providing the target information, route, enemy defences along the track, anticipated weather, any particular landmarks along the way, method of attack, and the return instructions, time check. After the briefing, we would be provided with any large scale target maps, or photographs to assist target recognition, then issued with our 'escape kit', which contained currency for the countries we would fly over, a silk map, tablets to purify water, and a plastic container to collect the water. There would also be energy tablets, perhaps a fishing line, a tube of condensed milk.

If we had already eaten our meal, the next step was to go to the adjacent crew equipment locker room, where we kept all of our flying kit under controlled air-conditioned environment. The only items not in our personal lockers would be the 'Mae West' [life-jacket] and parachute, which were subject to frequent checks for safety reasons. Firstly we would empty our pockets of anything that may be of use to the enemy, even used bus tickets, letters, notes, photographs. We would dress ourselves according to the anticipated weather conditions, and heights that we would be flying. Remember that the temperature falls 2° F for every thousand feet you climb, and our aircraft heating was very primitive and inefficient. On a nice evening in England with a temperature of 60°F, it would be 20°F at 20,000 feet over Berlin. Twelve degrees below freezing!

As crews became ready, collecting their Mae West and parachute, they would make their way to the transport waiting outside, and . . . out to the selected aircraft. Once more the crew would carry out checks before entering the aircraft. As air bomber, I checked that the bombs were the correct types specified in my orders, and in the allotted positions, also that the fusing wires were in position. The pilot would check such things as free movement of aircraft control surfaces, that the pitot tube cover had been removed, wheel covers removed, chocks in position. Each man carried out his own checks inside the aircraft, the gunners that they have sufficient ammo, and that it has been fed to the guns, safety catch on. The engines would be run up again, and when satisfied that all was OK, would be shut down to await the final 'go' in about an hour's time. This was usually preceded by the flight/squadron commanders driving around the airfield checking with each pilot, and mentioning any last minute changes, such as the runway in use, due to a wind change.

The 'off' was signalled by firing a green Very cartridge from the Control Tower at a pre-arranged time. A red would signify a cancellation or postponement. Each aircraft would now start up and proceed around the perimeter track to the runway, and await the signal from the caravan at the starting point. The aircraft would be signalled at about thirty-second intervals, take their position on the runway, rev up, get a second green, release the brakes, full power, maximum revs and boost; then as it moved forward sufficiently, the next would be signalled to take its place on the runway.

On 16 June 1944 just over 5,000 Bomber Command aircrew busied themselves with preparations for operations that night. Nearly 3,000 of these men attended briefings showing them operational routes to targets in France. In addition to the aircrew preparations, thousands of men, the groundcrews on the RAF stations, would be checking over and preparing the aircraft, and bombs would be retrieved from the bomb stores and loaded onto the heavy bombers.

The weather forecast for the night's operations to France indicated considerable cloud cover over the English bases and the targets. The method of attack for the four targets was as follows:

Target and aircraft despatched	Plan of attack
Domleger 5 Mosquitos, 49 Halifaxes, 54 Lancasters Bombload 385.2 tons	Zero hour – 0150 hours Using Oboe groundmarking, 5 Mosquitos to mark the target with red TI. The main force was to approach the target using GEE, confirming with H2S, then aim their bombloads at the centre of the markers.
Renescure 5 Mosquitos, 70 Lancasters Bombload 264 tons	Zero hour – 0055 hours (as Domleger)
Sautrecourt 5 Mosquitos, 100 Halifaxes Bombload 332 tons	Zero hour – 0315 hours Using Oboe groundmarking, 5 Mosquitos to mark the target with red TI. The main force to aim their bombloads at the centre of the markers.
Beauvoir 5 Mosquitos, 112 Lancasters Bombload 444.5 tons	Zero hour – 0040 hours (as Sautrecourt)

On the same night Bomber Command despatched a large force of 321 aircraft to attack the oil refinery at Sterkrade/Holten, Germany.

The force attacking Beauvoir experienced weather which was poor for accurate bombing. The post-raid report of 619 Squadron Lancaster 'U' ND 932 piloted by Flight Lieutenant Howes details the conditions encountered and is very similar to the other reports from aircraft on the raid. It does differ in one small way and gives an early indication of one of the problems the bomber crews would be experiencing on these types of raids.

> The primary target BEAUVOIR, was attacked and bombed from 11,000ft at 00:41 hours. Weather conditions: 10/10ths cloud; tops about 6,000 ft. The target was identified by orange glow and bomb bursts under cloud, bombs being dropped on the southern end of the glow. H2S not used. Leading edge of starboard tailplane damaged, thought to have been caused by bomb from another aircraft. Photographic failure due to weather conditions.[46]

The force attacking Domleger experienced considerable cloud cover, most bombing on the glow of TIs with very little opposition from ground defences. Attacking crews at Renescure also experienced complete cloud cover and at Sautrecourt there was reported 6 to 8/10ths cloud cover. At all the targets accurate and concentrated bombing was reported but the cloud cover made bombing photographs pointless. Subsequent day reconnaissance indicated severe damage at Domleger, Sautrecourt and Renescure, and several buildings at each site destroyed. The site at Beauvoir appeared to escape unaffected, but groups of craters were visible just outside the target area.

The force sent to Domleger had had an unfortunate start when the 10 Squadron Halifax LV825 ZA-G crashed into farmland in Yorkshire just 30 minutes after take-off. It was believed that a fire in the starboard outer engine caused the aircraft's demise. The pilot, Pilot Officer Leitch, and five of his crew were all killed. The rear gunner, Flight Sergeant Coleman, baled out without suffering any serious injury.

On the raid to Domleger the 78 Squadron Halifax 'X' LV957 piloted by Flight Lieutenant Hoffman was attacked by a single-engined fighter; the rear gunner returned fire and claimed it as damaged. The Halifax received considerable damage and the wireless operator Sergeant Barker was hit in the leg; his tibia and fibula were fractured. Hoffman brought the aircraft down at RAF Ford, owing to the damage (the home base was RAF Breighton). Barker was taken straight off to hospital.

Flying Officer Dennett piloted a 425 Squadron Halifax on the raid to Sautrecourt, which had a crew of eight. The additional crew member to the more usual crew of seven was a mid under gunner. Dennett was bringing his aircraft back from the attack when they ran into trouble. Sergeant Morrison, the mid upper gunner, was able to make out an Me109 on his aircraft's port beam at a distance of about 900 yards dead astern. Neither gunner had yet fired. There was always the possibility that they had not been seen and would avoid combat. However the Me109 closed in to attack at which point Sergeant McLean, the rear gunner, sighted another Me109 on the starboard quarter level at 400 yards. 'Corkscrew starboard' was barked down the intercom and the pilot reacted immediately, throwing the four-engined bomber into evasive manoeuvres. As he did so, McLean opened fire on the nearest Me109, on the starboard quarter. Morrison was initially unable to bring his guns to bear, but managed to get off two short bursts while the bomber started to climb as part of the evasive manoeuvre. The Me109 broke away from starboard to port quarter up at 100 yards. By then McLean was firing at the enemy aircraft directly astern, following it as it broke away to port quarter up. Morrison was able to get a short burst in as the fighter sped past. The two Me109s disappeared into cloud and were not seen again. Both gunners were convinced they had scored hits but no damage was seen. Dennett brought the aircraft out of the evasive manoeuvres and they continued on their way home. However the night had further action in store for the crew. As the Halifax crossed the English coast another single-engined aircraft was seen 900 yards astern. Despite being unable to identify the type of aircraft, its movement demonstrated hostile intent. Dennett threw the Halifax into evasive action once more and managed to lose the unwelcome company.

These were two of the very few encounters with enemy aircraft on the raids to the flying bomb targets, raids that had notably also met with very little opposition from ground defences. Bomber Command received reports of eight combats on the Beauvoir raid, although none of them involved any enemy fire. Two were found to be cases of Lancasters firing on friendly bombers. A Ju88 attacked a Lancaster on its homeward route from Domleger, with three other attacks over the target. Several bombers on the raid to Sautrecourt were also engaged. Despite the engagements, all the bombers despatched to the flying bomb targets returned. The force despatched to Sterkrade/Holten had drawn most of the nightfighter attention. The flak defences also exacted their toll on this force and a total of 31 aircraft did not return from the raid.

There was also one extremely unfortunate incident involving a 425 Squadron Halifax on one of the raids against a flying bomb target. Pilot Officer Harold Romuld of the Royal Canadian Air Force was bringing his aircraft and crew back from the raid against Sautrecourt when at 0325 hours gunfire was seen to be coming from the middle of another Halifax positioned above them. Tracer from the 'friendly fire' tore through the starboard window fatally injuring 21-year-old Romuld. The bomb aimer took control of the Halifax so that his pilot could receive attention, but Romuld died a few minutes later. The bomb aimer successfully brought the aircraft home, landing at Woodbridge, Suffolk.

On the night of 17/18 June two forces were sent to continue the attack on the supply sites at Oisemont (19 Lancasters, 90 Halifaxes and 5 Mosquitos) and St Martin l'Hortier (90 Halifaxes and 5 Mosquitos). The Oisemont main force bombed either on the glow of markers seen through cloud, or on a Gee fix. The site was to receive further attacks before a reconnaissance was made. Similarly at St Martin l'Hortier the crews either bombed on Gee or at the markers visible through the cloud cover. Subsequent reconnaissance revealed severe damage to the site; several buildings and installations were hit, with the attack centred 500 yards west of the aiming point.

What is noteworthy in these attacks is the use of Gee as a bombing aid. Indeed on a number of future raids Gee would be adopted for bombing particularly when cloud cover made other forms of bombing difficult. Flying Officer Frank Leatherdale was a navigator with 115 Squadron at the time of the flying bomb counter-offensive bombing:

> While Gee was a very accurate navigational system over Britain it became less accurate the further you were away from the transmitting stations. Over England the lattice lines produced by the intersection of the radio waves from the 'A', 'B' and 'C' stations were often at right angles, but at a distance these lattice lines would become much less acute – making it difficult to read the true time elapse as shown on the time base on the cathode ray tube. Some observers seemed to be able to read the CRT more accurately than others. Nevertheless, by the time we were over northern France and experiencing some jamming from the Germans, Gee did not provide a wholly reliable method of

bomb aiming. It had never been intended to use it as such – it was primarily a navigational aid. Its use was only resorted to because the situation was desperate and there was no other means of attacking these sites. We could not afford to wait until the sky cleared of clouds.

We would fly to a position from which we could fly along one of the lattice lines which passed through the point at which we would need to release our bombs on that particular track to hit the target. The navigator then directed the pilot by words such as 'left, left' or 'right' to keep the bomber flying along the chosen lattice line. Meanwhile he would be watching the pulse from the intersecting lattice line, this would be creeping along the time base until a point was reached at which the bomb doors would be opened. Then when the exact reading was reached the bombs would be released in a short stick, which would cover approximately 100 to 200 yards.

In daylight the crew could watch the other bombers in the gaggle, and would compare the time they released their bombs with what was happening in their own crew. This was a bit of a test for the navigator if any of the other planes dropped their bombs before you thought the right reading had been reached.

The use of Gee as a bombing aid made each bomber independent. There would be slight differences in when to bomb as each navigator, in each aircraft, stared at their cathode ray tube. As the bombers flew at high speed over a target, split second differences in bomb releases could lead to differences of hundreds of yards in where the bomb came down.

At this stage of the overall bomber offensive against Germany, it was soon thought that crews sent on raids to 'easy' targets, i.e. not raids to Germany, were under less risk than those that had been or were going to be sent to the harder targets. It was recognised that a crew could finish their tour of operations quite quickly, compared to the bomber crews of previous years. Bomber Command and the groups decided to count certain raids as less than one operation against a tour.

> *Sergeant Bert Kirtland, wireless operator, 76 Squadron:* The attacks on the V1 launching sites began for us on 16 June 1944 which happened to be my 21st birthday, when, less than 24 hours after bombing a fuel dump at Fouilard, we attacked a V1 site at Domleger. . . My log book shows that we did seven such targets in the next few weeks . . . They were not long trips, about 4 hours usually. The downside was that Bomber Command moved the goal posts and those of us who were almost 'tour expired' found that we sailed past the 30-trip mark without pausing for breath. In the case of our crew we had done 35 trips (the skipper 37) before we were screened [i.e. completed tour] at the end of July.
>
> *Flying Officer John Dyer, navigator, 54 Base:* The reasons

were, there was a shortage of trained aircrew following the heavy losses suffered during winter 1943 to 1944 (Berlin, Nuremberg etc.), and although the factories could produce sufficient replacement aircraft, the heavy conversion units were not producing sufficient new crews to man them. The trips just over the Channel were short in duration thus reducing the chances of being shot down. Over the invasion period it was possible for crews and aircraft to be turned around to enable two trips to be flown within a 24-hour period.

Flight Sergeant Ronnie Hunt, pilot, 75 Squadron: Bomber Command had the opinion that these operations were easy ops. In some cases they were, but some were against considerable opposition from both flak and fighters and significant 'failed to returns' occurred. Therefore many of us felt that counting these ops as ⅓ was unfair.

Sergeant Jack Watson, flight engineer, 156 Squadron: We were told that French trips would only count 3/5ths of an operation and there was a comment that if one 'bought it' over France one was completely dead, not 3/5ths. It was seen, however, as one of those things.

Flight Sergeant Ernie Drake, wireless operator, 77 Squadron: We took a poor view of not being accounted a whole op for these trips, because the Germans realised after a couple of such raids what was going on, and moved a lot of their defences to the west.

Pilot Officer Russell Gradwell, pilot, 9 Squadron: If you didn't go beyond about the middle of France it only counted as a third [of an op]. But on 3 May we attacked Mailly-le-Camp where we suffered horrendous losses [42 Lancasters out of a force of 346 Lancaster and 14 Mosquitos] and of course this idea . . . was scrubbed. I had done three trips, which only counted as one op.

Even though many of the Bomber Command airmen were not best pleased with the lengthening of their tours they still applied themselves to the task in hand.

CHAPTER 7

DAYLIGHT RAIDS

In Barnet, North London, in the summer of 1944, a young girl gained first-hand experience of the flying bomb menace:

> Look out! It's coming down!' I heard my father shout. The next moment there was a bright flash of light through the window, and then the house crashed down around us. I curled myself into a small ball as the bricks and mortar tumbled down, burying us in a sort of cave. The stairway still stood, making a roof. The bricks stopped falling and there was silence except for my father's faint voice calling. He had ducked under the sink. I sat still as I could and listened to my sister reciting the Lord's Prayer. I kept thinking about my chocolate cake and wishing that I had eaten it. Gradually the sound of digging came nearer until I could hear my father's voice telling me to sit still. At last there was a light in the hole near my head. Slowly it grew bigger until I could see my father's grimy face through it. A few minutes more shoveling and my father was lifting me out into the sunlight. All that was left was a heap of rubble, except for the chimney, which was still standing.[47]

Now that the flying bomb offensive had begun, the defences established on the approaches to London would be tested. In December of 1943 the Allied Chiefs of Staff had decided that, in part, to counteract the flying bomb threat, direct defensive measures would be looked in to. Air Marshal R.M. (later Sir Roderic) Hill (Commanding Air Defence of Great Britain) and General Sir Frederick Pile, Bt, (Officer Commanding-in-Chief, Anti-Aircraft Command) outlined a plan to Air Chief Marshal Leigh Mallory recommending that the traditional methods of air defence would still apply. As the bombing of the ski sites was believed by the Allies to have set back the German plans for the flying bomb offensive, this plan became adapted to fit with preparations for operation Overlord.

Leigh Mallory had received an 'Overlord/Diver' plan in February 1944 (Diver being the codeword for attacks by flying bombs) which was subsequently approved by the Chiefs of Staff and the Supreme Commander General Eisenhower. The plan, based upon radar and the Royal Observer Corps being able to track the flying bombs, called for fighters to patrol specific areas covering the flying bomb flight paths. These would be supported by light anti-aircraft guns, searchlights and balloons defending London. Bristol and the Solent had also been identified as areas for potential flying bomb attack. Whilst not having specific fighter defence these areas would have searchlight and anti-aircraft gun defence.

Following the 'full' opening of the German flying bomb offensive on 15 June, Air Marshal Hill began the implementation of the full deployment necessary for the 'Overlord/Diver' plan.

On the night of 15/16 June 23-year-old Mosquito pilot Flight Lieutenant John Musgrave and his observer Flight Sergeant Frederick Samwell were the first airmen to shoot down a flying bomb. Soon after midnight and within seconds of the warnings being given of the approach of flying bombs, Musgrave took off and intercepted the flying bomb over the Channel.

> *Flight Lieutenant Musgrave:* It was like chasing a ball of fire across the sky. We took off half an hour after midnight and . . . minutes later sighted a ball of flame and sparks. It flashed by us on our starboard side a few thousand feet away and at the same height as we were flying. I quickly turned to port and chased it. It was going pretty fast, but I caught up with it and opened fire from astern. At first, there was no effect so I closed in another hundred yards and gave it another burst. Then I went closer still and pressed the button again. This time there was a terrific flash and explosion and the thing fell down in a vertical dive into the sea. The whole show was over in three minutes.[48]

On the afternoon of 16 June a conference held by the Prime Minister requested redistribution of the gun, searchlight and balloon defences. By 21 June all the balloons and virtually all the guns were in place, and eight single-engined and four twin-engined fighter squadrons were involved in flying bomb patrols.

Bomber Command, in addition to bombing requirements, was also required to divert some of its Mosquito forces to flying bomb patrols. In June 85 Squadron and 157 Squadron were diverted away from 100 (Bomber Support) Group activities to conduct anti-flying bomb operations. Both squadrons had joined 100 Group in May 1944 to conduct Mosquito Intruder operations. Having only just started upon the campaign of hunting the German Air Force the diversion was not greeted with great enthusiasm by the squadrons. No. 85 Squadron started on its first Intruder operations on 5 June and claimed some success with seven kills recorded in a fortnight.

> *100 Group review of operations, 85 Squadron:* We were naturally encouraged by this start and the defensive bogey was not only scotched but forgotten. What then was our dismay when a small voice from north London whispered; 'Don't forget the Diver.' At this critical moment we were snatched from the job of putting 'round holes into square heads' and our status and cast shamefully, and I think unjustifiably, reduced to that of

airborne ack-ack. From the point of view purely of personal comfort we had the pleasure of returning to our old love, West Malling, from 21st July to 28th August, and on this very second eleven work managed to shoot down 33 whizzers.[49]

No. 85 Squadron would complete 326 sorties conducting anti-flying bomb patrols. No. 157 Squadron would claim 39 flying bombs destroyed from their 214 sorties. In addition 169 Squadron also claimed 1 flying bomb.

As the flying bomb offensive continued defensive reinforcements were made; the balloon defence was extended and made more dense and additional guns were applied. By 28 June 363 heavy and 422 light guns were in position on the Downs, by mid July this had changed to 376 heavy and 392 light guns. Also 600 light guns were positioned on the south coast. In addition 13 single-engined and nine Mosquito squadrons were in action, with the fighter defences claiming destroyed nearly a third of all the attacking flying bombs reported.

Defensive results were not as expected, however. Weather and interference between the fighter and gun belts proved problematic. A decision was made to implement exclusive areas of responsibility. All the guns were to be removed to the gun belt with fighters not permitted to enter. Following further debate it was also agreed to move the gun belt to the coast. By 17 July all the heavy guns which had been moved to the south coast, were ready, the light guns arriving two days later. Over the next month this was added to until 800 heavy guns and more than 1,800 light guns and 700 rocket barrels were in defensive positions on the south coast and round the Thames Estuary. This change proved wise. The whole success rate of the defensive system improved. The ratio of flying bombs destroyed to those observed rose in favour of the defenders.[50] But of course if the numbers of flying bombs reaching the English coast could be kept as low as possible it would make it that much easier for the defences to keep their success ratios high, and it was the Allied bomber forces which had the task of lowering the German launch rates.

Following Bomber Command's six raids on the four flying bomb supply sites between 16 and 18 June, which had been combined with raids by the American heavy bombers on the same sites, Harris expressed his reluctance to continue hitting these targets without reconnaissance proving the need. However with the numbers of casualties from the menace growing in England, notably from an incident on Sunday 18 June when 121 people were killed and 68 seriously injured at the Royal Military Chapel (Guard's Chapel) at Wellington Barracks, the Supreme Allied Commander General Eisenhower stepped in to re-emphasise that attacks on Crossbow targets would be of priority over everything except the direct requirements of operation Overlord. Despite the reservations of some of the senior Allied airmen, Eisenhower was supported by both the British War Cabinet and the British Chiefs of Staff. Leigh Mallory was particularly concerned on the diversion of the air forces away from supporting the land battle. His diary entry of 22 June recorded:

I am not, however, allowing the pilotless aircraft to interfere with my main strategical direction of the battle. I have no doubt that the Germans would like me to use big bomber forces on the sites launching pilotless aircraft, and they may even have begun to bomb London by this means in order to get me to do so, but I refuse to be diverted from my purpose. I shall wait for a day of fine weather and then I shall plaster them, but I am not going to attack them now, not while all this railway movement is taking place. That must be stopped in the interests of the battle, and if it means that London gets 40 or 50 pilotless aircraft shot at it, it must just take it, as I am sure it will.[51]

A new Crossbow Committee was set up by the Cabinet on 19 June to oversee defensive and offensive counter-measures against the flying bombs. Ski sites remained in the priority list during the opening week of the flying bomb attacks, since the Allies remained unaware that the sites were to all intents and purposes really now redundant. Intelligence was beginning to identify more and more modified sites, and 44 had been located by 18 June in the Calais-Somme area, of which 24 were believed to be operationally ready. The decision was made to prioritise the modified sites. However owing to the fact that no modified sites had been identified in the Somme-Seine area, ski sites remained in the targeting list.

Further problems now arose with the targeting of the modified sites. Owing to the relative ease with which the Germans could make available a modified site, Allied Intelligence struggled to keep pace identifying the sites. To maintain adequate reconnaissance and locate sites was far beyond the resources then available, and improvements in German camouflage techniques made the task even more daunting.

Whilst Allied Intelligence dealt with the targeting priorities the aircrews of Bomber Command continued to prepare for and attack the flying bomb targets allocated to them, some of the airmen welcoming the opportunity to strike back against the flying bomb menace.

Pilot Officer Russell Gradwell, pilot, 9 Squadron: We knew what dreadful things these were so we were quite happy to attack them.

Flight Sergeant Ernie Drake, wireless operator, 77 Squadron: Those of us who lived in the southern counties were very pleased to be bombing V1 sites, largely because it appeared to offer a good short term dividend. Having seen one of the first 'doodle bugs' arriving I found it quite a frightening experience, and it was heartening to feel that we might be able to smash the launching ramps and put them out of action.

Sergeant Ron Winton, wireless operator, 207 Squadron: My home was at Dagenham in Essex at the time, and as it was in the direct line with London it was being heavily attacked by the V1s. So my feelings about bombing were of great satisfaction, as I felt that I was directly helping to protect my family.

Flight Sergeant Tony Harris, bomb aimer, 50 Squadron: These ops were not necessarily less hazardous than the deeper night penetrations of the recent past but were certainly more interesting, and we were helping to protect our friends and families at home.

Sergeant Fred Fossett, bomb aimer, 463 (RAAF) Squadron: In August 1944, whilst on leave, I visited a factory at Ember Court near Molesey, in Surrey, and adjoining it was the Mounted Police Training centre. In the large sports field of this centre, a military band were playing, and the troops were having a sporting gala. A siren sounded, everyone in the factory took to the shelters, a V1 came over, the engine cut, and the bomb fell right in the centre of the band. The factory first aid services swung into action, and soon the Americans from Bushey Park were on the scene with their ambulances. I knew that as I was untrained in this type of work the best thing for me to do was get out of the way. I returned to base early, longing for the opportunity to repay the Germans for that bomb. I did, many times over. Of course the German bomb had been pure luck on their part, it could have been an empty field.

The importance of targeting the flying bomb menace was certainly made clear to the aircrews.

Warrant Officer Ronald Claridge, wireless operator, 7 Squadron: The first indication I had about flying bombs and rockets was 20 June 1944. A few hours previously I had driven to London from Oakington with my skipper Squadron Leader G.B. Frow DSO DFC on a 48 hour stand down. We parted at Northolt tube station having exchanged telephone numbers. I had been at my parents' house in Essex for about 12 hours when I had a call from Brian [Squadron Leader Frow] to say we had been recalled with immediate effect and he would pick me up in a couple of hours at Northolt. He told me that on his arrival home he had been given orders for our recall with immediate effect and that we were starting daylight raids immediately on our return, and that we were in a very grave situation and our orders were to destroy what had become a grim reality, *Hitler's Secret Weapon!* Two had already hit London with devastating results, whole streets had been demolished at a time with many deaths which I believe had never been released to the public. At first these were explained away to the public as being caused by faulty gas mains resulting from previous bombing.

On our return to Oakington we found a great 'flap' and we were rushed to the briefing room and were airborne in an hour. We were told that unless these launching sites were destroyed we were in the position of losing the war.

After the initial raids against the supply sites Bomber Command shifted emphasis for the next few days, attacking large sites. On 18/19 June 10 Mosquitos, and on 19 June, 11 Mosquitos and 19 Lancasters, with a fighter escort, attacked the large site at Watten in what was believed fairly accurate attacks. Ralph Briars DFM, at the time a flight sergeant, was a rear gunner with 617 Squadron and recorded his experience of the attack on 19 June:

> Took off about 6 p.m. in true fighter style, one each side of runway, flew over in formation of five, weather perfect. Fighter cover of Spits met us at Orfordness. Target 10-12 miles inland, saw results of Marauders work in lots of places; a little flak outside target area didn't trouble us. Circling for about 20 minutes before Wingco gave OK to bomb, target difficult in clearing on edge of wood. Bombing fair, BAs [bomb aimers] a bit disappointed with results, pity. Watched rest of bombing and came home. Believe bandits turned up as Mosquitos left – good show! 17,000 feet.

Reconnaissance later revealed a large number of craters around the target but with very little damage visible to any of the buildings. On 20 June 17 Lancasters and 3 Mosquitos were despatched to attack the large site at Wizernes but the raid was abandoned owing to bad weather.

On 21 June Bomber Command returned its attention to the supply sites. St Martin l'Hortier and Oisemont were targeted in a daylight raid, 41 Lancasters, 66 Halifaxes, 5 Mosquitos and 2 Lancasters, 99 Halifaxes, 5 Mosquitos were respectively despatched. At St Martin l'Hortier a master bomber directed the bombing, although some crews bombed visually. A good concentration of bombing was reported. The target was also attacked by American heavy bombers the previous day and this day by a total of 57 aircraft. Subsequent reconnaissance, however, revealed poor results from the raids; there were only a few more craters in the target area and the odd near miss but no hits on buildings. At Oisemont the bomber force experienced poor weather, and the master bomber called off the attack after 20 aircraft had bombed. This target was also attacked by 43 American heavy bombers this day and the day before. (Reconnaissance of the target will be detailed after further attacks.) A force of 99 Lancasters and 5 Mosquitos was also despatched to Domleger on the same day but the raid was abandoned owing to the inability of the main force to see any Mosquito markers, although the master bomber did manage to drop his load in the vicinity of the target, through a gap in the clouds.

These three raids were Bomber Command's first large-scale day attacks on the flying bomb targets. It was a new experience for many of the crews to be operational in daylight. Some regarded it with apprehension recalling the considerable daylight losses Bomber Command had suffered earlier in the war. Some men preferred it.

> *Flying Officer John Dyer, navigator, 54 Base:* Daylight raids were 'unknown territory' for crews brought up on bombing Germany at night and therefore were regarded with apprehension.

Flying Officer Ron Biggs, navigator, 44 (Rhodesia) Squadron:
Of course we were nervous about the daylight raids because we
still had only light machine guns in the turrets and the losses
had been heavy in earlier raids. However, we were assured that
there would be fighter cover, although we couldn't see any.
Sergeant Bob Riches, rear gunner, 9 Squadron: As a tail gunner
I preferred it! At least no one was creeping up on me in the dark.
Flight Sergeant Ken Grantham, wireless operator, 35 Squadron:
Because most of the daylight raids were to France I rather think
we thought they would be a doddle as most of our targets were
not far from the French coast and they were construed as a
'quick dash in and back for tea' sort of raid. How wrong could
one be?

One other 'new' experience for the crews was that they could see other
aircraft:

Flight Sergeant Walter Braithwaite, bomb aimer, 77 Squadron:
It was more hairy than night as we could see all the other silly
buggers.
Flight Sergeant Ernie Drake, wireless operator, 77 Squadron:
The air superiority the Allies enjoyed at the time made these
operations far less hazardous than night-dos or, for example, the
Big City [Berlin]. The biggest threat came from the descending
bombload from aircraft above, and we did witness an aircraft in
front of us disintegrate for this reason . . . The daylight raids
made us realise how hazardous the night mass raids were, as for
the first time we were able to see aircraft converge from all
directions as well as from above and below.
Flying Officer Alan Carter, pilot, 78 Squadron: . . . after the first
daylight raid which I took part in when I stayed at the briefed
bombing height, I saw all the other aircraft above me and bombs
falling very close to my aircraft. After this I bombed from as
high as I could get the aircraft.

American Sergeant Rick Green, navigator with 44 Squadron, took part in a
daylight raid against a flying bomb target in early August 1944:

. . . what excitement, a daylight raid! I believe take-off was
originally scheduled for 10.30 a.m. We piled into T-Tear
impatiently waiting for take-off. Then the word came that there
was a delay. Then another delay. Then the word came to go to
the mess and eat lunch. We finally took off at 14.20 hours. We
were in a gaggle (loose formation). As navigator I was in my
'office' and did not see out. Over the target area I hear Barry
Lillywhite (the tail gunner) call out, 'Oh, the poor bastards';
'What happened?' I yelled (intercom discipline had not been
established yet), 'The bombs from a plane up above tore off the
wings of another Lanc' was the reply. Ever since I have

maintained that a gaggle is an unhealthy way to fly.[52]

Flight Sergeant Norman Turton, a navigator with 207 Squadron, recalled a particularly tragic incident on a raid to a flying bomb target in August 1944:

> As navigator, when I got near the target I used to put on paper my courses out of the target and then go and stand up at the front. With this being daylight I could see aircraft all above us and there were bombs coming down like leaflets. I thought 'bloody hell'. There was an aircraft at the side of us just disintegrated. It was there one second and at the blink of an eyelid it was gone.

The crews could also see the defences attempting to bring the bombers down.

> *Sergeant Jack Watson, flight engineer, 156 Squadron:* One thing did show on daylight trips – we were much more aware of the flak bursts. They did look close together . . . At night it was a quick bright flash but in daylight the smoke puffs just hung in the sky like hundreds of little clouds.
> *Warrant Officer Ronald Claridge, wireless operator, 7 Squadron:* A bit worried at first but we felt that at last we could carry out daylight bombing as well if not better than the Americans with less losses. Flak seemed less dangerous as we could only see the smoke puffs. Rather silly but it seemed less dangerous than at night where there was always a flash before the bang.
> *Flying Officer Frank Leatherdale, navigator, 115 Squadron:* At night all you saw was the flashes of the shells bursting --mind you that was quite frightening – but in daylight you saw the puffs of smoke filling the sky as each successive shell burst added to those already there; you had to tell yourself that there was no danger in all those puffs – the one that was dangerous had yet to explode.

However it would not just be the aircrews whose lives were at risk. Once more the French civilians would suffer from the Allied bomber attention. On the night of 17/18 June the inhabitants of St Martin l'Hortier were awoken by the rumble of Halifax and Mosquito engines and flares lighting up the sky. Then the locals' nightmares were realised as for the next twenty minutes high explosive bombs rained down on them. Many, in their haste, didn't actually feel there was the need to get dressed before running to their air raid shelters. Many witnessed numerous houses collapsing. It wasn't until the next day that the full extent of the damage was revealed. All the local hamlets were in a very poor state. There were dead cattle littering the countryside. Incredibly no inhabitant of St Martin l'Hortier was killed. However at nearby Fresles one couple along with their child lost their lives as their house burnt, and one young man who had only just arrived in the area for the haymaking was killed.

The Germans evacuated the target area and most of the local families moved away to surrounding villages, delayed-action bombs going off being one of the persuading factors. There was also a local report that the Germans did indeed have some flying bombs in the supply site and a few hours after the raid these were transported to a castle at Saint Germain-sur-Eaulne. There would be no peace over the next few days as the Allied bombers continued to target Saint Martin l'Hortier. On the afternoon of 21 June Bomber Command attacked again. All the stained glass in the local church was blown out. The apple trees were turned upside down. By then the supply site was extensively cratered.

On 22 June three Bomber Command forces were despatched to Crossbow targets. One raid to Wizernes was abandoned owing to adverse weather. One raid was made to the large site at Mimoyecques. Although not known to the Allies at the time, this large site was being constructed for a long-range multi-barrelled gun (the V3), to fire specially designed shells across the Channel. Allied Intelligence suspected the construction as being part of the German secret weapon programme and hence included it in Crossbow target lists. A large force of bombers was also sent to Siracourt.

The large site at Siracourt lay approximately 130 miles from London. Activity at the site was first observed by the Allies in September 1943, and an eye kept on the progress of the construction. The main building on the site was rectangular, 625 feet long and 132 feet wide and was orientated at right angles to a bearing on London. The Germans built a single branch rail track to the site and a number of rail branches and sidings were also constructed. Early in 1945 an investigation was conducted to look at the heavy sites in northern France, the Sanders Mission,[53] and the Allied investigators found a building constructed from very heavy reinforced concrete offering considerable protection. Although the whole building was 132 feet wide, the main chamber was only 48 feet wide with a height of 20 feet. The roof was 18 feet thick. It was believed that a launch ramp would start at the large rectangular building, aligned on London, and flying bombs would be put on the ramp and launched under cover. As such only the ramp would be susceptible to bombing. A similar site had started to be constructed at Lottinghem but had been abandoned, after heavy bombing, in April 1944. The Sanders Mission investigators interrogated locals at Lottinghem, who indicated that the site was for the launch of flying bombs. As such it was clear that the site at Siracourt was also intended for launching flying bombs and the Sanders Mission would later report that the installation had the potential of launching two flying bombs an hour.

In June 1944, however, the exact purpose of the site was unknown to the Allies but its construction suggested that it was still worthy of attack. American heavies attacked on 30 May (35 Fortresses), 20 June (20 Liberators) and 21 June (39 Liberators) dropping a total of 275.5 tons. On 22 June Bomber Command was called in, sending 2 Lancasters, 100 Halifaxes and 5 Mosquitos to the large flying bomb site. Amidst heavy flak the master bomber initially called on the main force to bomb visually but later in the raid told them to bomb on red TI which had been assessed as being right on the aiming point. The bombing would eventually be recorded as scattered and Siracourt would need a further visit from the heavy bombers. The 466 Squadron Halifax piloted by Squadron Leader McMullan was lost on this raid. The pilot and five other men were killed. Two men survived; one then was captured, the other successfully evaded.

Two other aircraft were lost as part of Crossbow operations, on the raid to Mimoyecques. Shortly after take-off a 12 Squadron Lancaster, piloted by Pilot Officer Leuty, suffered severe problems with the inner port engine. It was decided to abandon the sortie and the bombload was jettisoned over the sea. To try and land a Lancaster with a full bombload and engine trouble would be extremely hazardous. On return to Wickenby the Lancaster over-ran the runway, fortunately with no injuries to the crew. The 550 Squadron Lancaster piloted by Flight Lieutenant Redmond, also on the raid to Mimoyecques, received flak damage. The crew brought the aircraft back to England and baled out over Kent with no injuries sustained.

American heavy bombers were also active on 22 June, notably attacking the supply sites at Beauvoir, Domleger and Renescure. The next day further American raids were made on Oisemont and St Martin l'Hortier.

On the night of 23/24 June, four forces were despatched by Bomber Command to flying bomb targets. The supply site at Oisemont was again raided, with considerable success, as the glow of some of the TI illuminated some of the ground detail of the target. Reconnaissance covering several raids, including all three Bomber Command attacks since the first on the night of 17/18 June, would reveal severe damage to the target area. The other three raids were Bomber Command's first to modified sites. At L'Hey 102 Lancasters and 5 Mosquitos, at Bientques 41 Lancasters, 65 Halifaxes and 5 Mosquitos and at Coubronne 81 Lancasters and 5 Mosquitos.

At L'Hey subsequent reconnaissance placed 15 craters in the target area, including a near miss on the launching point, although some of the craters may have been the result of an American attack on 16 June. There was one loss on the raid. The 622 Squadron Lancaster piloted by Flight Sergeant Cooke RNZAF did not return, three of the crew becoming POWs, two men evading capture, and the pilot and his mid upper gunner losing their lives. At Bientques the main force bombed through cloud onto the glow of the TI; later reconnaissance revealed a fairly successful attack with damage to both the square building and the launching point.

At Coubronne crews were requested to bomb through cloud by the master bomber, although many attacked using Gee. The attack was unsuccessful, and reconnaissance showed only three fresh craters in the target area, although two of them were near misses on the launching point. The raid to Coubronne was the last of the four raids to the flying bomb sites on this particular night. It is particularly noteworthy as it is really the first time that the German nightfighter force reacted strongly to raids against launching sites in the coastal area of the Pas de Calais. Bomber Command intelligence later identified that six nightfighter *Gruppen* had been active during the night. Two Lancasters from 7 Squadron, one piloted by Flight Lieutenant Irwin DFC, RNZAF and the other by Flight Lieutenant Wakefield, were lost with no survivors. The 156 Squadron Lancaster piloted by Pilot Officer Langford DFC was also lost; six of the crew, including the pilot, were killed, and the one surviving crew member became a POW.

Flight Sergeant Kenneth Grantham was wireless operator on a 35 Squadron Lancaster that took part on the raid to Coubronne. This was his crew's first raid to a flying bomb target: 'The feeling among the crew toward attacking flying bomb targets was pretty neutral, they were just another target, perhaps viewed, erroneously, as pretty easy i.e. less dangerous.' He recalled the raid and the note he made in his diary following the raid:

> P/O Marsden in F for Freddie mixed it with a fighter and were badly mauled, the aircraft being a write-off! The mid upper gunner lost an eye and the rear gunner an arm. Pilot Officer Ingram was reported missing (so much for the easy French targets!) On June 24 I went to inspect 'F' in the 'graveyard'. What a mess, it's a wonder they lived at all. The gunners' turrets are completely smashed and twisted. Fuselage peppered with holes, starboard wing was hit in the petrol tank and set on fire.

The 35 Squadron Lancaster piloted by Squadron Leader Ingram DFC was shot down by a nightfighter near Dunkirk. The pilot and his rear gunner were killed and the six other airmen on board became POWs. Fortunately the raids on flying bomb targets on this night had only required a small penetration over occupied territory, otherwise the losses may have been greater.

Following the night's efforts a further four daylight operations were ordered on Crossbow targets; three of them were modified sites at Les Hayons (102 Lancasters and 5 Mosquitos), Noyelle-en-Chausee II (2 Lancasters, 101 Halifaxes and 5 Mosquitos) and Bonnetot (2 Lancasters, 99 Halifaxes and 5 Mosquitos). The fourth Crossbow target was the large site at Wizernes; 16 Lancasters (617 Squadron) and 2 Mosquitos were despatched, with nine bombs later plotted in the target area and one building demolished just south of the aiming point. Clear weather was encountered at all the flying bomb targets, and good marking and concentrated bombing were reported. Reconnaissance at Bonnetot and Les Hayons revealed some buildings destroyed (although no important units were hit) and craters in the target area. At Noyelle-en-Chausee II reconnaissance only revealed five craters in the target area with the main concentration to the west. The 300 Squadron Lancaster piloted by Flight Sergeant Badowski of the Polish Air Force was hit by flak on the return route from the attack on Les Hayons. Badowski did manage to bring his damaged aircraft and Polish crew back to the skies over England but their fortune ran out and the Lancaster crashed in Lincolnshire with no survivors. One other aircraft was lost on Crossbow attacks this day. The 617 Squadron Lancaster piloted by Flight Lieutenant Edward DFC on the raid to Wizernes was hit by flak and crashed in the Pas de Calais. Flight Sergeant Hobbs was the wireless operator on the fated Lancaster:

This was to be my 35th operation. . . We were the only squadron then equipped to deliver the 12,000 lb 'Tallboy', the Barnes Wallis bomb that could penetrate 50 ft of reinforced concrete. They were in short supply and we had to identify the target visually or bring the bombs back. On this day reconnaissance had reported light cloud cover over the target area earlier so that take-off was delayed until late afternoon.

In a cloudless sky we climbed over the Channel and as we headed towards the target the English coastline could still be seen. We were on our straight and level bombing run when two flak bursts hit us and both port engines were set on fire. The flight engineer was killed instantly and but for the huge bomb beneath us the flak may have claimed more victims. The navigator, after checking the flight engineer, assisted the pilot in trying to extinguish the fires but to no avail and the pilot ordered him to jump. I was the wireless operator and I returned to the intercom when I saw the engines alight, to hear the pilot call 'Abracadabra, jump, jump', which was our pre-arranged signal to abandon aircraft.

There was a split second of panic whilst deciding to remove my flying helmet, but I took it off and then the drill took over and I moved aft to the rear door. I clipped on my parachute pack and I noticed some of the silk was showing so I kept my arm across it to prevent any further spillage. (In retrospect I can only assume that a piece of flak must have hit it in its stowage, immediately behind my seat.)

I climbed over the main spar and met the mid upper gunner who shouted in my ear that the rear was alight and that we couldn't get out that way. Forward again over the main spar and now the aircraft was shuddering violently. I stepped over the flight engineer just as the pilot was leaving his seat. He didn't see us and I didn't distract him but I remember releasing his oxygen tube as he made his way down to the front hatch. I saw him checking his harness and then I passed out through lack of oxygen.

I 'came to' in a cornfield with some German soldiers and French civilians looking at me. I recall seeing some burning wreckage in the next field, but things were hazy as I must have banged my head on landing as I had a broken nose as well as a broken right arm and leg. My parachute must have dragged me too as my face, legs and hands were covered in cuts and grazes.

I looked at the Germans and asked 'Deutsch?' and one answered, 'Ja', and that was the limit of our conversation. I indicated my top pocket and a Frenchman took out my cigarettes and lit one for me.

Splints were put on my arm and leg and a lorry, with a layer of straw on the floor, took me to the hospital in St Omer. Beside me lay the mid upper gunner wrapped in his parachute with a lot of blood on it.

Flight Sergeant Hobbs stayed at hospital a short while and was then transferred to a POW camp. The Frenchman who gave Hobbs his cigarette was André Schamp:

> At about 5 p.m. (German time) I was working in the school garden in the village of Leulinghem, near St Omer, where my wife was the schoolmistress. I heard the bombers and also the DCA (flak) and then I saw one of the bombers coming down in flames. I ran the 200 or 300 metres across the fields and I was terrified as the aircraft was right above me and whichever way I ran it seemed to follow me. At a height of about 100 or 150 metres it exploded and changed direction, crashing about 200 metres away and after the explosion some parachutes came down like candles. In spite of the exploding ammunition I searched and found the officer [Flight Lieutenant] Edward [DFC] dead near the plane and also [Flight Sergeant] Isherwood but [Flying Officer] Johnston [DFC RCAF] was still alive although unconscious. I ran home to get my first aid kit and took Johnston's revolver with me. On my return the Germans had arrived and were suspicious that the holster was empty but that there was ammunition in the pouch. However I got away with it. I found the 'radio officer' sitting in the field of oats, his head barely visible. He had fractures to his right arm and leg and superficial face wounds. He indicated his top pocket and I took out his cigarettes and lit one for him. He thanked me in English and then said in French, 'Vive la France', but I never knew his name. Both he and the unconscious Johnston were put in a lorry and taken to hospital in St Omer.

Flying Officer Johnston DFC RCAF would later die from his injuries. In addition to the injured airmen, Flying Officer Pritchard DFC RCAF and Flight Sergeant Brook were also captured. André Schamp continues:

> The rear gunner was dead in his smouldering turret and I waited till late at night when the Germans said that my presence was no longer desirable. Next morning after church services I was confronted by a German army truck and ordered to empty its contents. They were the bodies of Edward and Isherwood and we laid them in cloth on the church floor and organised the funerals for the following day. My wife and I tried to bribe the guard with snacks and drinks to release the gunner but it took three visits to the main office in Longuenesse to get the necessary permission for burial. He was in a terrible condition and difficult to remove from his turret but my courageous wife laid him out as best she could.
> Three graves were dug in the churchyard and we made oak

coffins for them. Due to the bombardment, the electricity was cut off and the coffins had to be made by hand, completing them at 1 a.m. A beautiful service was read in my own Roman Catholic religion and help was numerous from everyone.[54]

André Rolin was a local farmer who also witnessed the demise of the Lancaster:

The following day I went up to the field next to the crash site to make out I was working there. This was just an excuse to see what was going on, and much to my surprise up the narrow road came Russian POWs, in lorries. They stopped at the site and jumped out. There would be about 200 in all. They looked most odd in their striped pyjama-type clothes. They were quickly directed to the remains of the Lancaster and they started digging. After about an hour they dragged out what appeared to be a large piece of aeroplane. It was manhandled on to a low trailer by the Russian POWs and taken away.

The Russian prisoners had been used to extract the remains of the Tallboy bomb, which might well have been the first the Germans had managed to obtain. With the Germans believing they had accounted for the Lancaster's normal seven aircrew (four captured and three dead), the crash site was cleared. André Rolin continues:

It was late July and I started cutting the cornfield that the Lancaster crashed in. There were no tractors in those days; we used horses to pull the small machine. At a point beyond the crash site the pair of horses stopped, and would not move again. They appeared to be under some stress. I jumped off the machine to see what the problem was, and to my horror there amongst the ripening corn was the body of a British flyer. I immediately stopped work and reported what I had found to the local policeman. He informed the German garrison in St Omer who sent a party out to recover the body.[55]

The Germans had not been aware that there had in fact been a crew of eight on the Lancaster. André Rolin had discovered the body of Flying Officer King DFC, the flight engineer. Warrant Officer Price RCAF, who lost his life, had been the extra person in the front gunner position.

The Crossbow Counter-measures Progress Report number 41 gives a summary of the bombing counter-offensive to 24 June,[56] and records that 27 attacks had been made by Bomber Command and the American Eighth Air Force against six of the supply sites in the Pas de Calais/Dieppe area. The 4,284 tons dropped, the majority by Bomber Command, resulted in three of the sites being assessed as having 10 to 50% visible damage. The other supply sites were assessed as having less than 10% visible damage. The report also mentioned suspected flying bomb supply depots at the underground cave complexes at Nucourt and St Leu d'Esserent being scheduled for attack. The American Eighth Air Force initiated the bombing on Nucourt when the 250 tons dropped by the heavies caused major damage to buildings and the railway. It was also believed that the roof of the underground caves had possibly collapsed, evidenced by subsidence on the surface. Allied intelligence had now placed the supply depots in the suspected transportation system of the flying bombs:

> From all the evidence it appears that flying bombs and components are moved by rail from Germany to the depots in the Paris and Rheims areas in the first place [St Leu d'Esserent, Nucourt and Rilly-la-Montagne] and that from these depots the bombs, after the assembly and testing of fuselages, are moved by road to the launching sites where the wings are put on, fuses set and final adjustments made before launching. It is probable but not certain that the launching rockets are filled at the supply sites and delivered thence to launching sites. It is probable that considerable stocks of bombs and parts are held in the depots and that apart from reductions caused by our destruction of the launching sites the rate of fire is governed as much by the road transport problem involved as by any other factor.[57]

It is important to note and re-emphasise in the above quote that supply sites are featured as 'probable' in the flying bomb transport system. A 'probable' that would receive further attention from the bombers.

Since the opening of the flying bomb offensive the Allies had dropped a considerable bomb tonnage, nearly 9,000 tons, on the French targets. Bomber Command had focused the vast majority of its attention, approximately a third of the total Allied bomb tonnage, on supply sites. Resultant damage to all targets fell below expectations and appeared to be having very little impact on the ability the Germans had in supplying their launch sites and their launch rates. Indeed this was the case and Flakregiment 155(W) was most optimistic about their offensive. Up to midday on 24 June they had fired 1,352 flying bombs at England (212 of which crashed), since the full opening of the offensive on the night of 15/16 June. An average of 150 flying bombs per 24-hour period. The regiment's diary is full of intelligence reports detailing the chaos that their activities were causing on the other side of the English Channel. This was not just enthusiastic optimism. Although the Germans would not know it, in the main owing to British censoring of incidents, 723 people had been killed and 2,610 seriously injured in the first week of the attacks. There was indeed major disruption in the English capital. Flakregiment 155(W) even started thinking about expanding its area of operation to cover the entire coastline from France to Holland.

Bomber Command was now called upon to conduct more sorties directly against the flying bomb launch sites. On the night of 24/25 June a vast armada of the RAF's heavy bombers, crewed by over 5,000 airmen, crossed the French coast to conduct a massive attack against the launch sites.

CHAPTER 8

NIGHT BATTLE

Graham Inward was eight years old at the time of the flying bomb raids in the summer of 1944. His father was an ARP warden in London.

> I can hear my father saying in mid-June 1944 'There's talk of a German pilotless plane.' I can remember thinking that that's impossible. This was the beginning of my biggest fear of the war – the V1, doodlebug or buzz-bomb. The sound of one of those still makes my stomach turn over. That dreaded deep throbbing sound that got closer and closer and louder and louder. You hoped it would pass over and the sound disappear before the engine cut and it plunged to earth with an almighty explosion. Sometimes the engine cut long before it reached us but the explosion was still loud, even more so in the middle of the night. At night I was always awakened by the sound of a V1 – it seemed so much louder and more eerie than during the day. I can recollect seeing one in the daytime flying northwards – not very high and belching flames from its rear. It was travelling quickly away from us and I felt no fear.
>
> One night I was sleeping downstairs with most of my body under my father's desk (that is where I slept during an air raid) when I was awakened by this fearful, horrific deep throbbing sound of a V1. It got closer, closer, closer until it was right overhead and the whole house vibrated – when the engine cut. I held my breath, curling into a tight embryonic position with my heart beating to burst. Then there was an enormous explosion – the whole house shook but remarkably no windows broke. The next morning we heard it had landed in a nearby park with apparently no casualties but leaving an enormous crater. That V1 sound and those ten or so seconds after the engine cut are still with me and will never fade.[58]

This event led to Graham being evacuated. His father also took the precaution of obtaining a Morrison shelter.

On 20 June 1944 Commander-in-Chief of the Luftwaffe Reich Marshal Hermann Goering sent a message to General Walter von Axthelm. As commander of anti-aircraft forces, under the auspices of the Luftwaffe, von Axthelm had taken a major lead in the planning of the flying bomb offensive.

> The first effective blow dealt by our weapon, on the development of which you and your staff have done such excellent work, has struck terror into the enemy and has earned the gratitude and admiration of the whole German people. By untiring labour and passionate devotion to this project you, my dear Axthelm, and your colleagues, have surmounted all difficulties and made possible the blows which are hammering the enemy with deadly effect and meting out terrible retribution for the crime of his terror raids.
>
> When the history of this unique German invention comes to be written, tribute must be paid to your exemplary achievement. But I wish here and now to express to you, one of my most praiseworthy collaborators, my wholehearted appreciation and sincere congratulation on the occasion of the successful accomplishment of your task. I am equally grateful to Oberst von Gyldenfeld and his staff and also to Oberst Wachtel, who formed an excellently disciplined unit for our new weapon. All have accomplished their task in secret. The success achieved is the best reward for their efforts.[59]

The message is indicative of the fact that there was great optimism throughout the Luftwaffe for the flying bomb offensive. An offensive that could possibly relieve some of the mounting pressure on the German air force.

The Allies had really achieved daylight air superiority in Western Europe by the middle of 1944, but at a significant cost. In the autumn of 1943 the United States Eighth Air Force had made deep penetration raids into Germany, relying on its tight defensive bomber formations to counter the Luftwaffe day fighters. The day battles raged with considerable (and by some deemed unacceptable) losses sustained by the American bomber force. In one week in October 1943 the Eighth Air Force lost 148 bombers on deep penetration raids, an unsustainable loss rate. It soon became clear to the Allied planners that fighter escorts were essential if deep penetration bombing raids were to be continued, but at that time these escorts were not available. The air battles did however keep the Luftwaffe attrition rates high and in order to maintain their defensive effort on the Western Front they began to transfer units from other fronts.

One means of extending the range of fighter escorts was the use of the drop tank and throughout November and December 1943 the escorts for the American bomber forces, equipped with their drop tanks and greater amounts of fuel, were able to reach further and further into the Reich. The attrition continued but the Eighth Air Force would be able to withstand the losses better than the Luftwaffe, particularly with regard to the supply of experienced and suitably trained airmen.

During the first three months of 1944 the availability of American bombers and crews grew. Germany's defensive daylight fighter forces still exacted their toll but continued to sustain losses. To compound the Luftwaffe's problems, the German aircraft industry was now under attack from the Allied bombers, a strategy that soon became clear to the Germans who despite their own attrition felt they had to engage the bomber formations and risk combats with the escorts. The problem was not actually the numbers of aircraft lost, as despite the targeting of the aircraft industry German fighter production actually rose, but what really mattered was their considerable losses from enemy engagements with the resultant unaffordable losses of experienced fighter crews. The American bombers and escorts kept the pressure on, and demonstrated their growing daylight air superiority in March 1944 when they reached and bombed Berlin. The Germans were quite clearly losing the daylight air battle.

In preparation for Overlord the Allies had begun to execute the Transportation Plan, targeting the transportation system in northern France, in particular the rail marshalling yards. Alongside this the importance of air superiority remained a priority and attacks were conducted on French airfields. Both Bomber Command and the American Eighth Air Force were required to play their roles in the attacks on the rail yards, but the Americans still managed to attack the German aircraft industry and synthetic fuel production. During May 1944 the Eighth Air Force attacked the oil targets, with evidence from Ultra (generic term used for intelligence obtained through intercepting and decoding German messages) decrypts supporting such attacks by indicating that the Germans were beginning to suffer a general shortage of fuel. Still attrition rates remained high for both sides; indeed the German fighter aircraft and fighter pilot losses achieved their highest point in the war.

Following the opening of the Allied invasion of Normandy on 6 June 1944, the American bomber forces again began raiding the aviation fuel targets, with considerable success and the German production rates plummeted. The air engagements continued and American and German losses continued, but the German pilot losses began to prove critical. Pressure was put on training schools to pass their trainee pilots quicker and calls were made on other Luftwaffe areas of operation to release their pilots to the day battles over the Reich. During the summer of 1944 the German wartime fighter production peaked, but the problems of who was left to fly the aircraft, how experienced they were and whether there was enough fuel to get the aircraft in the air remained. The Allies had achieved general daylight air supremacy and the progress of the Allied land forces in France was hardly threatened by German air attacks. There would still be daylight bombing raids with high losses but the Luftwaffe was not allowed to recover from the attrition rates suffered in the second half of 1943 and the first half of 1944.

However the German nightfighter force could on some nights still be a most formidable opponent to Bomber Command. On the night of 21/22 June 1944 two forces of RAF heavy bombers were sent to synthetic oil plants at Wesseling and Scholven Buer. At Wesseling the German nightfighters penetrated the bomber stream and from a force of 133 Lancasters and 6 Mosquitos, 37 Lancasters failed to return, a staggeringly high casualty rate of 27.8%. On the raid to Scholven Buer, 8 Lancasters from the force of 123 Lancasters and 9 Mosquitos failed to return. Of course these raids required penetration by the RAF bombers into the defended air space over Germany. The attacks on the flying bomb supply and launch targets were of a shorter duration over northern France, giving the nightfighter controllers less time to vector their defending aircraft into the bomber streams. Time was a key factor. The longer the bombers spent on reaching, bombing and getting away from a target, the greater the opportunity for the prowling fighters to locate their prey.

The night of 24/25 June 1944 saw a massive effort by Bomber Command against flying bomb launch sites in the Pas de Calais area. Eventually 739 aircraft, and over 5,000 airmen, were despatched.

Target and aircraft despatched	Plan of attack
Prouville	Zero hour – 0015 hours
103 Lancasters, 9 Mosquitos	Using the 5 Group technique, 5 Oboe
366.1 tons high explosive	Mosquitos to mark the aiming point with
1.7 tons incendiary bombs	yellow TI at z-3 (to burn for 3 mins). A
	Controller was then to direct the attack.
Pommeréval	Zero hour – 2355 hours
102 Lancasters, 9 Mosquitos	(as for Prouville)
388.5 tons high explosive	
2.1 tons incendiary bombs	
Middel Straete	Zero hour – 0125 hours
80 Lancasters, 5 Mosquitos	5 Oboe Mosquitos, ground marking, to place
319.6 tons high explosive	red TI. The main force to aim at the centre of
1.3 tons incendiary bombs	the TI.
Le Grand Rossignol	Zero hour – 0300 hours
2 Lancasters, 100 Halifaxes,	As for Middel Straete, with the addition that
5 Mosquitos	backers up to aim greens at the centre of the
363.1 tons high explosive	reds. The main force to bomb the centre of the
1.3 tons incendiary bombs	reds, or greens, or blindly.
Rimeux	Zero hour – 0030 hours
78 Lancasters, 24 Stirlings,	As for Le Grand Rossignol.
5 Mosquitos	
438.1 tons high explosive	
3.4 tons incendiary bombs	
Bamières	Zero hour – 0145 hours
40 Lancasters, 65 Halifaxes,	As for Le Grand Rossignol.
5 Mosquitos	
389.3 tons high explosive	
3.1 tons incendiary bombs	

Flers

102 Lancasters, 5 Mosquitos
393.3 tons high explosive
2.7 tons incendiary bombs

Zero hour – 0315 hours

As for Middel Straete, using controlled Oboe ground marking, except that a master bomber, or deputy, to keep the aiming point marked with greens, the centre of which was the aiming point for the main force. If the Oboe marking was accurate, the master bomber would remain silent, but use yellows, if necessary, to distinguish the aiming point.

Good weather conditions were forecast for the bases in England. Little or no cloud was expected in northern France. Indeed the skies over the targets were all reported later as cloudless, with only a slight haze. There was a new moon, setting at 0045.

Early on in the night's activities the German nightfighters were airborne and directed to radio beacons in the Lille, Cambrai, St Quentin area. This resulted in a number of contacts with the bombers on the first three raids of the night, searchlights and flak adding to the bombers' worries. On the raid to Pommeréval, the first attack of the night and while the full moon was still up, four Lancasters were lost. Bomber Command ascertained from returning crews' post-raid reports that two were lost to fighters and two to flak. Two of these were the 44 Squadron Lancasters, piloted by Pilot Officer Aiken RCAF (pilot and crew killed) and Flight Sergeant Oswald (pilot and three of his crew killed, two evaders and one POW). The 49 Squadron Lancaster of Flying Officer Taylor was lost (pilot and two of the crew became POWs, one man evaded and three men were killed) and the 106 Squadron Lancaster of Pilot Officer Wright RAAF also failed to return (pilot and four of the crew killed, one evader and one POW).

German nightfighters were then able to engage the bombers involved on the next two attacks to Prouville and Rimeux, again while the moon was up. The searchlight operators assisted the nightfighters by lighting up their enemy. One bomber was actually held by searchlight cones passing it on for as long as 25 minutes with no flak fired.

The following quotes are from Bomber Command airmen who took part in the Prouville raid:

> *Sergeant Bob Riches, rear gunner, 9 Squadron:* I recall that we went into briefing on that night and when the curtain was pulled back it looked like a doddle – an hour and a half each way – 15 minutes over France. We arrived at the French coast and were told to hold although there were TIs burning on the ground. The flak was not very heavy, but searchlights were wandering all over the sky.
>
> *Sergeant Fred Fossett, bomb aimer, 463 Squadron:* I remember the mass of searchlights, and flak, as we ran up to the target, and the constant instructions from the Controller, for the pathfinders[60] to illuminate the target, and get the TIs down. I visualised having to go round again, but suddenly we received

the instructions to 'bomb the red'. I was relieved at that, and completed my run up, pressed the release, when the instruction came to cease bombing. We were able to continue our run out, and return to base, but there were some fighter flares dropping as we pulled away.

Pilot Officer Don Street was piloting the 61 Squadron Lancaster 'Y' Yoke:

From the time the Lancaster force crossed the enemy coast it was running the gauntlet down a corridor of searchlights through to the target area . . . 'Y' Yoke was detailed to fly in the second wave of the attack and thus we were able to observe a frightening spectacle as we approached. A number of blue/white master beam searchlights, radar controlled, it was said, moved across the sky in positive movements. One would fasten onto an unfortunate aircraft and was immediately backed up by four or five white searchlight beams. Once coned it was difficult to evade or slip away into the comparative safety of the dark night.

My mid upper gunner, Sergeant Peter 'Jock' Haddon, had good all round vision from his turret: 'Skipper. They are using nightfighters!'

I blinked upwards from the flying panel instruments to the scene ahead and just caught sight of a line of orange dots in the dark sky disappearing into an aircraft held in a searchlight cone.

'Pilot to crew. I'm going to drop my seat now and concentrate on instruments.' Directional gyro, artificial horizon, airspeed, altitude, turn and bank – rate of climb and descent, the panel so familiar to all night fliers. I fiddled about with the seat controls and it dropped with a bit of a thud. When I had re-aligned my sight on the panel I called:

'Pilot to crew. Now if we are coned, gunners try and shoot down the beams, you might knock some out. We'll go into corkscrew, they won't get us.'

Although the sky was crowded there was still plenty of airspace and I knew that other crews would keep clear of an aircraft caught in a cone, happy, as I would be, that someone else was claiming attention from the enemy.

'Y' Yoke, lumbering along at a steady 155 mph indicated airspeed, was now well into the forest of light beams and we were hoping that we might have the luck to sneak through. There was an almost audible click as a blue beam locked onto our aircraft and the cone was immediately completed as the white slave beams swung into position. A white void held our aircraft suspended, vulnerable and helpless. Inside the plane everywhere was a blinding glare, picking out rivets, scraps of aluminium, shiny where paint had worn off, every nook and cranny not noticed before, all seen in an instant of time. Shoot down the beams I had said, but where was down, where were the searchlight batteries?

Except for the navigator, Warrant Officer Dave Grant RCAF, who always kept his head in the office with the curtains securely drawn, maintaining that he had problems enough without worrying about what was going on outside, the rest of the crew experienced a momentary shock. The sudden change from comparative safety of darkness to the total exposure in a light too bright to look at was a physical blow. It was however but a split second in time before the survival instinct surfaced.

'Hang on everybody. We're going down.'

A terse comment as I rammed the control column forward and dropped the port wing in a diving turn to the left. The altimeter unwound losing height by 500 feet – 1000 – 1500 – 2000. I rolled the aircraft over to a starboard turn still losing height. The dammed searchlights still held us. 2500 – 3000 – 3500 – 3700 feet then they were gone as suddenly as they came, blackness all around. I reached forward and turned on the orange shaded cockpit light and hauled the aircraft back onto course.

'Everyone OK?' I asked. The 'OK Skip' reassured me that I still had an operational crew. Well almost. My navigator complained. He would be as soon as he had found his goddam pencil and a few other tools of the trade.

A 97 Squadron Lancaster ND 501 was caught in the searchlights and would soon have the company of a German nightfighter. The crew's post-raid report detailed the subsequent combat in which the mid upper gunner Flying Officer Jones would fire off 350 rounds at his adversary:

We were still in a cone of approximately 20 searchlights, at least 6 of these seemed to be directed on the rear turret. The rear gunner called out that he was blinded, the mid upper saw the enemy aircraft, Ju88, on the starboard quarter up, he ordered 'starboard corkscrew', the enemy aircraft pointed its nose down for the attack as our own aircraft was rolling. This gave the mid upper gunner a pointblank shot. He opened fire and gave a very long burst; hits were observed and pieces seen to fall off the enemy aircraft. The mid upper was then blinded by the searchlights and could not see any final result or report the position of the enemy aircraft.[61]

Sergeant Bob Riches, rear gunner, 9 Squadron: We were told to bomb, but when on the run-in with the bomb doors open the signal came to hold again. Flares were dropping and the whole area was like daylight.

We circled for a while and were caught in a searchlight, but after diving and weaving violently soon lost it. The defences were using searchlight with a smoky blue beam, possibly radar-controlled, and when it picked up and locked onto an aircraft six or eight 'normal' ones coned the plane and nightfighters came in to destroy it. With the crew blinded they had no chance. At one time it appeared that aircraft were burning and crashing all over the place, but we were not attacked and I cannot recall seeing a German plane at all. All we felt was the violent turbulence of the slipstreams from all the aircraft that were milling around.

When at last we had the go-ahead to bomb Al Carr [bomb aimer] could not find the target, so he dropped our stick of bombs across the searchlight battery and then we got the hell out. I think we must have been one of the last to leave because we bombed at 00.43 hours

Sergeant Fred Whitfield, rear gunner, 9 Squadron: While we were waiting over the target for the pathfinders to drop flares and mark the target, we were caught by 30 to 40 searchlights, which held us for six to eight minutes . . . The moment I spotted an Me109 coming down the searchlight beam from the starboard, I gave the skipper [Pilot Officer Ron Adams] instructions to corkscrew starboard, which he did. I fired my four guns and could see four lines of tracer bullets ploughing into him. He broke away in flames.

The second fighter to attack was a Junkers 88, a twin-engine fighter. He tried following us through the corkscrew; my bullets didn't seem to be making any impression on him, he still kept coming on, although my tracer bullets were ricocheting off him in all directions. He fired one long burst at us which appeared to me to be a long sheet of flame, which passed over my head. The next I knew I could feel cold air on my face. I appeared to be sitting outside. The turret had been hit but I was OK and continued to fire at him. The next I knew there were flames coming from one of his engines, he rolled on his back and passed below us.

The next to come in was another Me109 and it was Frank Stebbings [the mid upper gunner] who spotted him first and fired. I could see the mid upper gunner's tracer bullets flying over my head. I fired my four machine guns and he also rolled onto his back in flames and passed beneath us. It was quite reassuring to know Frank was there.

The Junkers 88 had hit one of our port engines and set it on fire. Jack Facheux, our wireless operator later remarked that when he saw the flames from the engine and the cannon shell holes stretching the length of the fuselage, he was sure the Skipper would give the instruction to bale out. He was quite cool and was working out in his mind the best escape method to use when he landed. (The order to bale out never came.) The Skipper and Larry [Brown] our flight engineer managed to put the fire out.

After Phil [Jackson] had bombed, Jim Lynam, the navigator, gave the Skipper a direct course for base. We hadn't flown very far, when the Skipper remarked that the controls were a bit heavy and it was at this point that the mid upper gunner, who could see the top of the aircraft, reported that we only had one fin and rudder. The starboard fin had been shot off as well as six feet of the port wing.

After crossing the Channel we were greeted with more anti-aircraft fire from our own guns. This we could not understand as we had our navigation lights on. It was only when I stood up in the turret and looked down that I spotted a buzzbomb flying on the same course as ourselves. The Ack-Ack gunners below were firing at the red glow of the flying bomb's engine, missing it and getting very close to us. We altered course in time to see it being shot down.

When we landed back at base we were amazed at the amount of damage our aircraft had sustained and how it had remained airborne was a miracle. It never flew again.

I shall always remember the Skipper's face when he removed his oxygen mask; it was quite drawn and I shall always maintain he is the greatest pilot in the RAF. Just how Ron Adams worked that night and got us back to base we will never know.

The attacks to Le Grand Rossignol and Flers were the last of the night's operations against the flying bomb launch sites. Many a bomber crew throughout the war had become victims of complacency. With the targets in France only a short distance from England, some felt they could relax a little. The 578 Squadron Lancaster, piloted by Sergeant Geoff Sanders, had a replacement rear gunner, a pilot officer, for the operation to Le Grand Rossignol. After bombing the target the mid upper gunner informed his skipper that he could smell smoke, which started to smell familiar. Climbing out of his turret he was amazed to see the rear gunner standing next to the Elsan toilet smoking a cigarette. Climbing back into his turret the mid upper gunner informed his captain, who decided to say nothing quite yet. Upon return to base the pilot gave his stand-in rear gunner a serious dressing down, emphasising the idiocy of his actions when still at risk of enemy attack and when standing next to a quantity of semi-volatile chemicals. Sergeant Sanders refused to fly with the higher ranking rear gunner ever again.[62]

Bomber Command would later note that the ground defences on the raids to the launch sites had been slight. Obviously any flak gunners that were there were giving the nightfighters the chance to engage their foe without running the risk of friendly fire.

At Prouville, with problems identifying the target, the attack lasted over half an hour and the waiting German nightfighters took advantage of the concentration of bombers. A total of 13 Lancasters did not return from the raid. No. 9 Squadron lost the Lancasters of Flight Sergeant Halshaw (pilot and five of the crew killed, two POWs), Pilot Officer Rae RCAF (pilot and five of the crew killed, one evader), and Pilot Officer Craig, whose aircraft was actually caught by searchlights after crossing the French coast and became a victim of flak (pilot and four of the crew killed, two POWs). No. 50 Squadron lost the Lancasters of Pilot Officer Wood, which was attacked by a nightfighter and exploded with the entire crew killed, and Pilot Officer Peters RCAF (six of the crew were killed, one evader and the pilot was captured). No. 61 Squadron lost the Lancasters of Flight Lieutenant Forrest RAAF, shot down by a nightfighter (pilot and five of the crew killed, one evader), and Pilot Officer Kramer RCAF (pilot and five of the crew killed, one evader). No. 97 Squadron lost the Lancaster of Flight Lieutenant Walton DFC, which was attacked by a nightfighter (three of the crew were killed, three became POWs and the pilot evaded capture). No. 463 Squadron lost the Lancasters of Pilot Officer Martin RAAF, which was a victim of a nightfighter (pilot and five of the crew killed, one POW), Pilot Officer Tilbrook RAAF, attacked by a nightfighter (pilot and five of the crew killed, one POW) and Wing Commander Donaldson RAAF (see below, pilot and three of the crew evaded capture, three POWs). No. 467 Squadron lost the Lancasters of Pilot Officer Berryman RAAF (pilot killed, two evaders and four POWs) and Flight Lieutenant Cowan DFC RAAF, which was hit by flak (pilot and four of the crew killed, two men were injured but later died). Monsieur Robert Davergne witnessed the demise of Flight Lieutenant Cowan's Lancaster:

> On the night of 24/25 June 1944 I was aware that aerial activity was more intense than usual. The sky was lit up by searchlights and there was the sound of machine-gun fire from fighter aircraft, anti-aircraft fire from the ground and bombers flying overhead. Suddenly I made out the moving white outline of a bomber coned by three searchlights. The aircraft managed to escape from the beams for about five seconds then was trapped again. The aircraft kept coming on into a stream of fire from the ground until it was hit. It caught fire and started to come down, passing over the roofs of the houses in the village about 1000 feet above me. The crew had some time to bale out before the aircraft crashed near some trees with a deafening sound several hundred yards away. The bomb load exploded and the aircraft was completely destroyed.
>
> In the night sky, I made out the shape of a parachute slowly descending in the glare. The airman ([Sergeant] Jack Sheffield) reached the ground alive near a neighbour's house, belonging to Mr Boitel.
>
> Mr Boitel watched the aircraft crashing in flames. He went back inside his house and was just about to close the bedroom window when a man appeared who proceeded to climb through the window into the room. At once Mr Boitel realised the man had parachuted from the blazing aircraft. Mr Boitel laid the airman on the bed in order to treat his injuries. The man was burned all over. Mrs Boitel put lard all over his body to soothe

him. Apart from his burned black clothes and parachute harness the man wore two crosses around his neck.

The airman indicated that he wanted to be taken to hospital. A doctor was sent for who came and looked after him. The airman died several hours later. His burns were too severe. Apart from being burned, he showed no other sign of being injured.

The following day I saw the dead bodies of five airmen laid out side by side in a room of a neighbouring farmhouse, not far from where the aircraft had exploded. Four days later the airmen were buried in the communal cemetery (at Mareuil-Caubert) where each year key figures and local people go to reflect on what happened that night.

The other airmen were certainly dead before they reached the ground. One was found with his parachute crumpled on his back, another fell near to where the aircraft crashed, two more were found on the plain (Villers-sur-Mareuil).[63]

Sergeant Laurie Boness, flying as flight engineer on a 463 (RAAF) Squadron Lancaster, recalls his experiences on the Prouville raid:

My crew arrived at Waddington on 15 June 1944. Our pilot, Flying Officer Bill Gossip, was killed flying with Flight Lieutenant Eric Smith and his crew on his second dickie trip in a raid on Gelsenkirchen on 21/22 June 1944. Wing Commander Don Donaldson had just joined 463 Squadron from 460 Squadron as squadron commander and he took us on our first operation – to Prouville – in Lancaster LM597, JO-W, a brand new aircraft.

Ours was the first aircraft of the thirty four to take off from Waddington that night. We had a fairly uneventful flight as far as the French coast near Abbeville, then we could see in front of us dozens and dozens of searchlights waiting for us. I was busy pushing bundles of 'Window' [metallic strips designed to fog German radar] out of the aircraft as we lined up to start our bombing run and I can remember Cyril Small, our bomb aimer, giving the Skipper instructions, 'Left . . . left . . . steady', when above the roar of the engines I heard the sound of a German flak burst. It stood the plane on a wing tip and the Skipper did well to stop the aircraft going over on its back. He righted it, but by this time both wings were a mass of flames streaming back past the tail and the order was given to put on parachutes. As soon as the aircraft was hit, the whole fuselage filled up with thick black smoke. It was practically impossible to see. I think we were very fortunate to be flying just high enough that we were on oxygen at the time, otherwise we would have choked. I always used to stow my parachute behind the pilot's seat, but on feeling for it I could not find it. Panic for a few seconds, then I found it. It had become dislodged from its usual place because of the violent movements of the aircraft. I made my way down the steps to the forward escape hatch to find Cyril struggling to get the hatch up and open. Cyril had been badly wounded in one arm and later, once he had parachuted safely, he was picked up by the Germans, taken to hospital and had his arm amputated. Anyway, Cyril managed to get the hatch open and baled out, followed by me – feet first – not the approved way. I can't remember pulling the rip cord and many years afterwards this lapse in memory still troubled me.

On the way down, once my chute had opened, the Germans shone two of their searchlights on me for a considerable time. I was very frightened that I would be shot at as I descended, but I have no recollection of this actually happening. However, talking to several crews back at Waddington months later, they told me they had seen the Germans shooting at an airman as he came down in his parachute lit up by searchlights. They were very annoyed about this, but I don't think it was me they saw. As it happened, during my descent I saw a Lancaster fly over just above me with flames streaming from one of its wings. In an instant the searchlight beams lifted from me to it and from then on I continued my descent in darkness. I did not see anyone bale out of the stricken aircraft and I have no doubt its presence saved me. When I landed I managed to bury my chute in the sides of a recently made bomb crater. Then I started to put as much distance as I could between me and my landing place.

Some time later I made contact with a French family who gave me shelter and helped me find further assistance until the area was liberated. As you can imagine, we became very good friends, although at the time I could speak no French. After the war my wife and I visited my French helpers many times and I studied French so I could communicate with them better. One of the first questions I asked the lady of the family was why she had done it in view of the risks to herself, her husband and her children, not to mention the cost of obtaining extra food on the black market to feed me. She said she had felt so sorry for me, I looked so thin and young (I was 19 at the time) that she felt she had to treat me as one of the family. Sadly the lady is dead now, but down the years we still keep in touch with her children who have visited us in England several times.

As I was being transported back to England, I learned to my amazement and overwhelming joy that all my crew had managed to get out of our blazing aircraft and had survived. In fact four of us had managed to evade capture, including Wing Commander Donaldson. Apparently, he had had some difficulty convincing the French Resistance of his identity, because flying with a 'headless crew', he had not known our names!

Cyril Small was repatriated in February 1945 because of the

severity of his injuries. He found his way to Liverpool on board a hospital ship called the *Letitia* steaming out of Marseilles. When he got to Liverpool, who should be standing on the wharf waiting for him but Don Donaldson. Some Air Force the RAAF![64]

The Prouville raid clearly highlights the potential difficulty of the 5 Group method of marking and then identifying the target. If there were problems in identifying the target as the main force crews arrived then the concentration of bombers over the target would increase as time progressed. If this coincided with the presence of nightfighters, as it did in this case, then, unsurprisingly, numerous combats would result.

At Rimeux, scheduled to be attacked just after Prouville, two Lancasters and two Stirlings were lost. No. 75 Squadron lost the Lancaster of Flight Sergeant Bateson RNZAF with no survivors. There were also no survivors from the 90 Squadron Lancaster of Flight Sergeant Mellors, which fell victim to a nightfighter attack. The 149 Squadron Stirlings of Flight Lieutenant Roe and Flying Officer Wunsch also failed to return with the entire crews of both aircraft killed.

At Flers, the last raid of the night, one Lancaster was lost from 576 Squadron, piloted by Flying Officer Alcorn RAAF with no survivors.

Information from returning crews indicated that the raids were accurate and well centred on aiming points. Subsequent day reconnaissance revealed the following:

Prouville	All the visible craters were to the north of the target.
Pommeréval	4 target buildings and 10 houses along with some other installations within a perimeter wire, were destroyed or damaged. Many craters could be seen in the target area.
Middel Straete	3 hits were made on the launching point, many new craters could be seen in the target area.
Le Grand Rossignol	5 bombs had hit a square building, 1 landed on the launching platform, 20 hit the road traversing the target.
Rimeux	2 bombs seriously damaged the base of the launching point, which also had 3 near misses. The square building received a damaged roof.
Bamières	The square building was destroyed. The launching point had a near miss, 60 new craters could be seen in the target area.
Flers	No apparent damage. Attack fell to the south and east of the target.

It is interesting to note that the air battle raging over northern France on this night was witnessed by a number of the units of Flakregiment 155(W). The regiment's diary recorded the event from the ground and suspected that their headquarters at Amiens was the target for the bombers:

> North, north-west and west of Amiens, the enemy aircraft dropped cascades of flares, but a surprise attack by German nightfighter formations prevented them dropping bombs. Our nightfighters intercepted and defeated it in 30 minutes of bitter fighting.[65]

It is also interesting to point out that on this night only 45 flying bombs were fired from 35 sites, 5 of them crashing. This is a major fall from the daily average of 150 firings since the main start of the offensive. This could possibly been due to supply but it may also have been due to the fact that firing units believed that a launch would identify the position of the launch site to the bombers flying overhead. The diary of Flakregiment 155(W) suggests that they thought that the Allies had not yet identified all the launch sites.

The very next day four forces were despatched to flying bomb targets, 3 of which were raids to launch sites: 102 Lancasters and 5 Mosquitos to attack Liegescourt, 2 Lancasters, 101 Halifaxes and 5 Mosquitos to Montorgueil and 2 Lancasters, 101 Halifaxes and 5 Mosquitos to Gorenflos. At Liegescourt the master bomber ordered the crews to bomb the markers that straddled the aiming point. Visibility was so good that half of the main force bombed visually. The returning crews reported the bombing as accurate and one of the fighter escorts reported shooting down a defending fighter. The force sent to Gorenflos was able to identify the target visually and a good concentration of bombs was achieved.[66]

Having taken part in, and returned from the raid to Noyelle-en-Chausée II the day before, Sergeant Thomas Fox, flight engineer with 77 Squadron, and his crew found themselves detailed for another raid:

> In a few hours we were over France again on our way to Montorgueil with weather very much the same as the day before, visibility was excellent and the trip out was very pleasant. Approaching the target we saw an aircraft above release his stick of bombs and very sad to say they landed on a Halifax, which was flying at our height just a few hundred yards in front of us. The aircraft disintegrated into very small fragments with no sign of life at all. We flew through the smoke and debris and onto the target; after 'bombs away' we turned for home feeling quite sick. The aircraft in question was one from our own squadron and the crew we knew very well indeed.[67]

What Sergeant Fox didn't see was that the struck Halifax then fell onto another Halifax. Sergeant Geoffrey Salisbury was a bomb aimer with 76 Squadron:

> The two aircraft disintegrated with a massive explosion on our starboard side. We were on the bombing run and I saw masses

of debris including the starboard wing of one of the stricken aircraft spiral down to earth. It was a horrendous business and did not help our powers of concentration on our bombing run.

The two aircraft involved in the unfortunate incident were the 77 Squadron Halifax flown by Flight Sergeant MacSteven and the 102 Squadron Halifax flown by Squadron Leader Treasure, whilst both were on their bombing run. There were no survivors from the two crews and the cause of the collision was soon reported by returning crews. The Melbourne Base records (10 Squadron) recorded the following:

> One of our aircraft stated that his bombs had hit another Halifax causing it to explode. Other crews reported seeing this incident and said that the wreckage of the aircraft hit fell upon another aircraft causing that also to go down in flames.[68]

One other aircraft conducted its last operation on this raid. The 102 Squadron Halifax, piloted by Squadron Leader Kercher, overshot the runway and was written off, fortunately with no casualties. Over Montorgueil, bombing had been carried out visually and on well-grouped TI. Reconnaissance of Montorgueil on 29 June indicated hits to all three ski buildings, to the concrete platform, to one other building, and slight damage to another building.

The fourth flying bomb target on 25 June was the large site at Siracourt, with 17 Lancasters, 2 Mosquitos and a single-engined North American P-51 Mustang Mark III despatched. This was the first raid against a flying bomb target in which a Mustang was used. Wing Commander Cheshire of 617 Squadron, in an effort to improve marking by giving him more manouverability over the target, had been able to persuade the Americans to allow him the use of the single-engined fighter. Cheshire also felt more comfortable with regard to the risky nature of his low level marking, as there was no responsibility for any other crew member.[69] The Mustang arrived on 25 June but would not be quite ready when the main force Lancasters took off, the first getting airborne at 0710 hours. Cheshire, who had never flown in a Mustang before and read the pilot's notes whilst waiting to take off, lifted the aircraft off the runway at 0753 hours and with his speed he was able to catch up with the Lancaster force. Conducting a dive attack from 7,000 to 500 feet he placed the red spot fires on the target at 0900½ hours. These were backed up by the two Mosquitos with smoke bombs and red spot fires. Cheshire remained over the target, assessing the subsequent bombing, and witnessing one direct hit penetrating the roof of the building with a large explosion. One further hit was made on the western wall with several other hits in the target area. The Lancasters all used 12,000 lb Tallboys for bombing. Invented by Barnes Wallis, the inventor of the bouncing bomb used on the Dams raids of May 1943, the Tallboy bomb's good ballistics, high blast potential and excellent armour-piercing qualities meant it was an appropriate weapon to use against underground or heavily concreted targets, such as Siracourt. The attacking bombers did not have it easy over the target, encountering heavy flak.

Several aircraft were damaged. One of the Lancasters, damaged by the flak, had a bomb hang up and had to jettison it over the sea. On return from the operation there was no rest for the aircrews as their aircraft were immediately prepared for another operation. However this was later called off.

On 27 June 2 Lancasters, 104 Halifaxes and 5 Mosquitos were sent against the large site at Mimoyecques. The 640 Squadron Halifax of Flight Sergeant Papple swerved off the runway on take-off and crashed. Fortunately the crew were able to get clear of the burning wreckage with no serious injury. Cloud cover caused problems over the target and crews were unable to see the TI, bombing on their ordinary navigational aids. As a result the bombing was scattered, although two large explosions were recorded. Reconnaissance did reveal limited success with some hits on the main unit. On the same day American bombers continued the attacks against the supply sites; at Beauvoir (33 Liberators, 74 tons), Biennais (21 Fortresses, 43 tons), Domleger (12 Liberators, 27 tons) and St Martin l'Hortier (26 Fortresses, 57 tons).

On the night of 27/28 June, 514 aircraft were despatched to flying bomb targets: 2 Lancasters, 103 Halifaxes and 5 Mosquitos to Mont Candon, 43 Lancasters, 65 Halifaxes and 5 Mosquitos to Ardouval, 99 Lancasters and 5 Mosquitos to Château Bernapré, 102 Lancasters and 5 Mosquitos to Biennais and 80 Lancasters and 5 Mosquitos to Oisemont.

The night started badly for the force sent to the Biennais supply site, as the 90 Squadron Lancaster of Pilot Officer Todd was believed intercepted by an intruder whilst over England and crashed. All the crew were killed. Over the target the main force experienced considerable cloud cover, most bombing on the glow of the red TIs. Bombing was scattered although crews witnessed three large explosions. The main force, sent to the launch site at Château Bernapré, had little problem with the thin cloud cover, although the early markers overshot the target. A heavy concentration of bombing developed and crews reported a successful attack. The 166 Squadron Lancaster of Pilot Officer Hunt DFC was lost on the raid with no survivors. At Mont Candon the main force bomb aimers looked down on a good concentration of TIs and although a few of the early arrivals undershot, the rest achieved a good grouping.

Flight Sergeant Ken Grantham, wireless operator 35 Squadron, was involved in the attack on the supply site at Oisemont:

> Briefed at 22.15 for a midnight take-off to a flying bomb [target, Oisemont]. They're paying a lot of attention to these flying bombs now the 'Heavies' seem to be used in attacking their launching sites quite a lot. Our route took us over part of London and saw several FBs [flying bombs] exploding there. Arrived at target 01.30 ish and suspected fighters about because of absence of flak and a few searchlights. Weather clear, visibility good. Target identified by GEE and H2S on Abbeville. Bombed woods at 01.29, 15,000ft, load 16 x 500lb GPTD, 2 x 500lb GPLD. Flak negligible, searchlights coning, fighters in evidence.

Over the target the main force pilots and bomb aimers were directed to bomb markers deemed to be well placed. Despite the presence of fighters, evidenced by the dropping of flares, there were no losses. Follow-up reconnaissance suggested fairly poor results for the raid with only one small building damaged by the blast from a near miss and a lot of fresh craters outside the target area.

The force sent to Ardouval found clear weather over the target area. Post-raid reports were optimistic, the marking believed accurate and some of the bombing photographs showing the aiming point. Follow up reconnaissance revealed that there was actually no damage to the target. The 425 Squadron Halifax of Sergeant Lavoie suffered an engine failure just after bombing the launch site. Lavoie managed to bring the aircraft back to base but as it came into land it hit another aircraft at its dispersal, which had been bombed up. Both of the aircraft caught fire and the bombs subsequently exploded. The Base Commander Air Commodore A. Ross was at the scene when the bombs went off. A piece of shrapnel cut into his left arm near his wrist and he would later have to have his hand amputated. Two ground crew, who were trying to get the aircrew away from the burning mass of metal, were also injured. Lavoie received serious injury. There were severe cuts to his lower back and it was suspected that he had fractured his spine. He was immediately taken to York Military Hospital. His injured flight engineer Sergeant Raper was also admitted to the hospital.

On the same night the large sites at Wizernes (104 Halifaxes, 2 Lancasters and 5 Mosquitos) and Mimoyecques (86 Lancasters and 5 Mosquitos) were also targeted. Both attacks were conducted in good weather. Accurate bombing was reported and follow-up reconnaissance on Mimoyecques revealed a number of hits on the target installations. The 44 Squadron Lancaster of Flight Lieutenant Merrick was lost on the raid to Mimoyecques and all the crew were killed.

On 28 June, just four hours after the night attacks, 103 Halifaxes, 2 Lancasters and 5 Mosquitos, with fighter cover, were again sent to Wizernes. The visibility over the target was excellent although dust and smoke later obscured the markers and a good attack was reported. The crew of one aircraft became casualties as a result of taking part in the raid. The 640 Squadron Lancaster of Flight Lieutenant Wisbey crashed at Hawkinge airfield in Kent and there were no survivors from the crew of seven.

CHAPTER 9

THE PRESSURE BUILDS

On 27 June 1944, Mr Herbert Morrison, Home Secretary and Minister of Home Security, sent a memorandum to the War Cabinet:

> The public have so far withstood pretty well the growing loss of life and prosperity and general inconvenience of flying bomb attacks. They have been buoyed up with the belief that the situation was well in hand and that in a short period the RAF would have destroyed the sources of mischief. This is proving a slow and doubtful process and I am apprehensive of what might happen if the strain continues and, in addition to flying bombs, long-range rockets are used against the Metropolis, producing wide areas of devastation and consequent heavy loss of life.
>
> I have a high degree of faith in the Londoners and the people of the small towns and villages of Southern England. But the Government and the Chiefs of Staff will be wise to be human. This is not 1940-41. The Anglo-American alliance is now a vast military power and the people, not unreasonably, expect a quicker and more decisive defence; people are asking 'Where is the air superiority they talk about?'; each 'incident' represents a considerable number of domestic tragedies apart from killed and wounded; the people have had nearly five years of war strain – they will resent this new trouble increasingly and want to know what we are doing about it, day and night they face the risk of death and horrible injury and the ruin of their homes. I assure my colleagues that I have done and will do everything to hold up their courage and spirit – but there is a limit, and the limit will come.[70]

The memorandum went on further to suggest that reports of the flying bombs attacks on southern England would be having an adverse effect on soldiers serving overseas. This memo gives a clear example of the growing political pressure to increase the scale of operations against the flying bomb threat. As flying bombs fell on London the public outcry increased in volume. In fact some quite drastic measures were being considered by the War Cabinet. One very serious plan was discussed to send bomber forces to certain German cities and attack them with gas. Churchill had always seriously considered the use of gas, since the German secret weapon threat first arose. As early as 10 January 1944 he had written to the Chief of the Air Staff Sir Charles Portal commenting on the poor results of the American high altitude attacks on the Crossbow targets. Churchill made a suggestion based upon the reconnaissance of the targets.

> The photographs certainly show that a liberal drenching with mustard gas would make all work, especially firing, very difficult. I am of the opinion that this matter should be further considered. What really surprises me about the photographs is how little harm we have been able to do with ordinary explosive bombs.[71]

In addition to the consideration of gas attacks, a target list was drawn up of small German towns, selected, for example, as being holiday retreats for high-ranking German officials. It was to be publicised that these towns would be attacked, by conventional bombs, if the flying bomb attacks continued, in an effort to dissuade the Germans from proceeding with their flying bomb offensive. Fortunately for the civilian populations of both Germany and England, and especially in terms of the probable escalation of gas attacks, these plans were never acted upon.

At the meeting of the Chiefs of Staff Committee on 27 June and bearing in mind the current political pressure, the continuation of attacks on the German flying bomb organisation received careful consideration. There had been no evidence that any ski sites had been used for firing any flying bombs. Suspicion arose that in the light of the fact there were no signs of repairs at the supply sites, they were in fact part of the ski site system and not part of the flying bomb supply line to the modified sites. Evidence from an inspection of the supply site on the Cherbourg peninsula at Valognes, which had by then been overrun by the Americans, did however suggest that the supply sites were still worthy of attack. Certain buildings contained aluminium or aluminium alloy tanks, which could be used for the storage of hydrogen peroxide, known to be used in the flying bomb launch sequence. This suggested that either the fuel was stored at the supply site to replenish the launch sites, or that the launching equipment received fuel at the supply site before being taken to the launch site. It was also surmised that certain buildings probably held spare parts and ancillary equipment. So the supply sites were still believed to play an important role in the flying bomb organisation. It is worth noting that the diary of Flakregiment 155(W) did record that on one attack on a supply site, flying bombs were being stored and 15 of them were damaged.

From 29 June to 4 July Bomber Command, acting upon the belief that the supply sites needed further attention, focused on daylight raids to these sites. In addition on 29 June the suspected large site and launch ramp at Siracourt was targeted by 101 Lancasters and 5 Mosquitos. Intense flak was encountered over the target; the 7 Squadron Lancaster of the master bomber Flight Lieutenant Clark was hit whilst approaching the aiming point, and the aircraft exploded. The pilot and five other crew members were killed, two airmen were thrown clear and survived becoming POWs. The main force was instructed to bomb a $^1/_2$ mile to the east of the back-up markers, but some bombs had already been dropped on the markers themselves. As a result there was scattering before correction was made. One other aircraft was lost on the raid, from 12 Squadron. Pilot Officer Underwood's Lancaster was hit by flak with only four men managing to get out alive; they became POWs. The pilot and the two other crew members were killed. The 460 Squadron Lancaster of Flight Lieutenant Critchley RAAF lost two engines owing to flak damage. Critchley managed to bring the aircraft back to the airfield at Manston in Kent and landed with the wheels retracted. The entire crew were able to get away from the aircraft with no injury.

Beauvoir was attacked on 29 June (85 Lancasters and 9 Mosquitos) and 2 July (121 Lancasters and 5 Mosquitos). On both raids bombing was believed to be concentrated and reconnaissance photographs taken on 8 July revealed a target area saturated with craters and considerable damage to many of the buildings. Pilot Officer Reg Dear was a pilot with 61 Squadron and remembers an incident on the 29 June raid caused by the flak defences.

> The bomb aimer was lying in the nose when a piece of flak severed the hydraulic line to the front turret and sprayed him with red hydraulic oil. The oil was red and so was the language! He was most peeved.

Other crews were not as fortunate and three losses were sustained on the raid. The 467 Squadron Lancaster of Flying Officer Edwards was hit by flak and set on fire. Four men became POWs, the pilot and two other crew members were killed. The 627 Squadron Mosquito piloted by Flying Officer de Platts was hit by flak after dropping markers. Both the pilot and his navigator baled out, the pilot becoming a POW and the navigator managing to evade capture. The 627 Squadron Mosquito piloted by Flying Officer Saint-Smith DFC, DFM was also lost and it is believed that it was brought down by the premature explosion of an in-flight flying bomb. Both Saint-Smith and his colleague Flying Officer Heath DFC, DFM were killed. The 463 Squadron Lancaster of Flight Lieutenant Buckham was hit by flak but the pilot managed to bring the aircraft back to England. However it was later deemed to be beyond repair.

Domleger was attacked three times, 29 June (100 Lancasters and 5 Mosquitos), 2 July (127 Lancasters and 5 Mosquitos) and 4 July (2 Lancasters, 105 Halifaxes and 5 Mosquitos), with a good concentration of bombing reported on each raid. Reconnaissance on 5 July revealed a mass of craters in the target area with near misses against some buildings.

Biennais was attacked twice, on 1 July (2 Lancasters, 101 Halifaxes and 5 Mosquitos) and 4 July (2 Lancasters, 99 Halifaxes and 5 Mosquitos); the crews experienced almost complete cloud cover on both raids and had to bomb on their navigational aids. On the 1 July raid, whilst homeward bound, the 420 Squadron Halifax of Pilot Officer Caine had a failure of both port engines. The pilot was able to crash land at Linton-on-Ouse with the wheels up, but the aircraft was written off. The pilot received a laceration over his right eye and the flight engineer sustained a compound fracture of his left tibia. The rest of the crew emerged physically unscathed.

St Martin l'Hortier was attacked twice. The first raid on 1 July (2 Lancasters, 102 Halifaxes and 5 Mosquitos) had to be made through almost complete cloud cover, crews were forced to bomb using navigational aids and it was believed that the bombing was scattered. The 10 Squadron Halifax of Flying Officer Rosen was lost, hit by flak, and only the rear gunner survived, managing to evade capture. On the second raid of 4 July (2 Lancasters, 103 Halifaxes and 5 Mosquitos), crews were able to identify the target visually, by means of the markers, and the master bomber's instructions were clearly heard. A good concentration was achieved and two large explosions were seen.

The raid to St Martin l'Hortier on 4 July was Warrant Officer Ronald Claridge's 56th operation. Acting as the wireless operator on Squadron Leader G.B. Frow's 7 Squadron Lancaster this was his first operation on an aircraft acting as master bomber. This was now becoming a regular feature of many Bomber Command operations with the master bomber, in a Lancaster, giving instructions to the main force over a target. However there were considerable dangers associated with such responsibility:

> *Warrant Officer Ronald Claridge, wireless operator, 7 Squadron:* As a master bomber crew we were in rather a different position to the rest of Bomber Command. We were a law unto ourselves. We could make our own way to the target and back we hoped! Navigation during my time was very accurate. We were expected to be marking the target about five minutes before the main force arrived, to guide them in and instruct them during the raid. This meant we would be over the target for sometimes as long as twenty minutes. A very long time compared with about three or four minutes taken for the average bomber to do its run in. We could only return after the main force had left.
>
> As a master bomber crew we were given a free hand to destroy these sites which resulted in what must have been some of the lowest wartime flying carried out by a bomber the size of a Lancaster. These sites were very hard to find as they were usually sited in woods. In fact we returned from one op with a tree branch stuck in an engine nacelle, much to the anger of the ground crew!

Oisemont was attacked three times, 30 June (102 Lancasters and 5 Mosquitos), 1 July (2 Lancasters, 104 Halifaxes and 5 Mosquitos) and 2 July (126 Lancasters and 5 Mosquitos), all of which raids were made through considerable cloud cover. Bombing was scattered, but subsequent reconnaissance did indicate some damage to buildings. The 156 Squadron Lancaster of Warrant Officer Clarke, on the 2 July raid, suffered a collapsed undercarriage on return to base with two of the crew slightly hurt.

The only real opposition the bombers were coming up against on these daylight raids was the flak. On 2 July Flight Sergeant Ken Grantham, wireless operator 35 Squadron, took part in the raid to Oisemont and recorded in his diary:

> Told to stand by for ops in the morning and we were called to briefing at 11.30. It appears FBs [flying bombs] are getting serious in London and we are switched to daylight bombing to try to keep them down until the Army reaches their areas. Take-off 12.30 and flew most of the way in cloud. Channel was clear however. We map read to the aiming point, which was identified without difficulty. There appeared to be quite a lot of a/c [aircraft] on this trip approaching in a broad front, from the coast, concentrating and narrowing at the aiming point, and fanning out again thereafter. They bombed, turned to starboard and doubled back to the coast. As we flew in, the bomb aimer, George, was instructing, and at the moment of release another Lanc swung in below, in line of aim. Dawson [the pilot] closed the bomb doors, then decided not to go home and report a 'no drop' trip. Rather to circle to port and come in again. By the time we had done a wide circle everyone else was off home and we were the only kite coming up on the target. Asking for it, we got it, lots of bangs and flashes underneath and the smell of cordite . . . drifting in. Straight and level on the bombing run, jinking was out. I saw several large holes appear in the wings and several ugly red flashes and smoke puffs out to starboard. As George released, the flak boys got us in their sights again. Rear gunner's turret controls were severed and the nose perspex shattered. Alan got a cut face and had to have first aid. Bomb doors were closed and Dawson started jinking and lost the next burst.

Despite the damage the pilot, Lieutenant Dawson Kornegay USAAF, managed to bring his aircraft and crew back to England and in recognition of his skill he received an immediate award of the DFC.

In addition to the Bomber Command attacks against the supply sites, on 2 July American heavy bombers targeted Renescure (21 Liberators dropping 54 tons) and Sautrecourt (13 Liberators, 34 tons).

Since the night of 24/25 June Bomber Command had conducted 2,742 sorties against Crossbow targets. Three-quarters of these were in daylight with very few losses resulting from enemy action (less than 0.4%), in the main owing to the short trips required, Allied daylight air supremacy over the target areas and the fighter escorts, something most bomber crews actually never saw.

> *Sergeant Geoff Gilbert, rear gunner, 61 Squadron:* Near Paris, on a daylight, we were flying in the usual gaggle, and it was just prior to the target. We couldn't see our fighter escort, the Spits

were up in the sun. This one Me109 came in all alone. All of a sudden six streaks came out of the sun and before we knew it the Me109 started to show smoke, caught fire and the chap baled out. The aircraft blew up and the Spits went back into the sun again. That was the only time I ever saw the fighter escort except for one other occasion. Back over the Channel and nearly into England this Spit came down and put his nose into my turret. I kept my hands up.

Low loss rates were, however, not the case with regard to the night raids in the period. On the night of 28/29 June 20 aircraft were lost from a force of 230 sent to attack rail yards at Blainville and Metz – a high loss rate of 8.7%. The railyards at Vierzon were attacked on the night of 30 June/1 July and 14 Lancasters were lost from the force of 118 Lancasters – a 12% loss rate. Quite clearly, at this stage of the air war the chance of a Bomber Command aircraft being shot down on a day raid to northern France was significantly less than on a night raid. If the German nightfighter controllers could vector their forces into the bomber streams they could engage the bombers without having to worry about fighter escorts. The German nightfighter force was far from beaten. However on 4 July Bomber Command heavy squadrons and their airmen, all 5 Group, began to prepare for another major night raid to a flying bomb target in the north of France. Some of these airmen, as had happened to thousands of their colleagues, would go to briefing not realising that on this raid their lives would end.

CHAPTER 10

CAVES AND COMBAT

The Allied invasion in Normandy had been experiencing partial success through to the end of June. The beach-heads had linked up but attempts to capture the key objective of Caen had so far failed. The Americans had been successful in capturing Cherbourg but overall achievements fell short of the pre-invasion expectations. As far as the Germans were concerned, though, the Allies were ashore and had not been thrown back into the sea, so they were in need of positive propaganda, something the flying bomb offensive could provide.

On the afternoon of 1 July 1944 the German war correspondent Oberleutenant Dr Holzmer, having obtained permission from LXV Armee Korps, visited a flying bomb launch site to record the firing of a salvo of flying bombs that night. The diary of Flakregiment 155(W) recorded his visit:

> The site lies in a thicket, excellently camouflaged. The ground round about is turned up with bomb craters. The edges of the craters show up white against the cultivated surface of the chalk. Dusk falls. The sky is overcast, it is raining very slightly. Best weather for firing.
>
> Beneath a tree on an embankment a war correspondent is waiting anxiously, a microphone in his hand. The recording machine is running in the radio van. It is just past 23.00. There is a sudden flash over the wood. The speaker raises his voice: 'Any minute now. All out V1 operations!' And the V1 thunders on its way, while the war reporter records the experience for the home front and for the ears of the world. Two more launchings, one after 40 minutes and the other an hour after that (delay because of enemy reconnaissance). Again the flash over the wood, then the bang and the familiar whine. A thunderbolt, and yet another, is launched into the night drizzle, slowly climbing in the direction of London![72]

The regiment was still quite clearly delighted with the progress of the offensive. On the night of 28/29 June the 2,000th flying bomb was fired, prompting a congratulatory signal from Hitler to Heinemann. The Allied bombing had had some effect however. On 27 June LXV Armee Korps had ordered two extra maintenance sections per *Abteilung*, be set up, to deal with the reduction in fire power caused by the Allied bombing raids, and to repair damaged sites quickly. The regiment, in summarising the Allied bombing attacks up to the end of June, noted in its diary that blind attacks above cloud, and large-scale night attacks using air and ground markers had been very accurate in most cases. It did also comment that fighter bomber attacks had been very inaccurate. The regiment did record a fair amount of damage to sites: 2 sites completely destroyed, 22 suffering heavy damage, 8 medium damage and 10 light damage. The regiment also lost 20 of its personnel either missing or dead and 71 wounded. However with their current set-up allowing for a maximum firing rate from 64 launchers, there was ample scope for the use of reserve sites. From the night of 15/16 June to 15.00 hours on 30 June an average of 150 flying bombs per 24 hours were still being fired. In fact if the average is taken every day of the previous week's firings, this was actually increasing steadily from 25 June. It was clear that the Allied bombing raids were causing a fair amount of damage to the flying bomb launch sites but Flakregiment 155(W) had enough reserve sites to maintain a relatively consistent rate of fire. The Allied land invasion was however starting to concern the regiment and plans were put in place to seek out new sites for an *Abteilung* north of the current area of operations.

Towards the end of June 1944 the Allies began implementing a change in flying bomb targeting priorities. Enigma decrypts (intercepts of German communications) had indicated that the link between the production centres and the launching sites was assembly depots, situated below ground. The production centres in Germany were linked to the assembly depots by rail with the flying bombs then being transported from the depots to the launch sites by road. In fact in March 1944 the Special Operations Executive (SOE) had produced a report indicating that there was an underground flying bomb store at St Leu d'Esserent. For whatever reason this report was ignored. During May Enigma decrypts had revealed that LXV Armee Korps had an interest in caverns at Nucourt. Further decrypts during the first half of June confirmed suspicions that these depots were being used, and added the name Rilly-la-Montagne to the two already mentioned.

On 29 June a cypher message was sent from the Air Ministry to the main headquarters of the Allied Expeditionary Air Force requesting that St Leu d'Esserent be placed on the targeting list as first priority. The caves were split into two distinct areas for attack, St Leu d'Esserent I and II. The cypher also stated that it would be necessary to use 12,000 lb Tallboy bombs owing to the nature of the target, i.e. the underground caves. The United States Eighth Air Force was the first heavy bomber force to be called upon. On 27 June 80 Liberators dropped 204 tons on the St Leu d'Esserent caves. On 22 June 24 Liberators released 63 tons on Nucourt, followed up by a further attack on 24 June by 70 Fortresses dropping 186 tons. Further information was gleaned from an Enigma decrypt which gave specific numbers relating effectively to 'goods in, goods out' at St Leu d'Esserent from 9 June to 2 July. From simple comparisons of these figures to the number of flying bombs thought by the Allies to have been launched, it became clear to the Allies that St Leu d'Esserent was the main flying bomb supply depot. It became clear that a major bombing attack was necessary, and Bomber Command was called on.

Madame Raymonde Carbon lived in St Leu d'Esserent. Aged 33 at the time of the raids against the flying bomb sites, she was looking after her own four children and one other child whose mother had died during the war. She was active in the Resistance movement in the area and Madame Carbon used to carry messages from one Resistance group to another, in pockets in her dress, on her bike. She also let small Resistance groups use her cellar but would only see them arrive and let them in. She did not know if they were Resistance members, but if they knocked on her door and displayed half a postcard, of which she had the other half, then she would let them in. Her husband also helped in the Resistance and part of his job was to steal gas (which the Germans used for lighting). In the caverns where the Germans stocked their material they also stocked the canisters which Madame Carbon's husband would steal and give to his friends in the Resistance movement so they could make small hand grenades.

> *Madame Carbon:* Security was most severe around the caves. On top of the caverns were ventilation ducts and all that area was out of bounds. The Germans did not treat the civilians too badly, as if there were any atrocities this could bring attention to St Leu d'Esserent and they did not want that. The German Commander was very humane and did not like the Gestapo.
>
> It was against the law to listen to the BBC but we did tune in to the news broadcast to occupied Europe, and knew we would be subjected to air attacks, but not when. As we were living in a house close by the caves, every evening we would see German lorries covered with tarpaulin leaving the caves. We did not know what was in them. At the same time we started hearing that London was being bombed by unknown bombs and we guessed that these bombs were being taken from St Leu d'Esserent.

The fact that some kind of secret weapon was being stored in, and transported to and from, the caves soon became quite clear to the local French population. On one occasion a lorry overturned revealing something rocket-shaped with tail fins. The German soldiers then made the civilians in the proximity of the accident evacuate the area and remain indoors with shutters closed.

> *Madame Carbon:* We knew the lorries were going in the direction of Beauvais and the Pas de Calais where the launching sites were situated. We knew this was something serious as the equipment was being delivered by train and taken into the caverns. We expected air raids.

Indeed the local Resistance had passed information across to British Intelligence. A Monsieur Bonaventure worked on the local railway line.

'Bonaventure' could be translated as 'good trip'. The BBC broadcast a message to inform the Resistance that their message had been received: 'Tonight we will come and wish you a good trip.'

For the night of 4/5 July, Bomber Command decided to send two forces to attack the supply dump and tunnels at St Leu d'Esserent. The two attacks were designed firstly to cave in the tunnels, and then heavily crater the area around the tunnel entrances and cause serious disruption on the road and rail supply lines to the tunnels. The first attack was made by 617 Squadron with 17 Lancasters, 1 Mosquito and 1 Mustang. The Lancasters were all carrying 12,000 lb Tallboys. Wing Commander Cheshire in the Mustang led the first attack on the caves, taking off at 0015 hours, about ¾ hour after the main force had departed. At the target Cheshire dived from 5,000 feet to 800 feet to drop his two red markers at 0130 hours. The supporting Mosquito was not called upon. Cheshire's VHF set had failed but the main force still carried out bombing. The first Lancaster bombed at 0131 hours, one of only 11 Lancasters that bombed, the last at 0144 hours. The six other Lancasters withheld their Tallboys owing to smoke obscuring the markers. Following this first attack the second, large attack followed almost immediately.

Target and aircraft despatched	Plan of attack
St Leu d'Esserent 231 Lancasters and 15 Mosquitos 1156.8 tons high explosive and 5.2 tons incendiary bombs	Zero hour – 0145 hours 5 Group visual marking with Oboe ground-marking. (8 Group Mosquitos to open the marking). Weather was forecast as good all night over bases with little or no cloud affecting the raid over the target. Time over France 0100 to 0211 hours.

Bomber Command combined the attacks on St Leu d'Esserent with major raids to the railway yards at Orleans and Villeneuve involving 287 aircraft. On the same night a force of 36 Mosquitos went to Scholven/Buer and 25 aircraft carried out RCM (Radio Counter Measure[73]) sorties. Sixty-one Mosquitos conducted operations over enemy territory, attempting to engage the enemy fighters and attack their airfields, some aircraft carrying Serrate, a device used to home in on radar transmissions of enemy aircraft. In addition to these forces, 6 Stirlings and 5 Halifaxes were sent for minelaying off Brest and St Nazaire, 16 aircraft were employed on resistance operations, dropping supplies and agents, and 30 aircraft took part in OTU (Operational Training Unit) sorties, which were to act as a diversion.

One feature of this raid was the use of a Mandrel screen whereby the Bomber Command forces would try to gain an extra edge against the German air defences. In December 1942 the device became operational with the jamming carried out by a ground device in England. However on the night of 16/17 June 1944 aircraft of 199 Squadron conducted the first airborne Mandrel screen. The German early warning radars were jammed by British aircraft each carrying up to eight sets of jamming equipment. These aircraft, usually flying over the sea, would fly a tight course transmitting their jamming signals, with the main bomber force 'hidden' behind until it was time to emerge. The effect of the jamming was to prevent giving the German defences early warning of the size, location and heading of a bomber force.

Some of the main force crews on the St Leu d'Esserent raid were given special roles in an attempt to silence the ground defences. It was well known to Bomber Command, from photographs of the area around the caves, that it was well covered by anti-aircraft positions. Two aircraft from 463 Squadron were involved in such a special responsibility, their role being to drop fragmentation bombs on the guns protecting the target, hoping, as the squadron operations record book puts it 'to fragmentate a few of the personnel manning the guns'.[74]

It will be important to note the timings of the raids to the railway yards as these had a direct bearing on the German nightfighter reactions and a subsequent influence on the force attacking the caverns at St Leu d'Esserent.

Orleans lay to the south of St Leu d'Esserent and Paris. The attacking force's scheduled time over France was 0020 to 0235 hours with a time over the target of 0110 to 0140 hours. Villeneuve lay just to the south-east of Paris and St Leu d'Esserent. The attacking force's scheduled time over France was 0030 to 0224 hours with a time over the target of 0115 to 0121 hours. St Leu d'Esserent lay just to the north of Paris. All three raids were scheduled to take place between 0100 and 0145 hours, the raid to St Leu d'Esserent being the last of the three; all the approaches suggested a major threat to the Paris area. The following details how the night's activity progressed:

2329 to 0029 hours
Orleans force: Over the sea to the west of the Cherbourg peninsula, then turning to cross the French coast to the south of the peninsula.
Villeneuve force: Over the sea and approaching the French coast near St. Valéry.
Main St Leu d'Esserent force: Assembling over England.
German reaction (from Allied Intelligence intercepts): 36 German nightfighters of II./NJG2 (meaning second *Gruppe of Nachtjagdgeschwader 2*) and II./NJG 4 make for the Dieppe area. At 0020 hours the German controllers pass on information of a bomber force crossing the coast near Fécamp (Villeneuve raid). At 0022 hours 10 nightfighters of I./NJG 5 are directed towards the Paris area. At 0023 hours 13 Ju88s from Florennes, having originally flown west to the Arras–Cambrai area, are redirected to the Creil area.
Combats (100 Group): At 0027 hours a 141 Squadron Mosquito picks up an Me410 between Arras and Lille. The Mosquito closes the gap, takes up position on the German nightfighter's tail and opens fire, registering hits on the port engine, fuselage and wing. The Me410 bursts into flames and dives down, exploding before hitting the ground.

0030 to 0045 hours

Orleans force: Well to the south of the Cherbourg peninsula and now flying east towards Chartres.

Villeneuve force: Crossing the coast near St. Valéry and proceeding south-east and to the west of Rouen.

Main St Leu d'Esserent force: At 0030 hours still over England and nearing the Kent coast.

Other forces: The Mandrel screen still in operation, the diversionary OTU force having just come back behind the screen following a brief show to the German early warning radar.

German reaction: At 0035 hours the German Controller identifies the Villeneuve bomber stream over the mouth of the Somme. There then follow numerous attacks and combats as the Villeneuve stream progresses, west of Rouen toward the turning point near Chartres.

0046 to 0100 hours

Orleans force: Continuing east to Chartres and beginning to turn south-east towards Orleans.

Villeneuve force: Continuing to, and starting turning, near Chartres.

Main St Leu d'Esserent force: Starts to cross the French coast.

German reaction: Further combats and attacks against the Villeneuve stream. At 0100 hours I./NJG3 are directed to Abbeville as the St Leu d'Esserent force proceeds south to Cayeux. After the Villeneuve force turns the number of enemy engagements against this bomber stream diminishes.

Combats (100 Group): A 169 Squadron Mosquito picks up a visual sighting of an Me110 at 0050 hours and opens fire. The German nightfighter starts to burn, rolls to starboard and plummets downwards.

0101 to 0115 hours

Orleans force: Turns toward the target and after a fairly short leg attacks the rail yards. The force then turns north-west on homeward route.

Villeneuve force: Proceeds on last leg and arrives at the target.

Main St Leu d'Esserent force: Proceeds south-south-east towards Paris.

German reaction: At 0105 hours some fighters directed to near Orleans. At 0107 hours the German Controller directs 'All fighters' to Abbeville. At 0115 hours some fighters directed towards Paris as the Villeneuve raid opens.

Combats (100 Group): A 214 Squadron Flying Fortress claims a Ju88 at 0108 hours.

At 0115 hours a 239 Squadron Mosquito closes on an Me110 and opens fire. The pilot witnesses his fire striking the enemy aircraft on the fuselage and wing roots with pieces of the aircraft flying off. He then sees two parachutists falling out of the stricken aircraft. He opens fire again at the aircraft sending it into a steep dive.

0116 to 0130 hours

Orleans force: Continues on north-west homeward route.

Villeneuve force: Attacks the target then after a short leg south turns west.

Main St Leu d'Esserent force: Continues south-south-east then turns towards and arrives at the target. Aircrews start to see some bombers, crewed by their colleagues, falling from the sky.

Flight Sergeant Futcher's 106 Squadron Lancaster crashes to the ground near Beauvais; the pilot and five of the crew of seven do not survive.

Flying Officer Carter RAAF is killed with his entire crew as their 463 Squadron Lancaster falls to earth near Aumale.

German reaction: Further plots made of the St Leu d'Esserent force. German Controller broadcasts 'Many bombers in the area Abbeville-Paris'. Combats and attacks against the St Leu d'Esserent force. A few engagements with the Villeneuve force.

0131 to 0145 hours

Orleans force: Continues on north-west homeward route.

Villeneuve force: Turns towards Rouen and then turns west.

Main St Leu d'Esserent force: Attacks target. The bomber force experience a clear night over the target and the supply dump and the tunnel are both marked accurately. Little flak is encountered but there are numerous combats between the airmen of Bomber Command and the German nightfighter force and more aircraft fall from the night sky. The force then splits into 3 waves for the homeward route.

Pilot Officer Wilson and his crew lose their lives when their 207 Squadron Lancaster falls to earth near Chantilly.

The 49 Squadron Lancaster of Flying Officer Dod falls victim to a nightfighter attack, near Aumale, with total loss of life.

Only two men survive from the crew of Pilot Officer Young as the pilot and 5 others die when their 44 Squadron Lancaster crashes and burns on the ground near Beauvais.

German reaction: Numerous combats against St Leu d'Esserent force. The first wave of the bomber force then followed by fighters northward and then westward. The second wave also followed but to a lesser extent.

No further action with the Villeneuve force once it turns west.

Combats (St Leu d'Esserent force): At 0132 hours a 617 Squadron Lancaster is attacked by a Ju88 and both gunners return fire. The Ju88 bursts into flames and dives down to the ground.

At 0139 hours a 207 Squadron Lancaster claims an Me109.

The rear gunner is injured in the attack. The mid upper gunner sees the enemy aircraft attacking from the port quarter up and fires, seeing strikes register on his opponent. The mid upper gunner continues to fire at the Me109 and his enemy bursts into flames and dives toward the ground (the experiences of this crew are detailed later).

At 0139 hours a 97 Squadron Lancaster crew become aware of what they think is an Me410 pursuing them, weaving on their port side. Both gunners open fire and the enemy starts trailing smoke and glowing as it dives down. The nightfighter breaks up in the air just before smashing into the ground.

At 0143 hours a 9 Squadron Lancaster claims an Me110 (see rear gunner Bob Riches' account later).

At 0144 hours a 630 Squadron Lancaster is shot at by what they believe is Do217. The rear gunner returns fire and his adversary breaks away, flames streaming from the port engine. Its downward path is followed by members of the crew and it plunges into the ground.

0146 hours onwards

Orleans force: Crosses French coast just south of Cherbourg peninsula then turns northward for Bridport, England.

Villeneuve force: Near the French coast the stream joins the same homeward route as the Orleans force.

Main St Leu d'Esserent force: First two waves join up and then proceed north-west crossing the French coast north of Dieppe. The third wave proceeds to a turning point north of Rouen and then north-west, crossing the French coast south of Dieppe. Further losses to the nightfighters.

Pilot Officer Ryan's 9 Squadron Lancaster falls near Montataire, with no survivors from the crew of 8.

A nightfighter shoots 57 Squadron Flight Lieutenant Grubb's Lancaster out of the night sky. The entire crew perish and their aircraft burns on the ground near the village of Cormeilles.

Pilot Officer North's 61 Squadron Lancaster plunges earthwards near les Andelys, but the crew manage to get out and all survive.

463 Squadron Pilot Officer Webb is killed with his other seven crew members as their Lancaster falls victim to a nightfighter over Lyons-la-Forêt.

Flying Officer Crosier dies but the rest of his crew survive as their 106 Squadron Lancaster is shot down over Sevis, midway between Rouen and Dieppe.

German reaction: Fighters engage the first two waves on the run up to the coast and for a short time over the sea.

Combats (St Leu d'Esserent force): At 0150 hours the mid upper gunner and rear gunner of a 61 Squadron Lancaster open fire on a pursuing Ju88. The gunners keep their triggers pressed until the enemy breaks away with its engines flaming and pouring smoke. The Ju88 plummets to the ground and explodes.

Over northern France there had been an uncompromising air battle taking place. Some Bomber Command airmen managed to defend themselves against their nightfighter foe:

Sergeant Bob Riches, rear gunner, 9 Squadron: On approaching the French coast the starboard inner engine started to vibrate badly and it had to be closed down. We pressed on to the target on three engines. We should have bombed at 15,000 ft but lost a lot of height and finished up actually bombing at 10,000 ft. On the actual bombing run the bomb-sight packed up, so we dropped our bombs manually! They were thought to have hit the target anyway. There was quite a bit of nightfighter activity and when we left the target the pilot decided to go as fast as we could in the circumstances and weaved violently from side to side until we were clear of the target area. This manoeuvre possibly saved our lives as we were attacked by an Me110, which gave us a long blast but missed. On recovering from the attack we spotted the aircraft coming in for another attack, took the appropriate evading action (a corkscrew) and gave it a good long blast from both the rear and mid upper turret, after which the attacking aircraft slid away to starboard with a stream of smoke coming from the starboard engine. We saw no fire but then it disappeared. At de-briefing when we returned we reported it damaged but five days later we were credited with a 'kill' as two other aircraft reported a twin-engined plane crashing in the vicinity.

Flight Sergeant Ralph Briars, rear gunner, 617 Squadron: Full moon, expected and had, reception as at Nuremberg. Search-light belt just outside coast annoying but no flak. Combats (seen) all the way in and out, at target turned and had moon dead behind, hardly helpful! Fighters came in from all directions, never seen so much tracer, got very mad and scared! Ju88 at last came near enough to have two long squirts and it appeared to go into one big ball of fire, lost sight of it but Skipper reckons it broke in half and hit the deck. Unable to bomb because markers indefinite, pity. Fighters followed all way to our coast, couldn't have any coffee till we got to Reading.

Shortly after bombing the target, Pilot Officer McIntosh's 207 Squadron Lancaster was approached by an Me109, which opened fire and the bomber's gunners responded similarly. The rear gunner Sergeant Burton was hit in the face and quickly blinded by the blood streaming across his eyes. He had to stop firing. McIntosh started to experience great difficulty in controlling his four-engined aircraft, the tail plane was damaged, the port elevator had been blasted off and the Me109 had registered hits on the starboard outer fuel tank. He had to employ considerable force on his controls, eventually having to use his knees. Sergeant Shannon, the bomb aimer, went to Burton's assistance, pulling his injured crewmate from his turret and quickly applying first aid. Despite the attention Burton fell unconscious owing to the blood loss. Shannon climbed into the rear turret and even though the doors would not close, risking being sucked out into the night sky, he swung it around to give the Lancaster back some of its balance. As far as the Me109 pilot was concerned his foe was little damaged and to get his kill he would need to attack again. This proved a fatal decision. The Lancaster's mid upper gunner Flight Sergeant Barker pressed the trigger on his browning machine guns, maintaining the pressure until he saw the Me109 going down in flames.

No doubt seeing the demise of the Me109 was of great relief to the Lancaster crew but they were certainly not out of danger and other enemy aircraft were seen. There were a few anxious moments as McIntosh headed for clouds and, once they entered, flares were dropped from a fighter trying to illuminate them. Damage to the Lancaster's controls prevented any evasive manoeuvres and McIntosh kept the aircraft in the clouds, out of sight, as he attempted to bring his crew home. Once the cloud cover broke McIntosh, in a further effort to avoid fighters, brought the aircraft down, to fly low across the sea back to England. Control was becoming more difficult and with the help of his flight engineer Sergeant Grint they used a rubber oxygen tube to take some of the strain of holding the controls. As the aircraft approached England the wireless operator tried to radio their predicament but they were at first too low. McIntosh eventually had to climb a little in order to send the message, which was received at Spilsby. They were to try and land at the emergency landing ground at Woodbridge, Suffolk. To carry on to Spilsby would have cost more time and McIntosh's rear gunner was in need of urgent medical attention. There was the possibility that apart from the pilot and injured rear gunner the remaining men could have baled out, but McIntosh would never have been able to trim the aircraft in order for him to get out, and Burton was in no fit state to jump. The crew decided to stay together and head for Woodbridge. On the approach to the emergency airfield the crew took up their crash positions except for Sergeant Grint who helped his captain wrestle with the controls. McIntosh brought his crew down, a little shakily, but safely. Grint slipped and injured his foot, the only injury to any of the crew in the landing. The base records for Spilsby, 207 Squadron's home base, recognised McIntosh's crew's teamwork: 'This crew has added one more to the long list of episodes in which a determined and capable crew show what can be done by co-operation and initiative to avert what might so easily have become a disaster and turn it to success.'[75]

Pilot Officer Don Street piloted a 61 Squadron Lancaster on the raid to St Leu d'Esserent on the night of 4/5 July 1944:

> It was my crew's twenty-third sortie; we were about two thirds
> of the way through our operational tour, the end of which was

not yet in sight but we were cautiously confident that we would become 'tour expired'. Briefing was completed, the trades knew their vital bits of information and all had been put together by myself, still stressing the need for vigilance whilst in the air.

The pre-flight dressing up took place in the crew room with the solemn, but no longer furtive little rituals (we knew each other well by now) of right or left flying boot first, the adornment of scarves not washed until the end of the tour, and good luck charms from girlfriends and mothers. Now we were standing near our aircraft each of us with our private thoughts about the flight to come. Whatever those doubts and fears were they would disappear as 'Y' Yoke lined up at the end of the runway and I would say,

'Right here we go – rear gunner all set in the turret – OK inner's up to 2,000 (rpm) engineer.'

The sortie commenced with a take-off time at 2304 hours setting course over base at 2346 hours to join the Lancaster force heading for the target. The first leg south, on a track of 163°, led to point 'A' east of London then onto a track of 150° to turning point 'B' on the mouth of the Somme, then onto the next leg, a track of 163° to a point 'C' just west of the target. The operational height was just under 10,000 feet which was unfortunate as the hazy atmosphere at this altitude reflected the light of a full moon creating very poor horizontal visibility. Vertical visibility was good, there would not be any bombing problems. As we progressed down the flight leg we were heartened to see the occasional – dit – dit – dit – dah V for Victory morse code sign flashed by the French patriots, plainly visible against the blackness of the ground.

As expected the objective was visible and despite enemy nuisances it was with a feeling of satisfaction and relief that we turned out of the target area onto a northerly track of 026° towards turning point 'D'. In a short time turning point 'D' arrived, then onto a longer run to point 'E' on a course of 349°. The aircraft was, as always, much lighter to fly after the release of the bomb load, the four Merlin engines were harmonized at 2,600 revs per minute, the pressures and temperatures were as they should be. I was not too unhappy with the situation as I put the aircraft through a gentle weave heading for home base.

By now after seemingly years of experience, only actually a few months, the run up to, through, and out of the target area, was a well disciplined drill. A far cry from the first time, when everything was strange and frightening, a difficult target with 42 aircraft lost [the raid to Mailly-le-Camp on the night of 3/4 May 1944], and after the thump of the 'bombs gone' there was the wait for the target photo-flash and getting out of the area. On our current operation it was with great dismay that I saw that our height was 2,000 feet above what it should have been, I had forgotten to trim the flying altitude when the bombs were released. Not really dangerous this time, but a lesson not to be forgotten. I had a mental picture of the flight plan and knew that after the next turning point a further few short legs would take us to point 'G', which was on the French coast some miles south of where we came in. It would be a slight nose down for an extra few mph heading for home base.

There was a hiss of an intercom and the navigator [Warrant Officer Dave Grant RCAF] called: 'Next course will be 280° , turn now skipper.'

I set the new course on the compass and turned to port onto the new heading.

'Thanks Nav, on course, how long to coast?'

My question was for the crew's benefit, to keep them informed of progress, and let them know how long they had to go before their bacon and eggs.

'About eighteen minutes', said Dave.

By now the moonlight reflecting against the haze was at its brightest and as I gave my eyes a rest from the instrument panel with a quick look up and around I wondered if our aircraft was clearly silhouetted to anyone flying above the haze level. No probably not, it isn't cloud, but a trail. I was about to call the rear gunner [Sergeant Geoff 'Gillie' Gilbert] when:

'Skipper, I've picked up a bandit 1,200 yards astern and to port.' The wireless operator [Sergeant Doug Boothby] was keeping a close eye on his small radar screen.

'OK thanks. Gunners, sharp look out now.'

My order wasn't really necessary but it established the rapport of the four crew members making up the defensive team.

'Still there. 1,000 yards now skipper, the closing rate isn't high,' and a few minutes later '800 yards'.

'Any sign of it rear gunner?' I asked.

'Can't see a thing.'

'Mid upper?' [Sergeant Peter 'Jock' Haddon]

'Not yet, skipper.'

'600 yards. Still there,' called Doug.

'Gillie, Jock. Any sign yet?' I was getting anxious.

'No.'

'No.'

'500 yards. Still there,' came Doug's steady voice, and again: '400 yards. No change. Could be one of ours with his IFF [Identification Friend or Foe] not switched on.'

'Yeah. Could be. Let's find out. I'm turning 90° to starboard. Now.'

As the aircraft swung onto the new heading I was aware that I was crossing the bomber stream so I held a steady altitude to lessen the chance of collision. I needed to identify the following aircraft; the poor visibility would leave no time for doubt. At the first glimpse the gunners would shoot or be shot! A few minutes had passed on the new heading when:

'I've still got him skip. Right behind 400 yards,' from Doug.

'OK, I'm turning left back onto course now. Any sign yet, Gillie, Jock?'

'300 yards . . . 250 yards.' Doug's voice was now anxious. Then:

'Got him! Corkscrew port go! Go!' It was the urgent voice of Geoff Gilbert, and as the Lancaster dropped down he added, 'It's a Ju88.'

There was no sound of gunfire, the evasive action had been too quick and the sighting was lost in the haze. When about 950 feet had unwound on the altimeter I turned the aircraft through 60° to starboard and into a climbing turn.

'Where is he, Doug?'

He replied, 'Was over the starboard up . . . now moving to rear . . . across to portside about 300 yards . . . 200 yards.'

The relative position of the enemy nightfighter was changing rapidly as I flew the bomber through the evasive pattern. I called over the intercom:

'Have you got it, gunners?'

Doug added, 'Still on port . . . slightly down skipper . . . 100 yards.'

'Corkscrew port, Go!' called Geoff.

The Lancaster was still climbing with a slight turn to starboard and as I pulled it straight to commence a diving turn to port:

'Hold it, skip. Hold it!' The Scottish voice of Peter 'Jock' Haddon came over the intercom, and I froze, holding the bomber straight and level. This all happened in a split second within which the Browning guns rattled.

Sergeant Geoff Gilbert in the rear turret met his foe eye to eye:

> We had gone into the violent corkscrew and he was underneath us. Then I saw the Ju88. He was so close. I was looking right at him and I could see the Ju88's crew looking right up at me. I just depressed my guns and fired. The next thing I knew he was going down in flames.

Pilot Officer Don Street, whilst taking his aircraft through the evasive manoeuvres, anxiously awaited news from his crew:

> 'He's breaking away underneath to port,' called Doug. 'Going down and away rapidly.'
>
> 'He's on fire. We got him,' shouted Jock.
>
> 'Are you sure?' I queried, not quite believing the change in circumstances.

'We've got him. He's on fire' came the excited voice of Geoff.

'I can see it. He's hit the deck and there's two parachutes,' from Doug who had stood up with his head in the astrodome and was getting his share of the drama and excitement.

'I can see it on the ground now, and the two parachutes,' shouted Geoff.

I had to be sure and cut across the excited comments: 'Where is it?'

All three chipped in with instructions to look over to port and slightly forward. I dropped the port wing and had a quick look. Nothing. Another look and this time yes, I saw a large fire visible against the black ground just slipping under the wing and yes, two grey blobs, visible in the moonlight, that were the parachutes.

'Good show. Well done! Well done! Dave, log the time and the position. A Ju88 destroyed.'

The relief and elation were there, expressed on the intercom in the back chat and reconstruction of how it happened. I said nothing allowing the excited tension to ease, then:

'OK, fellas, let's settle down now, well done! Let's get home, there may be some more about.'

Back at base on the dispersal pan with the engines stopped, parking drills completed, the sudden silence deafening everyone, little was said about the victory. It was quietly suggested to the ground crew that a swastika would be joining the bomb symbols painted on the side of the aircraft's fuselage, then we were away in the crew bus to the debriefing room. Before sitting down with the de-briefing officer we grabbed a mug of tea perhaps with a shot of rum for those inclined, and I then walked over to the squadron commanding officer, a down to earth, approachable Australian, doing his second tour of operation.

'Well, sir, we finally got one tonight. A Ju88. Saw it hit the ground.'

I was tired after the flight, like all of the aircrew in the room, but people in general were weary, war-weary, and the drama of Lancaster 'Y' Yoke's fight for life had happened before, many times to many people. It was only important to those involved, but even we would quickly forget as each subsequent flight presented its different emergencies.

So we were de-briefed and claimed an enemy fighter destroyed. This was confirmed and was mentioned in the bomber group's news sheet some weeks later.

Sergeant Geoff Gilbert would receive a DFM for his actions on the night. Sergeant Doug Boothby and Sergeant Peter Haddon would also be later decorated with DFMs. Pilot Officer Don Street would receive the DFC.

Some Bomber Command airmen would not be returning from the raid.

In addition to the St Leu d'Esserent force losses detailed in the above description of the night's operation, 57 Squadron lost the Lancaster of Pilot Officer Smith RAAF, falling to earth near Foucarmont, with the entire crew killed. No. 207 Squadron lost the Lancaster piloted by Flight Sergeant Gibbs, which plummeted into the sea near Dieppe, with only one man surviving, to become a POW. The 630 Squadron Lancaster of Pilot Officer Taft added to the loss count, near Abancourt, with no survivors from the crew of seven. Thirteen Lancasters went missing on the St Leu d'Esserent operation, from which 77 men were killed, 8 men became POWs and 9 men evaded capture. Bomber Command attributed 2 of the losses to flak, 8 to enemy fighters, 1 to fighters and flak and 2 unknown.

In addition to these losses, the Villeneuve force suffered 11 aircraft gone, the Orleans force three aircraft (and one Lancaster written off shortly after take-off) and one Halifax was lost on an RCM sortie. Bomber Command intelligence surmised that the probable factors in the high losses were twofold. The early withdrawal of the diversionary force failed to hold enemy fighters north of the French target areas for very long. This was then compounded by the ability of the German nightfighters to maintain contact with the forces due, in part, to the moonlight. But the German nightfighters had not had complete control of the skies that night. Mosquitos from 100 Group carried out Intruder patrols over the nightfighter airfields. The hunters were also hunted.

It had been a successful night for 100 Group. In addition to the four successes detailed in the night's activities above, the Group also claimed an Me410 and FW190 as damaged. One more German nightfighter would receive the attentions of a Mosquito long after the RAF bomber forces had returned to the skies over England. Warrant Officer Preston took off from Little Snoring airfield in his 515 Squadron Mosquito on the night of 4/5 July, bound for Coulommiers airfield. He arrived at 0205 hours but found the airfield inactive. Preston then decided to search briefly elsewhere for targets. He returned to the airfield ¾ of an hour later and this time was rewarded. On approach to the target he saw a flare fired into the air and instantly the airfield lit up its double flare path. Preston brought his Mosquito down to 1,000 feet and his navigator, Sergeant Verity, sighted a Ju88, flying a southerly course, at approximately the same height, at a range of between 300 and 400 yards. Preston gave chase.

Immediately the pilot of the Ju88, realising he was being pursued, started weaving, then turned starboard and dived. Preston continued the pursuit and as the Ju88 pulled out of its dive, at tree-top height, it came into the sights of the Mosquito. At a range of 200 yards Preston fired a 3-second burst of cannon fire and the Ju88's starboard engine exploded in flames. Almost instantly the Ju88 blew up, burning pieces falling to the ground. Preston went back and circled the area and, as his combat report stated, 'adding insult to injury' he dropped his two 500 lb GP (general purpose) bombs on the south end of the airfield. He was still not finished then as on the return to base he took the opportunity to shoot up a small freighter moored in a Dutch canal.

In total Bomber Command claimed 17 enemy aircraft as destroyed on the night's operations (two of which were probables) and six damaged. ADGB (Air Defence of Great Britain) had also sent 14 Mosquitos to patrol enemy airfields on the same night and they claimed one Ju88 as destroyed. A costly night of attrition for the German nightfighters but they had managed to account for most of the 28 Bomber Command aircraft lost.

Initial raid assessment indicated accurate marking and bombing in perfect weather. Day reconnaissance of the target area at St Leu d'Esserent showed considerable damage to parts of the supply depot with numerous craters visible. A very large section of earth registered 20 hits and appeared collapsed into the underground workings immediately to the east of the tunnel entrances. The railway tracks were also damaged, those leading north to the yards at Thiverny cut in 20 places. A section, half the width and a third of the length, of a bridge alongside these yards was destroyed. Reconnaissance photographs taken on 6 July also showed that the Germans were devoting a lot of energy to repairs.

The raid also had an effect on the civilian population of St Leu d'Esserent:

> *Raymonde Carbon:* The first serious air raid took place on 4 July, which is the American national holiday so we made jokes amongst ourselves that it was the presents that the American air force were sending us as part of their festivities. When the raids started we were allowed into some of the caves that were reserved for civilian use.
>
> Our house was destroyed on 4 July, so my family and I had to find somewhere else to live. Many houses were destroyed so the people who had lived in these houses were placed in temporary lodgings in a park close to the town centre. When the air raid alarms sounded we had to find other shelter.
>
> There were not too many civilian casualties as they were able to take refuge in the caverns. Those who watched [the bombing] were the ones that were killed and injured. There was no animosity as we knew it was necessary to do it. I was in the Resistance and knew it was the price we had to pay. We understood it had to happen. There were some civilians working for the transport company on the railway sidings and as they had volunteered to work for the Germans they knew the danger they were exposing themselves to, and they became some of the victims.
>
> I was able to see that the main destruction from the bombing was on the railway and road network giving the Germans great difficulty in moving the equipment from this assembly point [the caverns] up to the launching sites.

Not only did the Allies have photographic reconnaissance on which to assess the success of the raid, they were also able to intercept a German signal summarising the attack. It should be noted that the times used in the signal were of course local French time.

> From field ammunition depot 10/XI [St Leu d'Esserent] to LXV
> AK [Armee Korps] issue 4 am 5/7.
>   Installation attacked by heavy bombers . . . Several hundred
> bombs of heavy and heaviest calibre dropped. Cavern entrance
> clear, approach roads, railway installations destroyed. Approach
> from St Leu probably repaired within 24 hours. Casualties
> among ammunition depot personnel 5 men missing. Among
> flak personnel 5 dead, 6 wounded and 6 to 7 missing. In cavern
> no penetrations. Communications out of action.[76]

A partial success could be claimed but it was clear that the caverns would need a further attack, which would be conducted as soon as the opportunity arose.

On the night of 5/6 July Bomber Command despatched 388 aircraft to four targets. A force of 81 Lancasters and 5 Mosquitos was sent to Wizernes. Marking and bombing were reported as concentrated in the target area and reconnaissance later revealed considerable disruption and damage to the supply roads and railways. One of those taking part in the raid was a 622 Squadron Lancaster piloted by Flight Lieutenant Hargreaves whose flight engineer Sergeant Chandler recalls his experiences:

> The outward trip and bombing run had been comparatively uneventful, we were cruising along at 8,000 feet, in very bright moonlight with not a cloud in the sky. Sometime after leaving the target another Lancaster formatted on us at about 500 yards, slightly below on our starboard side, and slightly astern. We were not too happy with this situation since there were rumours floating around that the Germans were repairing some of our shot down aircraft and mixing them in with our bomber stream and shooting down our unsuspecting aircraft. Since the other Lancaster was on our starboard side my position as flight engineer put me in a very good position to keep an eye on its movements. Its position relative to ours remained unchanged for seven or eight minutes.
>   Suddenly, without any warning whatsoever, it disintegrated in a vast explosion and ball of fire. Almost immediately the gunners and myself saw an Me110 which seemed to appear from nowhere. (From information acquired since the war it's quite apparent that this unfortunate crew was the victim of a *Schräge Musik* attack. At the time the appearance of the Me110 was a complete mystery.)

Schräge Musik[77], was proving a deadly weapon for the German nightfighters. Since the autumn of 1943, installation of the weapon (a pair of upward-firing cannon) on a nightfighter aircraft, had enabled the pilot to creep up in the darkness beneath the bombers. He could then aim his cannon fire at the petrol-carrying wings of the bomber silhouetted against the brighter night sky. Bomber crews were often totally unaware they were being hunted until fire broke out in one of their wings and by then it was usually far too late to do anything. There is no doubt that *Schräge Musik* gave the German nightfighters an important advantage and accounted for numerous RAF bombers. Sergeant Chandler continues his story:

> The Me110 positioned itself for an attack on our aircraft; as it came in, we corkscrewed violently and both gunners opened fire on our attacker. Unfortunately only one gun was firing in the rear turret and one of the guns in the mid upper was loaded with daylight tracer. Result, a great blaze of light and loss of night vision. Until such time as the mid upper gunner was able to disconnect the offending belt of ammunition he restricted himself to a running commentary of the enemy aircraft's position. The Me110 made three attacks before breaking off and was claimed destroyed by our rear gunner.
>
> Almost immediately we were again attacked, this time by a Ju88. By now the mid upper gunner had managed to return fire from his one good gun. Again three attacks were made before our assailant broke off the engagement and the rear gunner claimed the attacker as damaged, probably destroyed.

The official report of the engagements tells of the gunners seeing both enemy fighters breaking away to port in flames. Chandler's position as flight engineer was on the starboard side of the Lancaster and hence he would have been unable to witness the flaming fighters. The rear gunner, Flight Sergeant Glynn, was given an immediate award of the DFM. Four aircraft were lost on this raid. The 15 Squadron Lancaster of Flying Officer Golub RCAF, the 582 Squadron Lancaster of Pilot Officer Manson RCAF and the 635 Squadron Lancasters of Pilot Officer Weaver and Squadron Leader Riches DFC and bar. There was only one survivor from the four crews: Pilot Officer Pack from Riches' crew managed to evade capture.

Watten was also attacked by 82 Lancasters and 5 Mosquitos during the night, with one concentration of marking confirmed visually as accurate and subsequently bombed. Reconnaissance revealed serious damage to supply roads and railway. The main building received some damage from a near miss and a light trestle bridge on the opposite side of it was demolished. The fact that Bomber Command had attacked the Watten and Wizernes sites at all, caused some consternation at the Air Ministry the following day. Sir Charles Portal, Chief of the Air Staff, sent a handwritten note to Bottomley, Deputy Chief of the Air Staff, noting that Bomber Command had attacked two large sites and saying that, 'I thought we had laid off for the present in favour of other Xbow [Crossbow] targets?'

Bottomley replied confirming that attacks on large sites had been suspended and that he was looking into the reason for the then current target priorities not being followed. Bottomley was, at that time, unable to speak to the Deputy Supreme Commander, Air Chief Marshal Sir Arthur Tedder, but did receive information that Bomber Command's Commander-in-Chief was 'taking a fatherly interest' in the big sites and 'thought they needed immediate attention!' Bottomley did eventually manage to discuss the matter with Tedder.

At an Allied Expeditionary Air Force meeting on the morning of 5 July Air Commodore Claude Pelly had expressed the opinion that within a week it was likely that Watten and Wizernes would be scheduled for attack again. Harris, noting that the weather conditions were suitable, took the opportunity to hit the targets early and Tedder described it as 'perhaps not a well disciplined act but well intentioned'. The matter was laid to rest, but 27 men had lost their lives on the 'well intentioned' act.[78]

Two other Crossbow targets were also attacked on the night of 5/6 July, both of which were flying bomb targets. A force consisting of 2 Lancasters, 99 Halifaxes and 5 Mosquitos was despatched to Biennais. The 431 Squadron Halifax of Flying Officer Harrison RCAF swung round on take-off and crashed. The wireless operator Warrant Officer Hooker RCAF and the mid upper gunner Flight Sergeant Content RCAF then put their lives on the line for their crewmates as they assisted their fellow airmen from the burning Halifax. The aircraft continued to burn and later exploded. All of the crew were injured with the bomb aimer Flying Officer Dumville RCAF so badly hurt that he later died. Those aircraft that proceeded to the target at Biennais were able to see the TI grouped to the west of the aiming point and bombing was reported as well placed on the TI. Day reconnaissance indicated a fairly unsuccessful attack with only 30 craters identified in the target area. No building damage was visible although the supply rail line was cut in at least two places. A local report confirms the inaccuracy of the raid. The majority of the bombing fell on the centre of Biennais. The surrounding area was well cratered and the church was destroyed along with numerous houses.[79]

A force of 2 Lancasters, 102 Halifaxes and 5 Mosquitos was despatched to St Martin l'Hortier. On approaching the target the main force crews saw two groups of markers about 500 yards apart, one to the east, the other to the west of the aiming point. Both groups were attacked, with more attention given to the easterly grouping deemed a little closer to the aiming point. Reconnaissance revealed considerable damage, one building receiving a direct hit and three other buildings with damage to their roofs. The railway lines, supply roads and main road were hit several times. Neither of the raids against flying bomb targets this night sustained any losses due to enemy action.

These raids completed Bomber Command's attacks against supply sites. American bombers attacked Renescure and Sautrecourt on 6 July, the last Allied attacks on supply sites. In all 12,224 tons of Allied bombs were dropped on the supply sites, of which 10,290 tons had been dropped by Bomber Command on 26 raids, and 1,934 tons by American bombers on 26 raids by heavy bombers and 2 raids by tactical bombers. This must be noted as a considerable tonnage of bombs, which actually had little effect on the German flying bomb offensive.

With the importance of the supply depot at St Leu d'Esserent now fully accepted by Allied Intelligence, and taking into account the German signal intercept following the 4/5 July operation, further attacks were called for. On 6 July some squadrons were detailed to prepare for another attack to the Oise valley caverns:

> *Sergeant Bob Riches, rear gunner, 9 Squadron:* . . . bombed up, keyed up and then fed up! The sortie . . . was cancelled as we sat in the aircraft a few minutes before take-off. I was then chastened by our superstitious crew for not remembering that it was my 20th birthday. We had taken wakey-wakey pills so had to play cards all night.

However five suspected German secret weapon targets were attacked, four of which were associated with flying bombs. At Siracourt (33 Lancasters, 59 Halifaxes and 5 Mosquitos), Forêt du Croc (102 Lancasters and 5 Mosquitos) and Coqueraux (54 Lancasters, 48 Halifaxes and 5 Mosquitos) accurate marking led to good bombing concentrations. Reconnaissance of Forêt du Croc on 9 July showed a cratered target area and hits to the launching ramp. At Croix Dalle (2 Lancasters, 103 Halifaxes and 5 Mosquitos), the initial bombing was reported as scattered but did improve with two large explosions witnessed. Day reconnaissance revealed many craters around the aiming point, some blocking of roads and two near misses on the concrete platform. The other Crossbow target attacked, by 130 aircraft, was Mimoyecques. This raid is of particular note as following Wing Commander Leonard Cheshire's return from directing the raid, he was ordered to leave 617 Squadron and rest, thereby finishing his fourth tour comprising 100 operations. He was subsequently awarded the Victoria Cross partly in recognition of his commitment and application in the development of low-level marking techniques.

Bomber Command lost six aircraft on the Crossbow operations. Three of these were on the raid to Croix Dalle. The 515 Squadron Halifax of Flight Sergeant Abell RAAF suffered severe flak damage. Abell managed to bring the aircraft back over England where the crew baled out. The 76 Squadron Halifax of Pilot Officer Mottram was diverted to an emergency airfield at Carnaby in Yorkshire owing to undercarriage problems. Mottram managed to bring the Halifax down but the aircraft carried on past the end of the runway into woodland. Fortunately there were no casualties. The 578 Squadron Halifax of Pilot Officer Parfitt crashed on returning from the raid near Nottingham and the entire crew of seven was killed. Whilst over the target on the raid to Forêt du Croc the 12 Squadron Lancaster of Flight Lieutenant Gray had the misfortune of losing its starboard fin and rudder when hit by a bomb from another aircraft. Gray was able to use all his skill in bringing the stricken aircraft back to England. However on the approach to Faldingworth airfield, in Lincolnshire, the Lancaster crashed. Two of the crew were killed and one other was so seriously injured that he later died. The 424 Squadron Halifax of Flying Officer Bannihr RCAF was hit by flak on the raid to Siracourt and there were no survivors from the crew of seven. The 347 (French) Squadron Halifax of Sous-Lieutenant Varlet FFAF (Free

French Air Force), sent on the Mimoyecques raid, crashed near Lindholme airfield in Yorkshire; there were no survivors from the crew of seven, all French airmen.

The attack on Siracourt on 6 July was the last by Bomber Command to this target. It is of note that no flying bombs were ever launched from the Siracourt bunker. The Bomber Command attacks, whilst not inflicting too much damage to the bunker itself, had devastated the surrounding area. The USAAF would actually carry out one further interesting attack on the target. Under the codename of Aphrodite, battle-weary B-17s were filled with explosive and, via radio control, directed onto targets. On 4 August the first Aphrodite missions, using B-17 'flying bombs', were carried out on Mimoyecques, Watten, Wizernes and Siracourt. However none of the targets was hit.[80]

CHAPTER 11

'YOU'LL KEEP GOING BACK'

The Enigma decrypt, which revealed the partial success of the 4/5 July Bomber Command raid to St Leu d'Esserent, and reconnaissance showing the Germans' feverish attempts to repair any damage, led the Allied planners to decide upon sending another large force of RAF heavy bombers to take out the flying bomb supply depot.

Flight Sergeant Ron Dent, a navigator with 463 (RAAF) Squadron, arrived at his new operational squadron in the summer of 1944. The squadron had been operational since November 1943:

> We, with five other crews, were new at 463 . . . and asked in the mess, 'How long does it take to get through a tour here?' Puzzled looks and dead silence, then: 'No one has yet mate.'
>
> The practice was to first send the pilot on an operation as second dickie to an experienced pilot. Zac [Flying Officer J. Tanner] went to St Leu d'Esserent and came back safely. One of the other pilots who started with us failed to return.

On 7 July Flying Officer Tanner was detailed to take his fresh crew to the St Leu d'Esserent caves. The importance of taking out the flying bomb supply depot was once more highlighted to aircrews briefed for the raid. At 463 (RAAF) Squadron, crews were informed that:

> You'll keep going back until you get this target. It is a flying bomb store and unless we get it, there will be up to 600 flying bombs a day falling on London at a cost of perhaps a million lives.[81]

Sergeant Len Barham was a navigator with 207 Squadron.

> Reconnaissance photographs taken after the previous attack at St Leu d'Esserent had shown that although considerable damage had been done, it was not complete. We were not surprised therefore to learn, at briefing, that our target was the limestone caves.[81]

For the night of 7/8 July Bomber Command despatched two large forces to French targets. One involving 123 Lancasters and 5 Mosquitos, to the rail yards at Vaires, 12 miles east of Paris, the other involving 208 Lancasters and 13 Mosquitos to visit the flying bomb supply depot at St Leu d'Esserent. One hundred and six aircraft (Lancasters, Halifaxes, Stirlings and Wellingtons) were sent on a diversionary raid over the North Sea to the coast of Holland, 32 Mosquitos were sent to Berlin and 9 Mosquitos to Scholven/Buer. Fifty-four aircraft were employed on RCM and Resistance operations. Sixteen Stirlings operated a Mandrel screen and 45 Mosquitos made Serrate and intruder patrols; 16 Mosquitos were involved in anti-flying bomb patrols.

Bomber Command planned an interesting ruse for the night's operations. The force sent to St Leu d'Esserent was directed to form three waves on the outward route. The largest wave, of approximately 100 aircraft, being half the force, would share their approach route with the Vaires force. Over France and to the west of Paris the Vaires force would then continue south whilst the St Leu d'Esserent wave would turn towards a rendezvous point for all the three waves to the south-west of St Leu d'Esserent. The aim of this exercise was to try and suggest to the Germans that raids involving 200-plus bombers were to take place to the south of Paris with smaller raids on flying bomb sites to the north.

Target and aircraft despatched

St Leu d'Esserent
208 Lancasters and
13 Mosquitos
1121.3 tons high explosive
and 4.3 incendiary bombs

Plan of attack

Zero hour – 0110 hours
Mosquitos to locate the aiming point at zero hour – 4. Then Oboe Mosquitos were to drop yellow route indicator TI. At zero hour, if the Controller required, the target was to be illuminated. The aiming point was to be marked with red spot fires and green red TI, and backed up if accurate. Yellows were to be used to cancel wide markers. In a further attempt to confuse prowling opposition nightfighters and draw them away from the real bombing target, RAF 'spoof' (diversionary) aircraft would drop red, green and yellow TI approximately 50 miles to the north-east of the St Leu d'Esserent target area, at zero hour – 12.
Time over France 0022 to 0158 hours, time over the target 0110 to 0125 hours.

The time over the target for the Vaires force was ordered for 0123 to 0136 hours with time over France as 0022 to 0158 hours. The diversionary force was ordered to be at a longitude position 3 degrees east, heading toward the Dutch coast, at 0100 hours, the hope being that this would draw the defensive German nightfighters north away from the actual main bombing targets. A Mandrel screen was also to be used, in an attempt to further confuse the German defenders' control of the nightfighters. Bomber Command's weather forecast for the night suggested good clear areas in France with little cloud at Paris. Below is the detail of the night's operations:

2330 to 0015 hours

St Leu d'Esserent force: The large force proceeds across the Channel and then splits into three waves mid way across. Approaching the French coast.

Vaires force: Proceeds across the Channel on the same route as the St Leu d'Esserent force and then with the St Leu d'Esserent third wave when this splits. Approaches the French coast.

German reaction (from Allied Intelligence intercepts): German controller starts assembling fighters at the beacons between Beauvais and Creil and between Creil and Paris. I./NJG 5 sent to the north of Paris and I./NJG 4 sent from the Cambrai area to the Beauvais/Creil area.

0016 to 0030 hours

St Leu d'Esserent force: The first two waves cross the French coast and proceed south-east towards the target. The third wave crosses the coast just to the east of Le Havre, with the Vaires force.

Vaires force: Crosses the French coast just to the east of Le Havre and proceeds south-south-east.

German reaction: At 0018 hours the RAF's bombers were plotted to the south of Beachy Head. At 0023 hours I./JG301 from St Dizier were readied and at 0029 hours sent to a concentration of searchlights in the Dieppe area.

0031 to 0045 hours

St Leu d'Esserent force: The first two waves proceed south-east towards the target area. The third wave prepares to turn eastward and departs from the Vaires force.

Vaires force: Continues south-east across France.

German reaction: At 0043 hours I./NJG 5 is positioned north of Paris and awaits orders. At 0044 hours I./JG301 is ordered towards the mouth of the Somme, receiving information that the bombers were in the area and at Le Tréport.

Combats (100 Group): At 0040 hours a 239 Squadron Mosquito closes in on an FW190, 8 miles north-west of Amiens. From dead astern the Mosquito opens fire, striking the single-engined nightfighter which explodes violently and scorches the Mosquito's port wing. The burning debris of the FW190 cascades to the ground.

At 0041 hours a 239 Squadron Mosquito sights an Me110 in the Meaux area and sends a two-second burst of cannon fire into the enemy aircraft's fuselage and port engine, which explodes. Smoke trails the stricken Me110 as it descends rapidly, with further explosions, and hits the ground.

0046 to 0100 hours

St Leu d'Esserent force: All three waves converge on a position just to the south-south-west of the target. Aircrews begin to witness the demise of some of their RAF colleagues.

The whole crew bales out of Flying Officer Mather's RCAF 106 Squadron Lancaster owing to fire in both port engines and in the rear fuselage. All men survive and their aircraft burns near Gournay-en-Bray.

Pilot Officer Monaghan RAAF and his crew bale out of its 106 Squadron Lancaster, over Anet, and all men survive.

Flight Lieutenant Ball DFC and his crew all lose their lives as their 44 Squadron Lancaster is believed shot down by friendly fire from another Lancaster. The aircraft burns near the village of le Chesne.

Vaires force: Proceeds south-east to turn north-east towards the target.

German reaction: Some fighters are held north due to the diversionary raids. Engagements between fighters and bombers begin against all three of the St Leu d'Esserent waves.

Combats (100 Group): At 0050 hours a 141 Squadron Mosquito stalks an Me110, opens fire and strikes are seen along the top of the German nightfighter's mainplane. A large explosion results and the aircraft turns on its back, dives to earth and explodes on the ground.

At 0053 hours the 239 Squadron Mosquito that had claimed a kill at 0041 hours sights another Me110, 5 miles south of Compiègne, and opens fire from dead astern and slightly below. The middle of the enemy aircraft is hit and it explodes; oil and burning wreckage fly back, the oil covers the victorious Mosquito's windscreen. What is left of the German nightfighter falls from the night sky and explodes on the ground.

Other forces: Spoof attack starts at 0100 hours with little effect. The diversionary force turns back over the North Sea at 0100 hours.

0101 to 0115 hours

St Leu d'Esserent force: The three waves converge, approach and attack the target. Stricken RAF bombers, going down, continue to be witnessed and recorded by more fortunate bomber crews.

All four engines on the 106 Squadron Lancaster of Flight Lieutenant Marchant RAAF are set on fire and the aircraft rapidly descends to smash into the ground near Anet. Only the pilot and two other men from the crew of seven survive.

Flight Sergeant Boyce is killed along with four of his crew (two men survive) as their 207 Squadron Lancaster falls to the ground near Haudricourt.

The 83 Squadron Lancaster of Flying Officer Griffiths DFC is shot down. The pilot dies and of the crew of seven only two survive. The fallen bomber burns near Bû.

A direct flak hit causes the explosion of the 61 Squadron Lancaster of Pilot Officer Passant RAAF. There is a total loss of

life as the debris cascades to the ground near the town of Mouy.
Vaires force: Proceeds north-east towards the target area.
German reaction: At 0105 hours the first bombers start to reach
St Leu d'Esserent, close to where I./NJG5 is assembled.
Bomber Command's radio intercepts start to pick up German
victory claims. Numerous engagements occur up to and over
the target.

0116 to 0130 hours

St Leu d'Esserent force: Over the target and then splits into
three waves for the return route with further losses.

A nightfighter attack results in the death of 207 Squadron's
Flying Officer Stamp and two of his crew. The four other crew
members survive the Lancaster's destruction in the sky over
Auvers-sur-Oise.

The 44 Squadron Lancaster of Pilot Officer Gowing crashes
near Neufchâtel-en-Bray. Five men survive, the pilot and the
other crew member are killed.

A nightfighter shoots down the 49 Squadron Lancaster of
Flying Officer Baker, over Beauvoir-en-Lyons, and there are no
survivors.

Flight Lieutenant Grantham is killed along with four of his
crew (the other two men surviving) as their 61 Squadron
Lancaster falls near Moliens.

Squadron Leader Marshall DFC loses his life along with his
entire crew as their 106 Squadron Lancaster falls to earth near
Ste-Geneviève, after being hit by flak.

Flying Officer Alderton and his entire crew manage to get out
and survive as their 207 Squadron Lancaster hits the ground
near Songeons.

Pilot Officer Milner dies and there is only one survivor from
his crew of seven as their 207 Squadron Lancaster falls to earth
near Gisors.

Wing Commander Deas DSO DFC and bar, is killed with five of
his crew, one man surviving, as their 630 Squadron Lancaster
falls near Villers-en-Athies.
Vaires force: Approaches and attacks the target.
German reaction: The battle over St Leu d'Esserent continues
and the bomber force suffers numerous losses. The fighters start
to give chase and engage with the bombers along the home
routes.

0131 to 0145 hours

St Leu d'Esserent force: Proceeds homeward in three waves,
still suffering losses.

57 Squadron Pilot Officer Owen and his crew manage to get
out of their Lancaster, and all men survive, before it crashes
near Montdidier.

Flying Officer Hordley is killed with four of his crew, two men survive, as their 207 Squadron Lancaster falls to ground near Sancourt.

Flight Lieutenant Johnston survives with four of his crew, the other two men dying, as their 619 Squadron Lancaster plunges to the ground near Précy-sur-Oise.

Vaires force: Attacks the target and then proceeds south-west and then west, away from the target.

German reaction: The air battle rages on the St Leu d'Esserent force homeward route. At 0131 hours I./JG301 is told to wait between Dieppe and some searchlights; at 0134 hours they were told that the bombers would be over the mouth of the Somme within 5 minutes.

Combats (St Leu d'Esserent force): At 0133 hours an 83 Squadron Lancaster is attacked by a single-engined enemy aircraft. The bomber's gunners return fire, seeing it hit their adversary's wing roots and fuselage. A glow appears which eventually bursts into flames and the German nightfighter plunges and explodes on the ground.

Combats (100 Group): At 0135 hours, south-east of Charleroi, a 239 Squadron Mosquito closes on an Me110 and opens fire. Strikes are witnessed in the middle of the aircraft's fuselage. The Me110 explodes and pieces of wreckage fly past the Mosquito. What is left of the German nightfighter aircraft hits the ground and burns.

0146 hours onwards

St Leu d'Esserent force: The three waves proceed, with a few burning bombers seen to fall, towards the French coast and converge on a point mid-Channel from where the bombers proceed on to Reading.

Pilot Officer Langford's 9 Squadron Lancaster falls to earth near Gamaches, with only the pilot and two other men surviving.

Flight Lieutenant Carnegie's 44 Squadron Lancaster is shot down by a nightfighter, crashing near St-Germer-de-Fly (detailed later).

A nightfighter shoots Sergeant Lloyd's 50 Squadron Lancaster out of the sky over Grandvillers, with a total loss of life.

RCAF Pilot Officer Laidlaw's 50 Squadron Lancaster explodes over Mesnil-Mauger, throwing clear the pilot, who is the only survivor.

Pilot Officer Rose RAAF is killed along with two of his 57 Squadron crew and one of the crew is fatally injured. Three men survive the Lancaster's demise, which comes to earth near Fresnay-le-Long.

The 57 Squadron Lancaster of Pilot Officer Findley falls to

the ground near St-Nicolas d'Aliermont with a total loss of life.
Vaires force: Turns north-west and crosses the French coast to
the north of Le Havre and from there proceeds on to Reading.
German reaction: There are a few engagements with the Vaires
force and a few further engagements with the St Leu d'Esserent
force.

Over the target the St Leu d'Esserent force had experienced variable cloud
3 to 10/10ths at 15 to 17,000 feet, clear below. The moon was up all night
and just past full, perfect for the prowling nightfighters. Bomber Command
believed the target was marked accurately, but there had been delay. It was
hoped that the opening markers could be placed using the light of the moon,
but flares were needed. This resulted in the main force having to orbit,
giving more time for the German nightfighters to intercept. Bombing was
believed accurate with a slight southerly drift towards the end of the raid.
Apart from the attention of the nightfighters there was considerable heavy
flak, much stronger than the force on the 4/5 July raid experienced. There
were no searchlights over the target. Subsequent day reconnaissance showed
concentrations of craters over the northern, central and southern tunnel
entrances, with buildings destroyed. The main railway was also hit and 13
craters were counted on the tracks from the tunnel entrances. A gun position
received a direct hit. In terms of damage caused this raid could certainly be
classed as successful. Colonel Walter, Chief of Staff to LXV Army Corps,
was later to recall the conditions in the caves following the attacks:

> You could hear a constant rumbling overhead, and began to feel
> that the very mountain was on the move and might collapse at
> any moment. It was asking too much of any man's nerves to
> expect him to hold out in caves like that.[83]

Air Vice-Marshal Cochrane, Air Officer Commanding 5 Group, wrote a
congratulatory note to his aircrews:

> All members of aircrew taking part in Friday night's attack on
> St Leu have reason to feel proud of their achievement. Day
> photographs show concentration of bombs on and around the
> Aiming Point, which would have been considered excellent had
> there been no opposition. In the circumstances, the accuracy
> achieved is a magnificent tribute to Captains and Crews. It is
> now known that the enemy ignored all other attacks that night
> in order to concentrate his whole strength in defence of this one
> target. He brought to bear some 100 Twin and 50 Single-
> engined Fighters, many being concentrated over the target.
> Losses would have been heavier had it not been for the excellent
> discipline and strict adherence to Flight Plan, especially the
> timing of the attack and the dispersal after leaving the target.
> The plotted positions of aircraft twenty minutes after bombing
> shows an even spread over a front of 60 miles, and in height
> between 5 and 20,000 ft. As a result, interceptions quickly

diminished after leaving the target. Although the cost of the operation was high, it achieved its purpose, and has received from the Press the recognition which you so fully earned. I believe it to be the best achievement yet put up by No. 5 Group, and an indication to the Germans that even under conditions most favourable to them, they are still unable to stop attacks on the targets they value most highly. Well done.

The cost to Bomber Command had indeed been high. The German nightfighters had been carefully marshalled and were able to get amongst the heavy bombers. Yet again they showed that they were far from defeated as the air battle raged.

> *Pilot Officer Russell Gradwell, pilot, 9 Squadron:* I don't know whether the Germans had got a fifth column over here or whether they had just assumed that as we had missed it on the 4th that we would be back again but the nightfighters were queuing up waiting for us when we crossed the French coast. Fights broke out all around us and we were lucky nobody bothered us until we got about half way towards the target. Then a nightfighter closed in on us. I was lucky I had a rear gunner who was a game keeper in civvie street and his night vision was exceptional . . . he spotted the nightfighter and we fought with it. I think that one of the gunners luckily got a hit on the fighter and knocked the pilot out, because I was corkscrewing and the gunner suddenly screamed to me 'level out', which I did and the nightfighter passed just underneath us. Obviously they had knocked the pilot out and he had flopped at the controls with his aircraft returning to flying straight and level.
>
> We then carried on to the target but upon reaching it I noticed that we had a wing on fire. We bombed anyway but as soon as we had bombed, I didn't bother about the camera, I just turned away and we decided to put the fire out. We couldn't do it. We tried everything. We switched all the fuel off on the port side (where the fire was) and shut both engines down. I was lucky that I had a flight engineer who had been an apprentice at AVRO's building Lancasters, and he looked for a few minutes and said, 'I think we've had it because the fire is going back, and when it burns the spar the wing will go, and when the wing goes, we go. So I think we had better go while the going is good.' I agreed with him and we baled out.

Unfortunately one of Pilot Officer Gradwell's crew, Sergeant Price, whilst managing to escape the burning aircraft, which fell near Beaumont-les-Nonains, did not survive:

> He picked his parachute up by the release handle instead of the proper handle and released the parachute in the aircraft. All we could do was tell him to clip it on and hang on as there was a

little umbrella chute that acted as the pilot chute. We said hang
on to that and when you get clear let it go and it should take the
parachute. Obviously it didn't and unfortunately his body
wasn't found until November.

The rest of Pilot Officer Gradwell's crew (consisting of eight men) all
managed to evade capture.[84] In addition to the loss of Pilot Officer
Langford's Lancaster mentioned above, 9 Squadron also lost the Lancaster
of Flying Officer Blackham, which fell near Ecquevilly; the pilot was killed
with five of the crew, and one man survived.

Sergeant Len Barham was navigator on Flying Officer Alderton's 207
Squadron Lancaster:

The trip was uneventful until near Beauvais we were attacked
by a German nightfighter, coming literally from out of the
clouds. We were flying at 10,000 ft just under the patchy cloud
(I have subsequently heard that the Germans had devised a way
of homing in on our airborne H2S navigation aid [German
codeword *Naxos*]). We had been hit amidships and there was
acrid smoke coming from near the W.Op's position. The
starboard inner engine was alight and feathering did not fully
extinguish it. The bomb aimer was unable to jettison our bombs.
We were therefore ordered to abandon. We were lucky in that
our pilot, Mike, was able to control the aircraft well enough for
us to bale out according to instructions. Fortunately we all
survived to tell the tale. In fact all but myself and Al [Sergeant
Chinn], the flight engineer, managed to avoid capture.

Lancaster 'P' of 44 Squadron had arrived at the target before any markers
were down and had to orbit. When the order to bomb was received, the
pilot, Flight Lieutenant Carnegie, had just taken his aircraft past the target
and started his second orbit, which was then completed before the bomb
run was made. As a result the bomber left the target late and after about five
minutes an aircraft, approaching from astern, was picked up by the
aircraft's tail warning radar, Monica. Flight Lieutenant Carnegie
immediately threw the Lancaster into a corkscrew to port followed by the
gunners opening fire. The German fighter returned fire but achieved no hits.
The fighter then followed this with a second burst hitting the corkscrewing
bomber in the bomb bay. Inside the Lancaster the lights went out, the
intercom failed, the fuselage filled with smoke and a small fire broke out
below the navigator's position, with sparks coming up through the floor.
After some difficulty opening the front hatch, the crew started to abandon
the aircraft. Carnegie asked his navigator to retrieve his parachute but did
not put it on. While he kept the Lancaster under control, gently diving, six
of his crew managed to get out of the burning aircraft, although the bomb
aimer Sergeant Holt was to die from his injuries. Some of the men then
witnessed the aircraft flying along with flames streaming underneath,
before finally going into a dive to end up burning on the ground. Flight
Lieutenant Carnegie had not escaped from the aircraft and it was believed

that this was as a result of being injured by the fire from the nightfighter.[85] Three of the crew then managed to evade capture whilst the two others were taken. No. 44 Squadron also lost the Lancasters of Pilot Officer Graaf, who crashed near Equennes-Eramecourt (the entire crew was killed) and Pilot Officer Gowing (mentioned previously).

In addition to the St Leu d'Esserent force losses detailed above in the description of the night's operations, there were the following: 49 Squadron lost one more Lancaster, that of Flying Officer McCracken, which was badly damaged by a nightfighter attack. McCracken was able to bring the aircraft back to base and land with no casualties amongst the crew. However the aircraft was later written off. From 50 Squadron the Lancaster of Flight Sergeant Davies went down with no survivors; the aircraft came to earth near Lalande-en-Son. The 467 Squadron Lancasters of Flight Lieutenant Reynolds (which fell west of Beauvais) and Flying Officer Ryan RAAF (near Courgent) failed to return with only two of Reynolds' crew surviving; they evaded capture. No. 106 Squadron had a particularly bad night, losing five Lancasters; in addition to those already mentioned, the Lancaster of Flight Lieutenant Clement DFC came down near Quetteville, with no survivors.

No. 207 Squadron had also had a terrible night; it too lost five Lancasters, one of which was Flying Officer Stamp's aircraft, adding to a German nightfighter's kill score. His wireless operator, Flight Sergeant John Fisher, recalls the experience.

> The flak near the target was light, which meant the fighters were around and they were expecting us. The combat with the nightfighter was brief as he came up underneath. We caught a blast of cannon fire under the aircraft and were engulfed in flames and had to bale out. I opened the door at the main spar to bale at the rear but was engulfed in flames and my face was burned, so I went to the front where the navigator, bomb aimer and engineer were all on the way out. I was last out and the two gunners and pilot went down in the plane.

The pilot and both gunners were killed. Flight Sergeant Fisher went into hiding with French helpers; he was eventually placed into an evasion line, but was captured and saw out the war as a prisoner. The flight engineer and navigator were also caught. The bomb aimer managed to evade capture.

No. 630 Squadron also suffered a considerable set back on the raid, not in terms of numbers of aircraft but owing to the previously mentioned death of the Lancaster of Wing Commander Deas DSO DFC and bar. The squadron's ORB recorded that it was, 'the saddest blow and the most grievous loss the Squadron could have. He was a most popular and efficient Commanding Officer, he was on his 69th trip.'

In addition to the aircrew losses from aircraft not returning from the raid, there were further casualties on aircraft that had been in combat. The 207 Squadron Lancaster flown by Flying Officer Oakes was engaged and shot at by a Ju88. The rear gunner Sergeant Hanson returned fire, his fellow gunner Sergeant John Butterworth, in the mid upper turret, was killed. The Ju88 then briefly held back before coming in for the second attack, exchanging fire with the Lancaster's rear gunner. The Ju88 broke away and disappeared. With little damage to the aircraft Oakes brought his crew back safely. The 22-year-old Sergeant Butterworth was buried at Manchester Southern Cemetery.

Bomber Command had lost a total of 32 Lancasters as a result of the raid to the flying bomb supply depot. One hundred and forty-two men were killed in these aircraft, 30 men became POWs and 47 men evaded capture. For a raid to a target in France these figures were extremely high. There were no casualties at all on the raid to Vaires. There had been a cost to the German nightfighter force for their success, however. On the night's operations 100 Group Mosquitos claimed five enemy aircraft and two main force Lancasters claimed an enemy aircraft each. In addition Air Defence of Great Britain Mosquitos claimed three Ju88s, one Ju 188 and one unidentified aircraft.

With respect to the success the German nightfighters could claim, most credit would go to the single-engined all weather fighters from I./JG 301, which shot down 20 of the Lancasters.[86] Leutnant Erich Jung (pilot), Feldwebel Walter Heidenreich (radio operator) and Oberfeldwebel Hans Reinnagel (flight mechanic) in a Ju88-R2 4R+AP of the 6th *Staffel* NJG2 took off from Coulommiers and destroyed two four-engined bombers. They had already claimed three four-engined bombers on the night of 4/5 July. Walter Heidenreich recalls the raids:

> The moon was very bright on these nights and it was teeming with enemy bombers. So our enemies and their staff must have been feeling great anxiety.

Heidenreich and his crew did not have it all their own way on the night of 7/8 July. After their two kills they began pursuing another four-engined bomber when:

> . . . all weapons failed. We immediately pulled away from the difficult position and tried to reload using compressed air. When we had regained a shooting position the securely attached weapons failed again. I then tried to engage our enemy with the mobile 12.7mm machine gun. However, after a few shots I had further weapon failure. It was very nerve-wracking.
>
> We set out on the way home to Coulommiers at a good height, travelling about 550 km per hour. I had reported to base and was told we could land as number 7. It was number 2's turn. Our height was about 130 metres when a shadow emerged in the horizon and at the same moment as I saw it it shot at us. It was precisely aimed, the burst of fire hit the left fuel tank, a good metre away from me. The tongue of flame shot far out beyond our tail unit. In the next second I left my seat and stood on the escape hatch. I called to the Mechanic on the intercom: 'Hans,

throw down the escape hatch' (the handle for this was right up on the underside of the fixed part of the roof). Hans immediately threw the panel down and in the same fraction of a second I let myself fall through the hole. My parachute went up immediately and threw me directly underneath our Ju88. As a result of the very high speed I received a violent blow. My throat microphone was still attached and it tore off causing a severe neck wound. But I was free from the plane. Straightaway I tried my flare pistol, as our enemy, the Mosquito, could be heard scarcely 10 to 20 metres away above my parachute and he shot for a second time at the hopelessly burning Ju88. That was superfluous and I politely describe it as unfriendly. My only thought at that moment was hopefully both my comrades had been quick enough and got out of the plane before this second burst of fire. So it was; both men had managed to jump as quick as lightning just before. They landed just a few hundred metres away from me. I have often tried to estimate how long it may have lasted from the hit until I was in the parachute. I think it was clearly under 10 seconds. From much observation and my own experience, I know what speeds means here, especially when one is as low as we were.

The night of 7/8 July 1944 takes its place in the history of Bomber Command as one of the fiercest air battles ever fought over French territory. Had the cost to the RAF in terms of aircraft and trained and experienced airmen been worth it? Had the attack on the limestone caves significantly disrupted the German flying bomb programme? Only time would tell and over the next few weeks Allied intelligence would closely monitor the German reaction.

CHAPTER 12

NO LET UP

In Barnet, North London, an eyewitness recalls the terror of the flying bomb offensive that summer:

> The noise woke me just before the explosion when a great flame burnt my eyeballs. There was dead silence from cut-out to explosion. The thing had caught on the telegraph pole opposite and brought it down, and the whole lot had landed in my neighbour's garden. The gas main caught light, which caused a big fire. The upstairs of the house fell on us bit by bit, also part of the outside wall. The wall seemed to float down like a feather, and yet we had an awful job to get it off the pillows. I started to struggle, but my husband pulled me under the blankets with him, drew it over our heads, held my hand tight and said, 'Wait till it stops dropping on us.' So we did, and by this time the children were sitting up and crying. The front door had gone and we were open to the street and the noise and the fire, which frightened them. So we all moved under the stairs and waited for help.[87]

The day and night after the St Leu d'Esserent raid the Bomber Command crews were not called upon to attack flying bomb targets. Indeed only minor operations took place. However on 9 July another major attack against the flying bomb threat was initiated when 347 aircraft were despatched to attack six modified sites. The forces attacking Linzeux (52 Lancasters, 5 Mosquitos), Château Bernapré (2 Lancasters, 53 Halifaxes, 5 Mosquitos), L'Hey (52 Lancasters, 5 Mosquitos) and Mont Candon (10 Lancasters, 42 Halifaxes and 5 Mosquitos) all experienced considerable cloud cover which disrupted the bombing. At Les Catelliers (2 Lancasters, 52 Halifaxes, 5 Mosquitos) and Ardouval II (2 Lancasters, 50 Halifaxes, 5 Mosquitos) the main forces were ordered to bomb the TI but the bombing was believed scattered. Follow-up reconnaissance on all targets, except Linzeux, revealed poor results. Only at L'Hey was any damage indicated: it was noticed that the launch platform no longer cast a shadow, the square building had disappeared and an auxiliary building had been demolished.

Bomber Command lost two aircraft from the raids. Warrant Officer Bamford's 622 Squadron Lancaster failed to return from the raid to

Linzeux, with no trace of the crew or aircraft ever found. Halifax LV799 'C' of 78 Squadron took off from RAF Breighton at 1136 hours, detailed to attack Château Bernapré. Very shortly after take-off a problem developed with one of the engines. The flight engineer Sergeant Price noticed that the oil pressure had dropped and the cylinder head temperature had risen, and suspecting a fire might develop, he watched the engines closely. Sure enough a small fire did start in the air intake of the port outer engine; it was immediately feathered and the fire went out. Pilot Officer Andrew, the pilot, decided to abandon the sortie, go out to sea and get rid of the bombload. He crossed the coast at only 1,500 feet and at almost the same time the port inner engine began to play up. This too had to be feathered. Meanwhile the aircraft lost further height, now at about 1,000 feet, and was 35 to 40 miles out to sea. The bombload was released on the fish.

Andrew set course for Carnaby but was still losing height. Wireless operator Warrant Officer Long sent an emergency message and received an acknowledgement. With the Halifax now at 250 feet Andrew decided to ditch close inshore rather than risk a landing and the crew was ordered to ditching stations. The Halifax touched the sea at an indicated air speed of 120 mph, with the H2S blister and the tail making first contact. Immediately the Halifax broke in two, 3 feet aft of the mid upper turret, the nose dipping down into the sea. The aircraft became vertical, with the mainplanes submerged, and the sea rushed into the nose of the bomber. Fortunately the crew all managed to make quick exits from their ditching stations. The interior of the Halifax filled with the sea and sank in about ten minutes. The crew was able to get to the dinghy and was spotted by another Halifax carrying out a training flight, which immediately reported the situation. The previous quick thinking of the wireless operator Warrant Officer Long had also alerted the rescue services and it was not long before a launch from Bridlington picked up the crew.

As before, the only major opposition the bomber crews faced on daylight operations was from the flak. Flight Sergeant Ken Grantham, wireless operator 35 Squadron, took part in one of the raids on 9 July:

> We were briefed at 0930 hours for a daylight to a Buzz Bomb site at L'Hey. Take-off was 1250 hours into cloud and icing started along the wings. This got thicker and thicker, then the port inner engine started failing. It got so bad that Daws [the pilot] feathered it until well over the Channel, where the cloud broke and we were in clear sunshine. Daws started the port inner again which continued giving only about half power. We came up on the target very quickly, having in fact started the bombing run at the coast. As last week, we copped it again. Some four shells burst in quick succession under the aircraft and made it jump. Once again large holes appeared all over the place. Dawson jinked but then steadied as George [the bomb aimer] started his litany. As the bomb doors opened they let us have it again. Another three right under the starboard wing. The cockpit perspex shattered and they reckoned a large piece of

flak passed between the heads of Dawson and Alan [the flight engineer]. Both starboard engines were hit and packed up completely. We continued over the target and bombed.

Then we sorted out the mess as we turned for home. Two engines out and one pulling half power. Could we make it home? Skipper ordered us to don parachutes, just in case! Alan got ready to jettison fuel and gunners to clear and dump ammo tracks. Ahead in clear sunlight we could see the coast, Channel and the cliffs of Dover. Another a/c saw our trouble, came alongside and kept us company. The aircraft kept losing height and we all sighed a sigh of relief as Dover slid below us. I called base, reported the damage and asked if we should make for the emergency drome at Woodbridge, or make for base. Was told to go for base. We arrived well after everyone else and were cleared for immediate emergency landing. All the crew went to emergency landing stations (we were not sure if the undercarriage hydraulics were severed or were working as no lights showed on the panel). The undercarriage went down – was it locked? Dawson strapped himself firmly in and made a long low approach. Much to everyone's surprise he made the smoothest landing he had ever done. The aircraft touched once and slid to a halt at the boundary. When I looked round at Dawson he was bathed in perspiration. There were 97 holes in the aircraft *and no one was hurt!* Miracles do happen.

Flight Sergeant Larry Melling, a pilot with 635 Squadron, also attacked the L'Hey launch site on 9 July:

We made our bombing run at 15,000 feet amid a few black puffs of flak and made a long slow turn to starboard to begin the trip back home to Downham [Market]. Just as we completed the turn the aircraft lurched suddenly, the port wing came up and there was rattling of shrapnel against the fuselage. A glance out of the port cockpit window showed white smoke coming from the port inner, meaning that we were losing coolant, but of the port outer there was no sign at all – just the bare firewall with some cables dangling loose. Blyth, the flight engineer, had already started the feathering procedure for the port inner engine and I immediately shut off the fuel cock to the port outer. Then began the struggle to trim the aircraft to fly on two starboard engines. Full right rudder trim and full aileron trim were not sufficient to accomplish this; it took full right rudder and a somewhat starboard-wing-down attitude to maintain anything like a semblance of a straight course. Having checked that all the crew members were unhurt, the decision was made in concert with my flight engineer to head for Manston, the emergency airfield in Kent, rather than return to Downham Market, as we had no way of being certain that we had not sustained any further damage from shrapnel.

During the flight to Manston, which took about an hour, Bell, my bomb aimer, suggested that he could relieve the pressure on my right leg by using the long bar of the control lock as a lever by putting it in front of the rudder pedal and across, behind the throttle control pedestal. Unfortunately the bar proved to be too short and all that was achieved was a slight bend in it. By placing both feet on the right rudder pedal I was able to relieve the strain to some extent. Thus we flew back to England in a slow descent, crossing the Kent coast at some 5,000 feet.

At this time I had a total of some 450 flying hours as a pilot, of which only 45 were on Lancasters, with a grand total of 21 landings! Accordingly, as we approached Manston I informed my crew that I was going to land the aircraft, but that if they wanted to bale out I would not hold it against them. They all decided that they would stay with me, which gave me a much-needed boost of confidence. I instructed them to take up their crash positions behind the main spar, with the exception of my flight engineer, whom I asked to remain with me to handle flaps until I was committed to the landing.

When I got down to about 800 feet on the approach I realised that I was lined up on a railway track, and the runway itself was about a mile off to port. With only the two starboard engines operating there was no way I was going to attempt a turn to port, so I had no choice but to do a 360 turn to starboard! This resulted in my being correctly lined up, but when I gave the order for full flap at some 500 feet on final, my flight engineer had already taken off for his crash position! He later told me that when I had to make the turn around to get lined up with the runway, he was convinced that I wasn't going to make it!

We did, however, land quite safely and there was no further damage to the aircraft.[88]

The aircraft was repaired later and continued flying until it was shot down on a raid to Trossy St Maximin on 4 August.

Following the American and Bomber Command raids to the supply depot at St Leu d'Esserent and the damage caused at the caverns, the Germans were forced to make an adjustment to their flying bomb supply lines. Further information from German signal intercepts indicated to Allied Intelligence that Nucourt would take those flying bombs that had been scheduled for St Leu d'Esserent. It is also likely that the Allies were being informed, from French contacts, about the activities at Nucourt. Certainly the French people who lived in or around Nucourt were aware that there was something important going on in their village and at the caves. All the large houses were requisitioned by the Germans for accommodation and in the mornings they would march down to the station, near the caves. Madamoiselle Dumont lived in Nucourt:

> A German, passing in front of my window, told me, 'You must go with the children. Here many aeroplane, no pilot.' I thought that they didn't have enough pilots. I didn't realise it was the V1s. We saw trucks but they were covered with sheets and we did see 'aeroplanes'.

The Germans enforced strict security around the quarry but all the secretive activity would not have gone unnoticed and information was passed through certain channels to agents who could then pass the information on to the Allies. Indeed in the nearby village of Cléry a transmitter was located in the bell tower.

Nucourt had been attacked twice by American bombers on 22 and 24 June, a total of 250 tons was dropped causing considerable damage to buildings and rail facilities, with three areas of subsidence indicating that parts of the roof of the caverns had probably collapsed. However intelligence information subsequent to the raids suggested that the caverns at Nucourt could operate. Bomber Command was called on.

On 10 July a force of 213 Lancasters and 10 Mosquitos, supported by fighter cover from 11 Group, was despatched to make a daylight raid on Nucourt. As the crews approached and arrived over Nucourt they experienced complete cloud cover. Under the instructions of the master bomber they had to bomb on navigational aids. There had been tragedy at 105 Squadron at the start of the raid. The Mosquito piloted by Pilot Officer Eaton DFC hurtled along the runway, at 4 a.m. in the morning, but just before take-off the port engine exploded. Eaton used all his skill to bring the aircraft round on one engine and land. However the navigator, Flying Officer Fox, suffered very serious wounding as he prematurely exited the aircraft. Despite being rushed to the station's sick quarters, the injury from the propeller strike proved fatal.[89]

On 13 and 14 July more Bomber Command aircraft were detailed for attacks on Nucourt, but the operations were cancelled. On 15 July another force of 47 Lancasters and 6 Mosquitos did actually take off to target the storage depot and, as on the previous raid, had to attack through complete cloud cover. Flight Sergeant Ken Grantham, wireless operator 35 Squadron, took part in the raid and recorded the cloud cover difficulties in his diary:

> At lunch-time the crew list was up on the board for ops today. At 1400 hours we were briefed and then went straight out to the aircraft. When we got there they were just putting the bombs on so we had a wait while the armourers completed the job. Today we are to do a pattern bombing raid and it will be the first we have done in tight formation. Because of the delay in putting on the bombs we took off well behind the others but managed to put on a spurt and take our place in the formation. We flew all the way in clear weather with an escort of Spitfires and just as we came up to the target area, near Paris, we ran into dense cloud, so dense that we could barely see beyond the windscreen. There we were, on top of the target in tight formation and

unable to see the other planes either in front, to port or starboard, or behind. Daws [the pilot], as usual hating to waste a trip decided to bomb on instruments and so after crossing the target he turned 180 degrees and came back over it, flying against the stream. Somewhere in that mist were other aircraft all converging on the same spot and it's only due to providence that we didn't meet any of them head on. Twenty minutes from the coast we came out of the cloud into clear weather and there wasn't another aircraft to be seen. We were worried about flak and fighters now that we were a sole aircraft, but nothing disturbed the peace of that summer afternoon in France.

That night a further 19 Lancasters, 162 Halifaxes and 9 Mosquitos were sent. The master bomber ordered crews to bomb from below the cloud and it was reported that a good attack developed. One aircraft was lost on the raid of 15/16 July, the 76 Squadron Lancaster of Flying Officer Steward, the pilot was killed along with three of his crew, the other three men were captured.

The Crossbow Counter-measures Progress Report for the 10 to 23 July summarised the results from the attacks on the Nucourt supply depot. In the three attacks 2,165 tons were dropped from Bomber Command aircraft. A study of reconnaissance photographs showed the target area covered with craters, which had caused a number of subsidences over large areas, some of which were 10 feet deep. The entrance to the tunnel was partially blocked, and in a few cases penetration by single bombs into the caverns below could be seen. The railway line to the north-east of the target had also been hit.[90]

A German signal intercept of 16 July, somewhat exaggerating the number of bombers involved, gave the Allies additional evidence of the success of the attacks:

> According field ammunition depot ZBV Nucourt Morning 16th
> A) Attack on Nucourt 1457 hours 15th by 3 formations of 200 to 250 bombers. 600 to 700 bombs dropped, including large number with D/A [delayed action]. Permanent way hit by D/A Bombs. 1 approach to east entrance badly damaged, lighting cable cut, lines partially out of order. All approaches endangered by D/A bombs lying nearby.
> B) 2350 to 0030 hours, heavy bombing attack on Nucourt. Casualties not yet established. Area of the caves very heavily hit. Roof collapsed in several places. Large number of 'apparatuses' buried. Rail installations, electric power supply installations and telephone lines destroyed.[91]

The series of raid against the supply depot at Nucourt had been a success in terms of the disruption and damage caused on the ground. However not all the raids had been on target, and even when they were, the French civilians in the area once more suffered. Madamoiselle Dumont experienced the bombs first hand:

The Germans came at midday to warn us. The Allies dropped
two or three bombs on the quarry [probably markers] and a lot
of people from Trama [a Belgian company operating in the
area] told us, 'We're running away and you too must go. The
village is going to be bombed.' It was a very warm day and the
children played in the garden. I asked them to go and fetch some
milk from Madamoiselle Prevot's farm. As they started to go I
saw a considerable amount of planes in the sky. We knew where
they were going to bomb so my mother-in-law took the children
to a safe shelter.

Mademoiselle Dumont then went to warn some other people. She then took
shelter in a trench, unwilling, as she was alone, to go into her cellar: 'After
the bombing I came out and I no longer had a house, it was all over the road.'
    Another local civilian recalled:

My parents had a small farm in Nucourt and when the planes
came over we didn't know where to go. We had a trench and a
cellar. Where to go? Because it was closer we went to the cellar.
There was an incredible noise, like a train had run over the
house. A bomb fell on the house, the stairway was blocked and
we had to clear away all the rubble.

During the last bombing, on the night of 15/16 July Madamoiselle Dumont
was in the nearby town of Magny:

I saw the bombing and it was an incredible fire display. That
time they bombed the caverns. The other times the Americans
destroyed the village but not the caves.

A Monsieur Benard also witnessed the night raid and the pyrotechnic
display from the nearby town of Serans:

I was at the window of my house and could see Nucourt as if it
were the middle of the day. That time all the bombs fell on the
caverns.

Not all the local people were able to escape the bombs. In Nucourt there
now stands a memorial to the six people killed by the Allied bombing.
    The attacks on the caves at St Leu d'Esserent and Nucourt certainly had
an effect on the flying bomb firing rate in the period following the attacks.
The average of flying bomb firings in the week leading up to 6 July stood
at 168 per day, but this steadily declined and on 20 July the previous week's
average stood at 80 per day.[92] This lowering of launch rates would also be
of benefit to the defences over England, lessening the chance of them
getting swamped.
    The diary of Flakregiment 155(W) recorded on 15 July that even though
there had been a considerable amount of enemy espionage they believed
that not much information had got through. Nevertheless it did assume that:

sufficient has already fallen into enemy hands for them to have effectively bombed the two field ammunition depots 'Leopold' and 'Norpol'. Treasonable material which has fallen into the hands of our Intelligence gives a very interesting picture of espionage activity in the Rouen area. It includes a report which gives accurate details of the 'Leopold' ammunition depot in a cave at St Leu in the immediate vicinity of Creil.[93]

It was now quite clear to the Germans that St Leu d'Esserent and Nucourt were known to the Allies as key elements of their flying bomb supply line. Either they would have to strengthen the defences around the caves or alternative depots would have to be used.

On 11 July, 26 Lancasters and 6 Mosquitos, all from 8 Group, were despatched to make two attacks on the modified launch site at Gapennes. This raid is particularly noteworthy as it was the first heavy Oboe raid of the war. The method of attack involved the bombers flying in formation and when the leader (or reserve) dropped their bombs on the blind bombing Oboe signal, then the rest of the formation were to do likewise. On the raids to Gapennes a 582 Squadron Lancaster, fitted with the Oboe equipment, was to lead the raid. Wing Commander G.F. Grant, from the Mosquito 109 Squadron, flew on the Lancaster, taking charge of proceedings. On arrival at the target the first attack by 7 Lancasters and 1 Mosquito was made through complete cloud cover. The following attack by 19 Lancasters and 5 Mosquitos experienced the same conditions, which prevented any initial appraisal of the bombing accuracy.

On 12 July a large force of 46 Lancasters, 168 Halifaxes and 8 Mosquitos was despatched on a daylight raid to Thiverny, just to the north of St Leu d'Esserent and under suspicion of being part of the supply depot organisation. The attacking force had to bomb on dead reckoning fixes owing to virtually complete cloud cover over the target. It was believed that the resultant bombing was scattered, but day reconnaissance on 17 July showed some new craters, mainly above the cave entrances, with one hit near an entrance; this appeared to have penetrated into the caves, but with no visible subsidence or damage. On the same day a force of 18 Lancasters and 5 Mosquitos attacked the modified site at Rollez with believed accurate marking and a reasonable concentration of bombing.

On the night of 12/13 July four modified sites were targeted. The attack on Bremont (2 Lancasters, 49 Halifaxes, 5 Mosquitos) was believed concentrated and subsequent reconnaissance would indicate considerable damage. Similarly at Les Hauts Buissons (2 Lancasters, 52 Halifaxes, 5 Mosquitos) and Acquet (10 Lancasters, 42 Halifaxes, 5 Mosquitos) the marking and bombing was believed accurate and concentrated. Photographic analysis of any damage caused at both sites was hindered by the presence of tall trees in the target areas, although many craters were visible. The master bomber on the raid to Ferme du Forestelle (2 Lancasters, 53 Halifaxes, 5 Mosquitos) was unable to see the TI and ordered the main force to bomb using their navigational aids. Analysis of reconnaissance was also hampered by the presence of tall trees. The 346 Squadron Halifax of Capitaine Gaubert FFAF was preparing to land

following the attack on Les Hauts Buissons when it hit another of the
squadron's Halifaxes. Gaubert's aircraft fell to earth killing the entire crew.
The other Halifax was able to land safely with no casualties. On 13 July 13
Lancasters were despatched to a launch site, but dense cloud cover
prevented any attack.

On 14 July a force of 19 Lancasters and 5 Mosquitos was despatched to
attack the modified site at St Philibert Ferme. Two days later the modified
site was again targeted by a force of 30 Lancasters and 3 Mosquitos. No.
105 Squadron was to provide the Mosquitos to lead this raid and a new
method was introduced. Each of the Oboe Mosquitos led a force of 10
Lancasters. As the bombers approached the target they found it covered
with cloud. The Lancasters were informed to close up on the bombing run
and drop their bombs with the leading Oboe Mosquito. Although the
success of this method on this raid could not initially be ascertained
because of the cloud cover, it would be repeated. Reconnaissance did
eventually reveal a cratered target area, one building destroyed and three
near misses on the launching platform.

On the night of 14/15 July, two Bomber Command forces attacked flying
bomb launch sites. There was scattered opening marking on the attack made
on the modified site at Anderbelck, targeted by 2 Lancasters, 50 Halifaxes
and 5 Mosquitos. The master bomber was able to make corrections and a
concentrated attack was reported by returning crews. Follow-up
reconnaissance would later reveal a successful bombing operation with the
target area well cratered, three near misses on the launching point, six
buildings with blast damage, all approach roads cut and an area cleared for
the square building covered in rubble. The modified site at Les Landes,
targeted by 2 Lancasters, 51 Halifaxes and 5 Mosquitos, was completely
covered with cloud when the bombers arrived and the crews were ordered to
use their navigational aids for bombing. Some crews did report being able to
identify markers, However reconnaissance would later reveal that the raid
had been a failure with no craters visible within a mile of the target.

On the night of 15/16 July, in addition to the attack on Nucourt,
previously covered, 42 Lancasters and 5 Mosquitos targeted the launch site
at Bois des Jardins. Some of the main force were able to bomb on the
markers, others had to rely on their navigational aids. Follow-up
reconnaissance revealed that a flying bomb had apparently exploded,
wrecking the launching platform. There were no discernible craters in the
target area, but it appeared that about half a mile away another flying bomb
had been destroyed.

Two modified sites were to receive the attentions of Bomber Command on
17 July. The attack on Bois de la Haye, involved 5 Mosquitos, 2 Lancasters
and 50 Halifaxes and post-raid reports placed the bombing as concentrated
and on the aiming point. One large explosion was reported. Sergeant Peter
Rowland, a flight engineer, describes the attack on the other site:

> On the fine warm summer evening of 17 July 1944 the Short
> Stirling four-engine bombers of 149 Squadron, now flying from
> their new base at Methwold, Norfolk, marshalled for an

operational take-off. Crews were briefed for the squadron's first bombing raid for some time, having specialized in sea minelaying and SOE [Special Operations Executive] operations to drop supplies to French Maquis groups in the length and breadth of France. This effort was to knock out an active V1 launching site just a short hop across the Channel, five miles south of Dieppe at Mont Candon. The raid was to be made in the broad daylight of early evening, to come out of the setting sun with a force of 28 Stirlings from 149 and 218 Squadrons, together with 22 Halifaxes at a slightly higher level in a quick concentrated attack. We were to have strong fighter cover [in addition the raid was led by 5 Mosquitos and 2 Lancasters].

'P' Peter was persuaded to leave the deck at 19.06 hauling herself up into the air under the able hands of Flying Officer Gerry Tenduis (from the Netherlands and now flying with the RAF), engines straining – full boost to build up flying speed, laden with a full load of twenty-four 500 lb bombs, almost 5 tons of high explosive, and some 1,000 gallons of high octane fuel on which the seven souls of its crew rode, once more feeling physically the tension and anxiety of a fully laden operational take-off dissipate as the engines held their power, flaps in, undercarriage folding and she soared on, rising gradually to a reasonable height and airspeed in the gentle curve to the left to bring us back over the airfield to set course on the first leg of the journey.

This trip was an easy one for the flight engineers for we were only tanked up in the two main tanks in each wing plus one of the smaller, so we weren't going to have the constant anxiety of all the consumption logging and calculations draining off all 14 of them.

Crossing our coastline I took up station in the astrodome, a bubble of perspex in the cabin roof which afforded a splendid view all round. I would have a grandstand view of the events and lend another pair of eyes to my mates in the three gun turrets. We spotted suddenly the tiny black spots in the far distance to the north, which rapidly grew into aircraft at about our height on converging course, then into four-engine Halifax bombers and the sky seemed full of them, actually only 22 but a most impressive sight as they slid relentlessly onto us on the same heading at the rendezvous point. We were all in the right place at the right time, and we had actually seen other RAF aircraft, which was unusual. It had been a tense moment as other aircraft had sort of jockeyed into position at random; mid-air collisions were not at all unknown and one shivered at the thought of what was happening unseen about you during the night raids, when one never actually sees another aircraft, hopefully!

Before the run-in to the target I have to check over all the engine instruments and gauges, everything is fine. I calculate the present fuel position and enter my log sheet before going into the astrodome again. The aircraft is now passing into the control of Ted Lukey, our bomb aimer from New Zealand, laying prone in the nose calling up directions to the Skipper. We have reached the left-left-right-right-back a bit!, situation. It is at this point that I became aware that one of the Halifaxes was jinking about directly above us only 400 to 500 feet away, and I felt a dreadful fear that this was going to be a very dodgy situation and waited to see that our tracks would separate slightly but he seemed to be following with deadly precision every move we made.

By now the bomb doors are opening and I can see very clearly the neat rows of bombs hanging in the belly of the aircraft right above my head. Gerry and Lukey were in intense concentration as we came up to the aiming point in perfect bombing conditions; an intercom silence was the strict rule for the rest of the crew during this critical stage regardless of anything until Bombs Gone!, so I had to keep silent, pray and put my faith in fate which all aircrew had to trust and live with one way or the other. Surely anyway the other bomb aimer must see us right underneath.

At the very moment I heard 'bombs away – bomb doors closed', with heart stopping suddenness I spotted the other load drop away lazily from the aircraft above and in an instant grow much larger.

Whilst writing this story I was able to ask our navigator Alex Crisp . . . of what immediate effect the next few moments had on him over the target. He of course, together with the wireless operator were the only ones effectively sort of shut off in the aircraft without a view outside. He said he could not really remember much except that I called something like, 'Watch out, we're going to be hit by a bomb!', and he thought, 'hit by a bomb? The bloke's gone bloody potty or something.' In fact I had forgotten after all the years that I had actually switched on and yelled out, but I still vividly remember grabbing my chute and banging it on the clips feeling great remorse and guilt at not warning earlier, but I know the Skipper would not have tolerated interference in the bombing run-in and would have pressed on anyway.

I simply crouched there standing by my panel expecting at the best that the aircraft would break up and with luck I would find myself thrown clear, and then a flash of abject dismay that we were over enemy ground and even if I drifted out over the sea the Germans would get me before our ASR [Air Sea Rescue] launches. I wouldn't get 'home', so near, yet – . I wonder now at the speed which these thoughts had passed through my mind in just an instant and are still extremely clear today. I must also reflect that not one thought of actually dying entered my head, only of danger and survival.

The bombs struck us with a most sickening crunch that was to haunt me for many years after. Jack and Bob in their turrets got the fright of their lives as dirty great bombs swooped past. One of them, I think it was Bob in the tail, sounded most indignant when he exclaimed with some emotion that 'a bomb's just passed me' and Jack said they were passing between the wing and tail.

The great huge Stirling was practically torn out of Gerry's hands and we plunged down as he struggled to regain control. The outer part of the port main plane had been hit, smacking it down, coupled with a lot of drag and loss of lift. Gerry Tenduis was a wonderful pilot, a professional before he joined the RAF; instinctively he had pushed open the throttles of the two port engines and applied opposite aileron and compensating rudder to lift up that wing. As he got his breath back he called out to ask if everyone was okay. Getting the affirmative answers he ordered us to stand by to abandon the aircraft and called Lukey to come up and help him hold her. Now this was something else, a few moments before I had learnt that I actually would have been able to jump out of a stricken aeroplane, no trouble at all given the chance in despair and panic of catastrophe, but to wilfully leave when necessity might be doubtful and a shred of hope remained, was a different matter.

The Skipper found he could hold her with the help of the co-pilot, their combined strength being needed the whole time to force the aileron controls against the drag of the damaged wing. Thank God, the dear old Stirling was built as strong as a submarine! She also had dual controls, two seats and everything, otherwise we don't think we'd have made it, and we had mercifully the four engines. We had lost 6,000 feet from our 12,000 feet bombing height by the time the Skipper regained full control and called Alex for a course back to base. We were just putting ourselves together when Bob Graves in the tail turret suddenly broke in with a quite unemotional voice: 'Hullo, Skipper, fighter approaching —prepare to corkscrew.' Of course we all thought he'd gone stark bonkers. Here we were with half a wing one side, just about under control, and now he wants poor old Gerry to start flinging it about all over the place! Poor old Bob, it really was textbook stuff to him anyway. 'Hullo, Skipper – Bob here, it's okay it's three Spits.' They flew back with us as escort, which was a very great comfort.

I didn't see anything of this for I was watching the gauges like a hawk, checking all the systems and assessing the damage. One bomb had taken a fair old chunk out of the leading edge just beyond the port outer prop and nearly back to the main spar, two others must have gone through the trailing edge breaking away a large area including almost all the aileron. There was just a little bit left inboard, perhaps about 18 inches with the cable control bell-cranks.

My main worry now was the fuel state: had we lost or were we losing petrol? I had started checking and rechecking consumption figures against the not too accurate or reliable gauges until I began to feel pretty confident that all was well, and that no fuel lines or tanks were damaged. The port engines, being 'opened up', were using more petrol from the two tanks feeding them than the engines on the other side of course. I resolved that I should discuss this with Gerry and open the cross balance cocks shortly before landing to ensure we did not lose power by engine failure on the damaged side.

Now well on the way home, Gerry's voice in our headsets told us that he thought he could land her on the emergency airstrip at Woodbridge. The pair of them were coping and holding her level with a lot of muscle power. With Lukey's help until the last moment he reckoned he could set her down. Felix, the young Aussie W/Op, was told to send out a 'Mayday' signal with our position and course to our intended destination. Now in my mind at least, there was a surge of elation that the prospect of getting my feet wet had suddenly receded. The chance that we might have been forced to 'ditch' had been very real.

Alex got us 'spot on' for Woodbridge; the Skipper called on the R/T to control that we were approaching with an emergency and he was coming straight in. We knew of course that all the emergency services were waiting for a chance such as this might be, and they had all the latest fire fighting and rescue gear. 'Roger, 'P' Peter Pancake lane 2', then the gen on wind speed and direction; we reply 'Roger 'P' Peter, Willgo, out.' The emergency strip was not only incredibly long, it was three times the width of the standard runway, its three lanes could handle three four-engined kites at a time, and had done so many times. We were going to have plenty of room.

We are 'coming in'. Throttles back a bit, IAS [Indicated Air Speed] 150 mph, flaps one third out, mixtures normal, undercarriage down. Too late to play with fuel cocks. I'm anxious not to have opened the cross balance valves and decided not to interfere with the pilot's concentration and prayed all was well. My dash down the fuselage to check the tail wheels are fully down, jack nut fully forward against the electric motor, was the fastest yet. The skipper and bomb aimer are really sweating it out, arms aching holding her level. 'Okay, all crew crash positions' and a little reluctantly we vacate our stations and scramble together behind the main spar, braced behind it squatting on the floor, knees bent, hands clasped behind head, elbows in, head down between legs, all feeling very much a mere passenger. We are plugged into the intercom of course: 'Finals – 100 ft, – full flap – 145 mph. Throttles back – 50 ft – 130 – 20 ft – 110 – okay I've got her – 10 ft – 105.' He's bringing her in on the fast side. She sinks so gently we are hardly aware of touch down. 'Okay, down now,' comes Gerry's unemotional voice in his rather quaint Dutch accent.

'Oh bloody good show Skipper', 'Wizard landing', 'Hurray bang-on Skip', – the crew's accolades spill out in a spontaneous torrent. The Stirling rumbles along terra firma with that comforting jogging, bouncing movement, the muted hush of the engines popping back in the exhausts at tick over revs, with a surge of power from one side or the other to keep the kite running straight. A squeal of brakes and the suppressed nervous anxieties lift and the airman begins to relax again. We've made it! Another of our aircraft returned safely.

Our first bombing trip, and the shortest, had lasted just 3 hours 5 minutes, duty carried out although we had got the aeroplane bent a bit! We were taken to see the MO [Medical Officer] for a quick once-over who asked if we were all okay, and dispensed our medicine in the shape of a dark evil smelling, to me, liquid. Navy style rum, yuk! Not for me thanks, I'm much too young. Gerry's eyes lit up through being an experienced liqueur and spirit man, especially his native Bols. He had more than his fair share but had earned it that evening. He phoned base to report in.

Next morning feeling a bit sour after kipping rough in our clothes, with not much of a wash, and unshaved, we took ourselves down the airfield to have a look at old LJ 623 standing forlorn and far from home and we wondered at the state of the wing and how it had stayed together; they were built those Stirlings.

After lunch our 'B' flight commander Squadron Leader Woolley came over with his 'N' Nuts to collect his errant crew. He told us how the chaps had cheered at de-briefing when he had announced that we were safely down at Woodbridge. We had been seen going down over the target. We were glad to get away from the strip and back to the squadron but sad to leave our personal aircraft behind. 'P' Peter had carried us safely through eight of our 12 ops so far, totalling 70.05 hours. The evening was spent celebrating with the ground crew in Feltwell village, finally staggering happily back via the fish and chip shop of course!

The master bomber on the raid believed that there had been a concentrated attack but subsequent reconnaissance would show that there had been no new damage to the targets. Wizernes was also attacked on 17 July by 16 Lancasters, 1 Mosquito and 1 Mustang of 617 Squadron, but despite finding a clear patch in the cloud over the target, no direct hits were achieved.

On the night of 18/19 July 2 Lancasters, 51 Halifaxes and 9 Mosquitos were despatched to the modified site at Acquet. Marking and bombing were reported as accurate but day reconnaissance photographs, of a poor quality, indicated no fresh damage. A 76 Squadron Halifax piloted by Flight Lieutenant Sinclair DFC failed to return, a victim of a German nightfighter flown by Oberleutnant Werner Hopf; it crashed near Abbeville. There were no survivors from the crew of seven. A 78 Squadron Halifax piloted by Warrant Officer Stratford came down to earth also near Abbeville, with no survivors from the crew of seven.

Pilot Officer Malcolm Buchanan, pilot in 78 Squadron, wrote to his father on 14 August 1944 detailing his experiences on the night of 18/19 July:

> It all happened on the night of 18/19 July on the crew's 29th sortie. The target was a flying bomb site and our total time over hostile territory was something like 20 mins, the least we'd had. Some of our targets in the past have been tough and long such as Stuttgart, Berlin, Düsseldorf , Karlsruhe, Aachen etc. but that did not mean that we were taking it easy on this one. In fact we saw several kites go down in flames before crossing the coast on the way out after attacking the target so there was no relaxing.

(Bomber Command had also despatched 253 Lancasters and 10 Mosquitos this night, to attack the French rail junctions at Aulnoye and Revigny. German fighters exacted a considerable toll on the forces. In addition to two Lancasters lost on the Aulnoye raid, a further 24 failed to return from the attack on Revigny. It is likely that Pilot Officer Buchanan witnessed the demise of some of these aircraft.)

> Something like three minutes after passing the coast we were attacked by a fighter which none of us saw before being hit. A cannon shell exploded beside the engineer's position wounding Bill Bailey, the engineer, fairly severely in the back of the thighs of both legs. It was some time before he realised he had been hit for immediately a serious fire broke out which would have taken precedence over almost any injury. It seems that a hydraulic oil pipe line was fractured and this oil was the fuel which caused the whole interior of the aircraft to become a sheet of flames. By leaning as far as possible out of the window I got as much relief as I could but it seemed that within just a few seconds the aircraft must 'go down' in flames. Indeed many aircraft on the same target that night returned and reported seeing the combat and the aircraft going down on fire. Although some ten to fifteen miles over the sea I gave the order to bale out. This point came less than ten seconds after the attack and without hesitation the whole crew commenced to leave. The navigator, bomb aimer and rear gunner got away, but the heat and flames had driven the engineer down into the nose of the aircraft, which was away from his parachute. But full of fight and determined to get his chute he grabbed an extinguisher and

battled into the flames until he got his chute, naturally suffering many severe burns to his face and hands in the process. The W/Op [wireless operator] in his haste accidentally pulled his ripcord thus delaying him for the few vital seconds and the M/U/G [mid upper gunner] likewise got snagged in getting out of his turret – just for a few seconds but it made all the difference. He too then had to use an extinguisher to fight his way towards an escape hatch and between them (the Eng. and M/U/G and soon joined by the W/Op), and also the fact that the oil had been mostly consumed, the fire was got under some control. During the brief seconds all blackout curtains had been incinerated and the astrodome melted and a hole forced through it to let out the heat and flames. Course was once more set for this country and a landing made in the south. The engineer even after beginning to suffer considerable pain performed all his duties, though losing skin from his burnt hands in doing so. Search was made for the missing men at daylight next morning but the weather wasn't good and nothing was seen. Very small possibility that the enemy may have picked them up. Very small possibility too but we're hoping. They would certainly find it hard to believe that the aircraft finally returned, and as for the rest of us we can just put it down as a miracle. Of course, those of us who returned are feeling very unhappy at the absence of the three others. The engineer will be in hospital for a month or two yet, and as you know I spent a week at his side, with 1st and 2nd degree burns.

The three men who baled out of the burning aircraft lost their lives. Rear gunner Sergeant J.R. Harmer is buried in Etaples Military Cemetery, bomb aimer Pilot Officer A.L. MacKenzie and navigator Flying Officer D.F. Rayment are both commemorated on the Runnymede memorial. Buchanan received a DFC for his efforts on that night and his engineer Sergeant Bailey the CGM. On the night of 21 November 1944 after returning from a raid to Sterkrade, Buchanan, now a flight lieutenant and nearing the completion of his tour, was the first from his squadron to approach the base at Breighton. He called up the base and as it was a foggy night the Senior Flying Control Officer asked him to fly down the runway and say whether or not it was safe for the squadron to land. Buck, as he was known to his squadron, obliged and reported that conditions were fine. His Halifax then plunged into a wood a half a mile beyond the runway and exploded. There were no survivors (Sergeant Bailey was not part of the crew).

On 19 July three further flying bomb targets were attacked: 13 Lancasters, 2 Mosquitos and 16 Lancasters, 4 Mosquitos were sent to the modified sites at Mont Candon and Rollez respectively. Both forces attacked in formation releasing their bombs as indicated by the leader. Reconnaissance at Rollez showed one hit on the launching platform and one building destroyed. Mont Candon would be attacked again before analysis of reconnaissance. The third flying bomb target was the suspected supply depot at Thiverny. A force of 103 Lancasters and 8 Mosquitos was despatched and the attack was made in clear weather and a number of bombs were reported as bursting around the aiming point. Reconnaissance made on 26 July showed many new craters on top of the cliff and an area between the cave entrance and a roadway. It appeared that there was no subsidence into the caves and no entrances were blocked. The roadway in front of the entrance was clear but the main road to Creil was blocked by numerous craters.

On 20 July Bomber Command launched another major attack on Crossbow targets. Seven modified sites and the large site at Wizernes were targeted; however the raid to the modified site at Forêt du Croc was abandoned. At Chapelle de Notre Dame (2 Lancasters, 53 Halifaxes, 5 Mosquitos), Ferme du Grand Bois (2 Lancasters, 50 Halifaxes, 5 Mosquitos), L'Hey (39 Lancasters, 13 Halifaxes, 5 Mosquitos), Anderbelck (6 Lancasters, 45 Halifaxes, 5 Mosquitos) and Ferme du Forestelle (2 Lancasters, 49 Halifaxes, 5 Mosquitos), the main forces all bombed on markers as instructed by master bombers/controllers. All the bombing was believed concentrated. Follow-up reconnaissance showed no fresh damage at L'Hey, near misses at Chapelle de Notre Dame and Ferme du Forestelle and substantial damage at Anderbelck and Ferme du Grand Bois. The force sent to Mont Candon (8 Lancasters, 2 Mosquitos) bombed on the leading Mosquito's release. There would be a further raid carried out to this target before reconnaissance was analysed. One aircraft was lost on the raids and two squadron leaders. A 582 Squadron Lancaster piloted by Squadron Leader Foulsham DFC AFC, and accompanied by Squadron Leader Weightman DFC, was leading the attack on Forêt du Croc, but on the run in it was hit by flak and exploded with considerable force. All eight men in the aircraft were killed. The force of 104 Lancasters and 5 Mosquitos sent to Wizernes reported a successful raid on its return and reconnaissance the next day revealed considerable damage. The cliff face beneath the dome had collapsed, with many cracks and gaps in the dome itself. The suspected firing platform was damaged as a result of the complete collapse of its foundations. It also appeared that the Germans were making no effort to clear any of the wreckage.

That night a force of 2 Lancasters, 54 Halifaxes and 5 Mosquitos took off to attack the modified site at Ardouval II, but over the target only a few crews saw any of the markers or were able to hear the master bomber, who abandoned the operation. One Halifax was lost, the 158 Squadron aircraft piloted by Flight Lieutenant Platten. There were no survivors and it was believed that adverse weather was to blame (although see later). Wizernes was also detailed to be attacked by 21 Lancasters and 5 Mosquitos from 617 Squadron but the bad weather resulted in the raid being abandoned. Bomber Command had had rather a bad night with regard other operations, losing a total of 38 aircraft on raids to the rail yards at Courtrai (9 Lancasters lost), Bottrop, a synthetic oil target (7 Halifaxes and 1 Lancaster) and the oil plant at Homberg (20 Lancasters). This provides another example of the fact that there was still a cost associated with conducting night raids at this stage in the war. The German nightfighter force remained a potent adversary.

CHAPTER 13

NEW POLICY, NEW TARGETS

The bombing activity resulting from the flying bomb counter-offensive continued to put the French civilians at risk, not only through operations conducted by the Allied bombers, but also as a result of flying bombs crashing to earth soon after launching. Gerard Dubord was living in the area where the flying bombs were being launched:

Little by little with certain astonishment, mixed with surprise and more than a little apprehension, we found out that they did not always work very well. Of course the launch was always successful, but the motors of the unmanned aircraft did not always start and the aircraft would fall back to the ground within about five minutes of take-off. That was about the time they would normally take to cross the Channel to Britain. The failure rate could be as much as one out of every three. Although most worked well there were also occasions when the engines would be alright but the guidance system was poorly adjusted and the aircraft would change direction after take-off. The most worrying was when they circled back around our village, as we knew they would crash and explode and it was impossible to predict where they would land. Fortunately they mostly landed in the woods or fields, but there was an occasion when this was not the case. On this particular evening, at dusk, we heard the sound of a V1 changing direction and it began travelling towards us with its characteristic noise. It got louder and louder and then cut out immediately over the trees near us. We did not have time to move so we just ducked our heads as it flew and then crashed and exploded about 300 metres behind us. The explosion demolished an old Norman single storey house, which was literally smashed to dust. By a miracle the two elderly people who lived there survived. At the same time, on a neighbouring road, a column of German transport vehicles, which included some horse-drawn carts, appeared to be hit. During that evening there was the sound of horses in distress and the screams of men. I think the horses must have bolted as they came looking for them the next morning.

The continual targeting of the launch sites and the difficulties in accurate marking and bombing led to many civilian and worker casualties. On 24 June the ski site at Bonnetot had been attacked by 106 Bomber Command aircraft. The site had been ruled out by the Germans as a launch site in part owing to the bombing on 14 January. Work was subsequently started on the site again in April by Russian prisoners as a bluff and it had worked. It was a public holiday in Bonnetot, the cows grazed in the fields, the farmer Henri Delacroix was working in the fields that were not too badly cratered from previous bombing. The construction work on the farm had practically finished. However that afternoon aircraft were heard and flares appeared in the sky. Destruction followed, and enormous craters appeared over the nearby countryside. The last sections of wall surrounding the farm were flattened. Problems for the local people did not end when the bombers departed as some of the bombs were delayed action. All this on a target that posed no threat at all.

On 9 July the Bomber Command attack on Les Catelliers had ended with particularly tragic results. Three families living next to each other had dug trenches either side of a hedge between their houses. One bomb fell right on to the hedge and buried one family in their shelter. The mother and daughter of one of the other families were buried and killed. In the nearby town of Richemont a mother and three of her children, hiding in their cellar, were killed. Allied reconnaissance after the bombing had suggested a failed attack, which indeed it was. An hour after the bombing the Germans launched the first of three flying bombs from the undamaged ramp.

Gerard Dubord: During the day we would see the many craters caused by the bombs and the remains of the incendiaries were like scattered silver paper. Anti-aircraft guns protected these sites and we would occasionally see an aircraft burst into flames and the crew jump out, parachutes bursting open. The anti-aircraft batteries were efficient and often on target. We were always apprehensive when we saw the aircraft coming towards the V1 sites.

One morning, very early, we saw a group of four-engined bombers flying towards the sites . . . I can remember wishing that I was able to warn them. As they approached the sites the guns opened fire and hit six of the nine aircraft in the first wave. Another time it was about midday when a group of bombers arrived at low level in a violent storm, with thunder and lightning. They dropped their bombs haphazardly in the fields. Unfortunately one of the farmers from the neighbouring village of Cropus was killed.

Generally the raids were at night and the German fighters would try to locate the Allied bombers and at the same time the searchlights would try and pick them out. When an aircraft was caught in the searchlight it was almost impossible to escape and the fighters would shoot them down. The spectacle of a bomber coming down in flames was horrible. One night we were taking refuge in our trench when one of them passed above us, the whole aeroplane was engulfed in flames and you could hear the ammunition on board exploding.

This aircraft was actually Flight Lieutenant Platten's 158 Squadron Halifax, lost with no survivors on the 20/21 July raid to Ardouval.

The Allied planners did, of course, realise that French civilian casualties were a risk of the bombing operations and there had been considerable debate concerning the pre-invasion bombing of French transportation targets and the possibility of high casualties. The German secret weapon threat was such that the expectation of bombing results outweighed by far the concerns over civilian casualties near the targets. In the conduct of all-out war this premise had grounding providing the targets chosen were suitable.

The choice of targets for German secret weapon counter-offensive bombing had until early in July been the responsibility of the Air Ministry, Director of Operations (Special Operations). However dissatisfaction with the choices made had been growing, particularly as it was believed that the choices were not being made by people who understood all the problems that all the bomber forces would face. On 8 July representation came from the American bomber force recommending a change and Air Chief Marshal Tedder then worked with the Air Staff and the Americans in devising a new structure. The outcome was that from then on Air Intelligence would deal with the intelligence, which would then be assembled by an officer selected by Air Vice-Marshal Inglis. This officer would then present this information to a committee, comprising representatives of both the Air Ministry and the United States Strategic Air Forces in Europe. This committee then had the responsibility of prioritising targets for bombing counter-measures.

On 21 July 1944 the Joint Crossbow Committee (JCC) met for the first time. The chairman of the committee was Air Commodore Colin McK. Grierson, Director of Operations (Special Operations); the other members were Colonel R.D. Hughes USSTAFE (United States Strategic Air Forces in Europe), Colonel A.R. Maxwell USSTAFE, Group Captain E.J. Corbally, Combined Operational Planning Committee, Group Captain A.P. Morley DDB Ops and Wing Commander W. F. Lamb, AD of Ops (Special Operations). The terms of reference eventually agreed for the committee (at the following meeting) were:

i) To survey and appreciate all intelligence relating to Crossbow.
ii) To examine the different components of the enemy's Crossbow organisation and to consider the order of priority in which these targets should be attacked.
iii) To consider the relative order of priority of individual targets within each of these systems.
iv) In the light of these considerations, to make recommendations as to how the effort of the air forces can best be applied in order to defeat the enemy's flying bomb attack and to prevent the launching of an attack with the long range rocket.[94]

The Committee set about reviewing the schedules of targets authorised for attack, made by the original Crossbow Target Priorities Committee. There was then recommended a considerable change in bombing policy with the supply sites, the headquarters and the electric power, transformer and switching stations suspended from attack and a review made of their importance as targets. This responsibility was delegated to a working committee, which had been set up to examine, in detail, matters referred to them by the main committee. The Committee also agreed to keep the launching sites on the target list as a second priority but that the COPC (Combined Operational Planning Committee) should look into the tactical aspect of the problems of the fighter bombers in locating the modified sites. It was also agreed that on the target list the launching sites were 'not for heavy scale attack but for harassing attacks only in visual bombing conditions or in "blind" conditions with the aid of "Oboe". A high percentage of delayed action bombs to be used.'

The Committee rearranged the first priority targets into two categories of equal priority:

Supply Depots	Industrial and Production Centres
Rilly-la-Montagne (a) and (b)	Ober Raderach
St Leu d'Esserent	Peenemünde and Zinnowitz
Bois de Cassan	Rheinfelden
	Düsseldorf (Henkel)
	Hoell Reigelskreuth
	Klausthal
	Fallersleben

However, despite the placing of launch sites as second priority by the JCC, Bomber Command would devote all its flying bomb counter-offensive bombing against launch sites during the next week. What is noticeable about the future attacks on the launch sites was that smaller forces of bombers were used to attack each target, as had been recommended by the JCC. Up until 21 July Bomber Command had been sending no less than about 60 aircraft on attacks against launch sites whereas from 21 July the attacks, with the odd exception, would be carried out by about 30 aircraft or less. A clear move from the 'heavy scale attack' to the 'harassing attack'. On 22 July Bomber Command continued its attacks on the modified sites. The raids on Linzeux (16 Lancasters and 4 Mosquitos), Noyelle-en-Chausée (8 Lancasters and 2 Mosquitos, aircraft in formation releasing bombs on deputy leader's lead) and Coulonvillers (8 Lancasters and 2 Mosquitos, similarly bombing on leader's lead) were all believed successful. Reconnaissance photographs taken of Linzeux revealed many craters in the target area and substantial damage. Two other launch sites, L'Hey and Acquet, were scheduled for attack by 20 aircraft but Oboe failure resulted in no bombs being dropped.

The next day Mont Candon (24 Lancasters and 6 Mosquitos) and Forêt du Croc (24 Lancasters and 6 Mosquitos) were targeted. Both modified sites were attacked in complete cloud cover by three waves of bombers, with bombing conducted on the leader's lead. Follow-up reconnaissance on both sites revealed many craters in the target area, buildings damaged and destroyed at Mont Candon and the launching platform destroyed at Forêt du Croc.

The night of 23/24 July had Bomber Command attacking the modified sites at Les Catelliers (2 Lancasters, 52 Halifaxes and 5 Mosquitos) and Les Hauts Buissons (2 Lancasters, 50 Halifaxes and 5 Mosquitos). On both raids a good concentration of bombing was achieved on the markers. At Les Hauts Buissons a vivid orange flash was witnessed by crews, followed by a fire. Analysis of photographic reconnaissance revealed many fresh craters in the target area with one crater near the elevated end of the launching platform and a building destroyed. At Les Catelliers photographic analysis of reconnaissance was hindered owing to the considerable number of trees in the area. One aircraft was lost on the raid to Les Hauts Buissons. A 102 Squadron Halifax piloted by Pilot Officer Donald went down into the sea and from the crew of seven only one man was recovered. The bodies of two of the other men were washed ashore; the other four men were never found.

Modified sites were again attacked on day raids on 24 July. Prouville (14 Lancasters, 4 Mosquitos) was attacked in two formations, bombing carried out on the leader's lead and concentrated bombing was reported. Indeed many new craters were seen in reconnaissance photographs of the target area, but no damage although a road was blocked. A similar attack was detailed for Acquet (14 Lancasters, 4 Mosquitos) but a failure of equipment resulted in only 1 Mosquito and 2 Lancasters actually bombing. Unsurprisingly reconnaissance revealed no damage.

On the night of 24/25 July two forces, both consisting of 2 Lancasters, 5 Halifaxes and 5 Mosquitos, targeted the modified sites at Ferfay and L'Hey. Only a few aircraft saw the TI and bombed on the Ferfay raid, with most of the force bringing their bombs back. No follow-up reconnaissance was taken. At L'Hey the bombing and marking was reported as accurate and crews witnessed a violent white explosion at the opening of the raid. Reconnaissance revealed a cratered target area and a near miss on a launch platform. The 420 Squadron Halifax of Flight Lieutenant Trickett RCAF failed to return from the Ferfay raid. The aircraft crashed into the sea and there were no survivors from the crew of eight.

Three further day raids to Crossbow targets were conducted on 25 July, of which two were modified sites. Bombing at Ardouval II (32 Lancasters and 5 Mosquitos) was reported as excellent and reconnaissance revealed near misses on the launch platform and one building obliterated. The bombing force at Coqueraux (33 Lancasters and 5 Mosquitos) tended to overshoot at the start of the raid but bombing was generally well concentrated. Reconnaissance showed no hits or near misses but a flying bomb could actually be seen with a damaged tail unit. The other Crossbow target attacked was the large site at Watten involving 16 Lancasters, 1 Mosquito and 1 Mustang. No marking was necessary and the Lancasters dropped their 12,000 lb bombs in what was reported as a good attack. Ralph Briars DFM, rear gunner with 617 Squadron and holding the rank of flight sergeant, took part in the raid.

Took off about 07.00, fairly clear, cool. Sky cleared nicely over Channel, target easily seen. Watched kites behind us as we ran up, so interested that I forgot about defences, and then they let go some very accurate flak just before bomb went down. Despite all this bombs were very well dropped, grand show on D.B.'s part. Weaved like hell for a few minutes till clear of area, never felt or heard flak so near – slung some Window myself, starboard tailplane slightly damaged. Saw one kite hit in engine, smoke poured out, engine was feathered and they got back OK. Spit escort.

In fact three aircraft were damaged by the flak. Flying Officer Cheney's Lancaster was one of those hit. The bombload was jettisoned, manually, seven miles south-south-east of the target. The intercom was wrecked and the mid upper gunner, Flight Sergeant McRostie, fearing the worst, baled out. Cheney, however, managed to wrestle his aircraft back to base in England.

Initial raid reports claimed outstanding success, four or five direct hits observed. Reconnaissance later showed three probable hits on the Watten complex, one of which had smashed away some of the concrete roof. Other buildings in the target area appeared completely destroyed.

That night the modified sites at Ferfay (2 Lancasters, 30 Halifaxes and 5 Mosquitos), Forêt du Croc (2 Lancasters, 33 Halifaxes and 5 Mosquitos) and Bois de Jardins (32 Lancasters and 5 Mosquitos) were targeted, with bombing at all three targets reported as accurate. Follow-up reconnaissance revealed no damage at Ferfay, but there were better results at Forêt du Croc where the launching point was destroyed by a near miss. Similarly at Bois de Jardins the launching point received a direct hit (although it had been previously destroyed).

The Joint Crossbow Working Committee met on 27 July to formulate recommendations to the JCC. They recommended that Rilly-la-Montagne and St Leu d'Esserent should remain as first priority for attack, and that following these as a priority, two probable flying bomb storage dumps should also be attacked; at Mery-Sur-Oise and Trossy St Maximin (sometimes referred to as Trossy St Maxim). L'Isle d'Adam and Bois de Cassan (a few kilometres north-east of L'Isle d'Adam) had been suspected as a German Air Force ammunition depot since December 1943. It was now also suspected, and only suspected, of a Crossbow connection, and remained on the list though below the other four targets. They also recommended that Nucourt should also be reinstated for attack if any evidence came to light of any repair or other significant activity. No direct link had been made with Trossy St Maximin and Crossbow activity but:

> . . . is at present the scene of great activity. The site consists of a quarry with tunnel entrances served both by road and rail and last cover (20 July 44) shows four large circular pits in one of which a tank has just been installed. Ground sources report this site as a fuel depot. Its situation 1 mile from St Leu d'Esserent and the general appearance of activity are consistent with the

hypothesis that this site is concerned in Crossbow either actively or prospectively.[95]

A special target, Forêt de Nieppe, approximately 30 kilometres west of Lille and just south of the rail junction at Hazebrouck, was also recommended by the committee because of 'generally ominous activities'. It was felt that attacks on German production targets would not be effective in the short term, and due to the dispersed nature of her manufacturing industries, any long-term effect would be doubtful. It did however recommend that the targeting of Fallersleben should be continued.

The working committee also noted that '. . . it was appreciated that the effect of the present attacks [on launching sites] was negligible and did not justify the continuing very large expenditure of effort.'

The recommendations were made to the second meeting of the Joint Crossbow Committee on 28 July, at which the priorities were agreed. It was noted that the recent reduction of the scale of flying bomb attacks appeared to have been linked to the previous raids on the supply depots, and it was recommended that further attacks on these targets should be carried out by Bomber Command. It was also noted that the flak defences of Rilly-la-Montagne, Mery-Sur-Oise and Bois de Cassan had been recently reinforced, and this was taken as further evidence to support attacks on these targets.

The Committee considered a report on the suspected activity at Forêt de Nieppe, with a number of points noted: there had been a considerable number of workers involved in construction in the area for almost a year, SS troops had recently been seen in the area, there had been considerable attempts at camouflage, security had been tight, and numerous reports had been received of 'torpedoes' at the site. The Committee recommended that the target should be raided in a heavy and concentrated attack on each of the three aiming points identified.

The Committee then went on to consider the damage to the launching sites. Group Captain Corbally outlined his conclusions about the attacks. He estimated that all the Allied air forces in England could inflict Category A damage to approximately 50 launching sites in one week. However, taking into account the requirement for good weather and the Germans' ability to repair the damage, an almost continual targeting would be necessary at the expense of all the other bombing operations. He had added that the COPC had consulted with representatives from the fighter bomber forces. They expressed their concerns about the 'uneconomical use of fighter bombers' resulting from their difficulties in locating targets and the large number of sorties required. They felt that medium or heavy bombers were better suited to the attacks on the launching sites.

Wing Commander Lamb informed the Committee that they were now able to use radar to track the flight paths of the flying bombs, enabling them to prioritise for attack the active sites. The Committee asked the working committee to analyse the results of the harassing attacks on launching sites, and also agreed 'to recommend that, while for operational reasons, it is not likely that harassing attacks would show profitable results, they should nevertheless be continued for political reasons, pending the receipt of the analysis.'

On 27 July Bomber Command despatched, on 'harassing attacks', 72 aircraft to the modified sites at Les Catelliers, Château Bernapré, Les Hauts Buisson and Les Landes. The forces raiding the first three targets, each comprising 4 Mosquitos and 12 Lancasters respectively, carried out their bomb runs in two formations. At Les Catelliers the formations were reported as rather straggled but bombs were observed to have straddled the target. Only one formation bombed the modified site at Château Bernapré owing to an equipment failure in the leader of the second formation. Some of the crews could see the target and were later able to report seeing the first bombload slightly overshooting, but subsequent bombs fell on the target. The attack at Les Hauts Buisson was reported as good.

The Les Landes attack by 24 Stirlings is of particular note. On this raid the G-H leader method of attack was employed for the first time. Similar principles to the Oboe leader blind bombing method applied. On arrival over the Les Landes launch site the bomber crews experienced complete cloud cover and the bombing was recorded as rather confused with the belief that the attack was scattered and unsuccessful. However the method was believed to be of value and further experiments were made, with attempts to tighten the bomber formations. On 28 July two separate forces of ten Stirlings were despatched to attack modified sites, the first to Wemaers Cappel, the second to Fromental. The first raid encountered the attentions of flak over the target with a resultant disruption of the formation, but it was believed that a fair concentration was achieved. The Fromental force attacked in formation, with the last aircraft across the target reporting the bombs falling well across the target. On 2 August 20 Stirlings were sent to attack the modified site at Mont Candon. The force attacked in clear weather with crews reporting the target straddled by the bombs. In fact these raids proved the G-H method extremely accurate. An average bombing error of 275 yards was achieved, and the Fromental attack actually achieved 150 yards.

Losses on raids to flying bomb targets had been very few since the heavy casualties on the St Leu d'Esserent raids. The Stirlings had been taken out of the front line for Bomber Command operations over Germany owing to high loss rates but the risks whilst attacking the flying bomb sites in France were not quite as high as penetrations into Reich air space. One young airman, Sergeant Roy Abbott, was to experience his first operation over enemy occupied territory as part of the Stirling force sent to Mont Candon.

> The 149 Squadron battle order on 2 August 1944 included the names of Flight Sergeant Keith Goldie RAAF and his crew. I was the flight engineer. This was to be our first operational flight. We did not say much, but I think we all had much the same thoughts; what would it be like going into action for the first time, flying through flak and perhaps being attacked by enemy fighters? I personally do not recall feeling nervous or apprehensive, just a feeling of exhilaration, our training was

over, now it was for real.

The morning dragged on all too slowly, then a pre-operational meal and eventually briefing. The target was Mont Candon, a flying bomb launch ramp site in northern France, just inland from Dieppe. We were briefed to fly a semi circular course around Dieppe which just missed a large patch of red on the wall map, denoting a heavy flak area. The route looked easy enough, but there was no fighter cover.

Our aircraft was a Stirling III, K – Kitty. She was a proud old lady, veteran of 69 operational flights over enemy territory when she became a part of my life. She was growing old, plenty of signs of wear and tear. The leading edges of the mainplanes had lost much of their camouflage paint, silver metal shining through; the soft metal of the engine cowlings bore dozens of dents from constant removal and refitting. Oil had stained the upper wing surfaces behind the four Hercules engines, black streaks to the trailing edges. Patches on the fuselage were evidence of earlier damage by enemy action.

On the airfield (Methwold, Suffolk) Kitty was ready to go with four and a half tons of bombs and 1,296 gallons of petrol. Contact and the powerful Bristol Hercules engines roared into action. And so at 15.35 hours we were airborne into a cloudless clear blue sky.

We could clearly see Dieppe as we crossed the coast of France; it all looked so peaceful. At last bomb doors open and away. A few bursts of flak sent us on our way. If the rest of the tour was going to be like this, I, for one, would not complain. Things did of course liven up considerably as we pressed on with our tour of 30 ops.

The results of these 'experimental' raids were most promising for the use of G-H in daylight precision bombing. Further statistical analysis by Bomber Command on the various methods of attacking small targets, however, demonstrated that Oboe formation bombing gave the best results, with the 5 Group visual and offset methods not far behind. But of course all this had to be weighed up with the disadvantages of each method. Only a limited number of aircraft could carry Oboe, thus limiting the scale of Oboe leader operations. Oboe's range was limited (as was G-H). The 5 Group methods were affected by adverse weather conditions, cloud cover. However in deciding the method of marking and attacking targets the G-H technique gave the operational planners another option.

Bomber Command had possibly been informed of the Joint Crossbow Working Committee targeting recommendations prior to approval by the main committee. On 28 July, the day the main committee met, Bomber Command initiated, over a period of 13 days, the first in a series of 11 raids, of varying size, on the suspected supply depot at Forêt de Nieppe. On 28 July two aiming points were targeted with 79 Halifaxes and 10 Mosquitos eventually despatched. The bombers were to attack at 1800 hours in three waves of 16 aircraft on the first aiming point and two waves of 16 aircraft on the second aiming point, with bombing initiated by the formation leader. However complete cloud cover was experienced over the target and crews were unable to make any assessment of the bombing accuracy. The second attacking force, 80 Halifaxes and 10 Mosquitos despatched, were due to attack at 1830 hours in a similar formation to the first force. By this time the cloud had cleared and an excellent concentration on both aiming points was reported. The force attacking the target, whilst achieving the excellent concentration of bombing, had to do so by risking the flak defences.

> *Sergeant Thomas Fox, flight engineer, 77 Squadron;* Frank (skipper) [Squadron Leader Frank Lord DFC] who was 'C' Flight Commander by this time was leading the squadron through the target. A few miles away from the target we could see a strong barrage of light flak, which was on our height and awaiting our arrival. Never, at any time, did Frank deviate from his course to a target unless, of course, we had to dive away as a safety measure. He flew straight through the flak expecting to be hit at any moment, but this was another occasion when someone else was on our side. After dropping our bombload we quickly turned for home with our fingers crossed and that was another tight corner we managed to get out of.[96]

There was a particularly tragic incident on this raid, witnessed by one of the local civilians.[97] A 78 Squadron Halifax, piloted by Flight Lieutenant Hoffman, was hit by the flak on the way to the target and began to get into difficulty. Hoffman and his crew had little choice but to jettison the bomb load. Three of the bombs fell into open countryside, with no houses hit. The first bomb exploded a short distance away from a married couple and their three young children. The father, holding his youngest daughter, was killed, hit in the back, and the child received minor injuries. The mother, who was pregnant at the time, was also killed, smashed up against a wall. The other children escaped unhurt. A witness saw some of the crew jump out of the stricken aircraft; one airman's parachute did not open correctly and he did not survive. This was probably the wireless operator, Pilot Officer Winter. The pilot also lost his life. For whatever reason he was unable to leave the aircraft, and he was found with the crashed Halifax. The Germans immediately arrived and the rest of the crew all became prisoners of war.

Later that night yet another large force of 5 Lancasters, 104 Halifaxes and 10 Mosquitos was sent to the suspected supply depot, again to attack as two separate forces. The first attack took place just before midnight and the second was made just over four hours later; Mosquitos marked the aiming point on both attacks. Both bombing forces reported perfect weather and an accurate and concentrated attack. No aircraft were lost on the raid. The German nightfighters were busy elsewhere. Bomber Command lost 39 Lancasters on a raid to Stuttgart and 18 Lancasters and 4 Halifaxes on a raid to Hamburg. Then the very next day yet another force (50 Halifaxes, 10 Mosquitos and 16 Stirlings) was despatched to follow up these raids. The supply depot was to receive its fifth attack within 26 hours. The attack, again, was made in two stages, all crews experiencing complete cloud cover over the target. The first stage involved the Halifaxes and Mosquitos bombing in formation, which became a little ragged owing to crews having difficulty in adapting to the speed of the formation leaders. However it was thought that a good concentration of bombs fell on the target. The Stirlings attacked in the second stage of the raid, bombing in good formation, and it was believed that a good concentration should have resulted.

Forêt de Nieppe was not attacked by Bomber Command again until the night of 31July/1 August when 100 Lancasters and 5 Mosquitos were despatched to the target, and attacked using the 8 Group visual marking method. The force reported an accurate and concentrated attack. One aircraft was lost on the raid, the 100 Squadron Lancaster of Flight Sergeant Tones RNZAF with the entire crew killed.

At the end of July the COPC presented a plan, codenamed Eiderdown, for a massive concentration of force against Crossbow sites. Air Chief Marshal Tedder had instigated the process in mid July, requesting the COPC, with representation from all the air agencies, to come up with a plan to reduce the number of flying bombs launched per day to 30. The COPC eventually came to the conclusion that it could not guarantee reducing the scale of the German attack to 30 flying bombs per day, but it could prevent the current scale of attack from rising.

The plan called upon all the available Allied bomber forces based in the United Kingdom at the time, with fighter support provided by 11 Group and the Eighth and Ninth American Air Forces. The American heavy bombers, expected to contribute 1,500 sorties, were allocated Peenemünde, Fallersleben, the hydrogen peroxide plants at Ober Raderach and Düsseldorf, the three suspected fuel depots at Vaas, Dugny and Pacy, the two supply depots at Mery-Sur-Oise and Rilly-la-Montagne, and 20 launching sites. Bomber Command, expected to contribute 1,000 sorties, were allocated the three suspected storage depots at Forêt de Nieppes, Bois de Cassan and Trossy St Maximin, and 22 launching sites. The Ninth Air Force, expected to contribute 380 sorties, would target 36 launch sites. The 2nd Tactical Air Force, expected to contribute 48 sorties (Mitchells), was allocated four launch sites. It was recommended that half the bombs dropped on the attacks on the launch sites should be delayed action. The plan was for all these attacks to take place within a 24-hour period but, importantly, good visual bombing weather was required at the target areas.[98]

Bomber Command's Commander-in-Chief wrote to the chairman of the COPC expressing concern over the extremely heavy requirement placed on his force but he was generally in agreement with the plan. The targets would receive considerable bomber attention but adverse weather and the demands of supporting the Overlord campaign extended the time required to action the plan.

Bomber Command had begun attacking Forêt de Nieppe on 28 July. Eiderdown called on the RAF heavy bombers to continue the attacks. On 2

August, 59 Halifaxes and 12 Mosquitos were despatched to attack three aiming points at the supply depot (two waves to each). The weather was clear and apart from the first-wave attack on the second aiming point a good concentration was thought to have been achieved. Photographic reconnaissance of the target was made on 3 August and revealed considerable damage to the target, affecting at least 46 buildings of which 12 were virtually destroyed. The roads and light rail lines in the area were also cut in several places.

Bomber Command also conducted another, and very large, raid to the suspected supply depot on 3 August, despatching 7 Lancasters, 308 Halifaxes, 5 Mosquitos and a Lockheed P-38 Lightning (the experience of the Lightning pilot is detailed later). Things did not start too well for Flying Officer Fox piloting a 578 Squadron Lancaster. On the outward journey he had great difficulty controlling the bomber and eventually the crew had to abandon the aircraft; the wireless operator was injured, and the bomber crashed near Beccles in Suffolk. Those crews that reached the target area experienced broken cloud but they were able to see the markers and identify the aiming point visually. The attack was reported as good. The target was photographed the next day with a good concentration of craters revealed and numerous storage units destroyed or severely damaged. Three Mosquitos were also sent, with only two bombing in clear weather. Photographic reconnaissance was also made on 5 August, on one specific area, which covered five previous attacks. The photographs revealed a well cratered target area with serious damage visible.

On 5 August the supply depot was yet again targeted with 8 Lancasters, 273 Halifaxes and 5 Mosquitos despatched. The main force clearly heard the master bomber and deputy over the cloud-free target and the subsequent concentration of bombing soon led to a smoke-obscured aiming point, hindering initial raid assessment. Photographic reconnaissance revealed a cratered target area with many buildings destroyed or seriously damaged. On 6 August yet another force (8 Lancasters, 105 Halifaxes and 5 Mosquitos) was despatched to attack the forest depot. The bombers found patchy cloud over the target and slight haze. The yellow markers were deemed accurate by the master bomber and he called on the bomber force to come below the cloud base at 10,000 feet to bomb. They duly obliged although some crews had their bombing distracted by some red TI situated to the north-east of the aiming point. As a result the initial raid assessment reported a scattered attack, which would be supported by partial photographic reconnaissance on 8 August showing only a few additional craters within the target area.

On the night of 6/7 August three Mosquitos attacked, bombing on Oboe and then the final Bomber Command assault on the supply depot took place on the night of 9/10 August (26 Lancasters, 95 Halifaxes and 5 Mosquitos). An accurate and concentrated attack was reported and reconnaissance revealed severe damage to certain areas of the target, with 20 buildings destroyed or seriously hit, and several roads in the target area completely blocked.

In total 4,781 tons of bombs had been dropped on the suspected supply depot. The damage had been considerable. The Crossbow Countermeasures Progress Report recorded the following concerning the last three raids conducted:

> An area in the south-west of the forest is covered with a very heavy concentration of craters and nearly every building there has suffered some damage. In the north of the forest two areas on the edge show many new craters and roads have been cut; in one of these areas no buildings remain undamaged and in places roads have been obliterated. Inside the forest 8 buildings have been destroyed and 6 severely damaged. In two further areas, damaged in previous attacks, no attempt has been made to fill in craters or to repair the nearby railway, which was cut in about ten places.[99]

The effect the raids against Forêt de Nieppe had on the flying bomb offensive will be considered when raids against the other suspected storage depots, as outlined in the COPC's Eiderdown plan, are detailed.

The JCC meeting of 28 July had kept the storage depot at Rilly-la-Montagne as a priority for attack. On 31 July 617 Squadron aircraft were part of the force of 97 Lancasters and 6 Mosquitos sent to the Rilly-la-Montagne rail tunnels. The pilot of one of the squadron's Lancasters was Flight Lieutenant William Reid, a holder of the Victoria Cross, which was awarded as a result of his actions on a raid to Düsseldorf on 3 November 1943 (whilst with 61 Squadron). On that night his Lancaster had twice been attacked by enemy nightfighters. He was injured in both attacks, his navigator killed, his wireless operator seriously wounded and the flight engineer also hit. Despite the damage to the aircraft Reid continued on the operation, used the stars to navigate, reached the target and managed to bomb. Things got worse on the return journey. Over the North Sea the four engines cut out, but it was soon realised that the petrol cocks needed to be switched over to full tanks. Reid then had to negotiate a landing, during which the undercarriage had to be pumped down, he began bleeding again and then the undercarriage collapsed. The Lancaster finally came to a halt. He recovered from his injuries in hospital, but his wireless operator did not pull through. Reid received the VC for his gallantry and was also to receive a posting to 617 Squadron.

On the raid to Rilly-la-Montagne Reid's aircraft had just released its bombload over the target, when another Lancaster directly above did the same. One of the 1,000 lb bombs went straight through the fuselage of Reid's aircraft, one of the port engines was lost and all the control cables were cut. He gave the order for his crew to bale out. As the aircraft began to spin the front nose broke away sending Reid tumbling through the air. He pulled his parachute cord, which opened successfully, and he came to earth suffering a broken hand and burned face. Reid was caught by the Germans very quickly and was taken to the nearby wreckage of his plane. The dead mid upper gunner was still inside the plane. The dead rear gunner was still in his turret, which lay 20 yards from the main wreckage. In fact his wireless operator was the only other person to survive and both men would see the war out behind German wire.

Returning crew reports led Bomber Command to believe that the operation had been successful. Both ends of the tunnel were hit, 473 tons dropped, and while the majority of the bombing force were able to crater the surrounding area, the Tallboys dropped by 617 Squadron caved in the entrances. In addition to the loss of Reid's Lancaster, the 9 Squadron Lancaster piloted by Flying Officer Worner did not return, with no survivors from the crew of seven.

CHAPTER 14

LONG DAYS AND NIGHTS

On 10 July the Allied Army achieved one of its D-Day objectives and occupied Caen, but operation Goodwood, an attempt to break through German defences south of Caen, stalled. The surrounding area became a pressure point and a focus for German reinforcement. Towards the end of July the Americans launched operation Cobra, to the west of St Lô and by the end of the month they reached Avranches. The situation for the German Army in Normandy was steadily worsening and the Allied advances would soon be threatening the flying bomb organisation outside the Cherbourg peninsula.

Following the attacks on supply depots in July 1944, Flakregiment 155(W) had seen a serious decline in its flying bomb firing rate. However towards the end of July there was a recovery, but not on the same scale as in the first few weeks of the offensive. In the period 1 to 15 July the regiment recorded 2 launch sites destroyed, 16 seriously damaged, 7 with medium damage and 14 slightly damaged. In the period 16 to 31 July: 5 launch sites destroyed, 5 sites seriously damaged, 6 with medium damage and 8 with slight damage. In the whole month the regiment lost 18 men dead or missing and 57 wounded as a result of the bombing.

From the opening of the offensive until 3.00 p.m. on 30 July Flakregiment 155(W) had fired 5,853 flying bombs (734 of which crashed soon after take-off). Information supplied to the British War Cabinet from Herbert Morrison, Home Secretary and Minister of Home Security, stated that up to 6.00 a.m. on 31 July, flying bombs had killed 4,640, seriously injured 13,571 and slightly injured 17,083 people. Whilst the flying bomb offensive was not producing the results the Germans would have hoped for in terms of civilian victims, although the occasional single flying bomb could cause substantial casualties, it was causing major disruption in London and civilian evacuation procedures had been introduced.

The men of Bomber Command certainly had their work cut out in the summer months of 1944, supporting the Allied invasion, maintaining attacks on German oil targets and conducting Crossbow responsibilities:

> *Sergeant Fred Fossett, bomb aimer, 463 Squadron:* The thing I most remember of all of the raids is being tired, for we could do a night trip, then a day trip, or a test flight on an aircraft, always having to make sure the aircraft was fit for the next sortie.

Frequently briefing would be about four hours before take-off, and we had to spend an hour at the aircraft before the take-off. They were very long days and nights.

On the night of 31 July/1 August, in addition to the force sent to Forêt de Nieppe previously mentioned, three modified launch sites were targeted. These sites at Forêt du Croc, Oeuf-en-Ternois and Coqueraux were to be marked by five Mosquitos with a master and deputy bomber in Lancasters to direct the main forces of 24, 26 and 26 Halifaxes respectively. All attacks were reported as accurate and concentrated but reconnaissance indicated failure at Forêt du Croc and Oeuf-en-Ternois. At Coqueraux there was limited success with three near misses damaging the square building, and other craters visible in the target area. One aircraft was lost on this particular raid: the 429 Squadron Halifax of Warrant Officer Irish RCAF with no survivors.

The next day a major Bomber Command assault on the modified sites was detailed, involving 777 aircraft. However bad weather stepped in to prevent this massive show of force, as complete cloud cover was experienced over the target areas. Only one of the 13 targets, Le Nieppe, was actually attacked, although the master bomber felt it necessary to abandon the raid half-way through.

On the return from the raid to Acquet, which was one of those abandoned on 1 August, the 431 Squadron Halifax piloted by Pilot Officer Skeaff overran the runway, skidded across a ditch and suffered a collapsed undercarriage. The aircraft was written off but at least no one was hurt.

On 2 August another major assault on flying bomb targets was detailed. Four forces, each of ten Lancasters and two Mosquitos, were despatched to Les Catelliers, Coqueraux, Les Landes and Château Bernapré. Excellent weather and visibility were experienced by the attacking force at Les Catelliers and a good concentration of bombing was reported. Analysis of reconnaissance photographs was hindered by the undergrowth in the target area but a few new craters were visible with some trees close to a building probably flattened by a bomb blast. The bombers over Coqueraux also experienced excellent weather and reported concentrated bombing; reconnaissance revealed numerous new craters in the target area and one building damaged by blast. The attack on Château Bernapré was reported as scattered across three distinct areas, fortunately one of which was the aiming point, and reconnaissance appeared to reveal a demolished launching platform. Tree shadows hindered further analysis but one building had disappeared as a result of a few near misses. Failure of the leader's blind bombing equipment led to the Lancasters having to bomb visually at Les Landes, but a good concentration was reported. Le Nieppe and L'Hey were both to be attacked by 20 Halifaxes and four Mosquitos respectively, each force bombing in two waves. Attacking crews identified both targets visually and at Le Nieppe a good concentration was observed. At L'Hey the bombing of the first waves was seen as slightly left of the aiming point. Scattered bombing reported by the second wave was put down to an extended formation. Reconnaissance at Le Nieppe revealed numerous craters in the target area but no important damage was identifiable. A force of 94 Lancasters and 7 Mosquitos was also despatched to attack the supply depot at Trossy St Maximin. The markers were reported as accurate and it was believed that the bombing was concentrated. Bois de Cassan was to receive the attentions of a Lightning, 5 Mosquitos and 100 Lancasters.

This was actually the second use of the Lightning. It had been employed on the aborted raids of the previous day. The diary of Group Captain C.B. Owen DSO and DFC, held at the Imperial War Museum, gives his experiences whilst piloting the Lightning, acting as controller (or 'shepherd' as he refers in the diary) on the Bois de Cassan raid. Owen had also flown the Lightning the day before, and was to fly the aircraft on the raid to Trossy St Maximin on 3 August. Owen's diary entries show the difficulties of trying to control raids, and fly and navigate in an aircraft single-handed.

> *1 August:* First trip in the Lightning. Curious sensation flying above cloud with no navigator to tell me where we were (or should be!) Thankful to pick up the Lancs on the south coast as cloud was getting very thick. 10/10 over the target so I called the show off and turned for home. Map-read back from Selsey Bill, which I found a bit of a strain after relying on a crew to do the dirty work. Found the Lightning very quiet and comfortable after a Lanc or Mossie.
>
> *2 August:* Another daylight to France. Got very bored stooging up and down the gaggle, except for a little excitement when the Spit escort got a little too interested in me for comfort. Good prang on the target and a fast trip home from the coast. First time I'd used VHF homing, and found it very efficient. Definitely a gentlemanly way of getting from A to B with a minimum of effort on the part of the driver. Good thing.
>
> *3 August:* Third trip in three days, and getting a bit cheesed with chasing Lancs across France. Country looked very deserted over the far side, but plenty of flak at the target. Gaggle very scattered on return and we were lucky not to get bounced by fighters. Got lost coming home above cloud and found Oxford instead of Reading, but managed it from there. Landed at dusk in time for a drink before dinner.[100]

The marking on the 2 August Bois de Cassan raid was reported as successful but the main force found bombing difficult owing to poor weather and the intense accurate flak. Two 467 Squadron Lancasters were lost on the raid to Bois de Cassan, one piloted by Flying Officer Bradley, the other by Flying Officer Dyer. The entire crew of both aircraft were killed.

On 3 August the largest number of Bomber Command aircraft of the whole flying bomb counter-offensive campaign was despatched. The raid to Forêt de Nieppes involving 320 aircraft has already been covered. A further 11 Mosquitos and 372 Lancasters were sent to Trossy St Maximin, and 5 Mosquitos, 221 Lancasters and 184 Halifaxes were directed to Bois de Cassan. A grand total of 1,114 aircraft.

The attack to Trossy St Maximin was to be conducted in two phases. On the first attack the markers were on time and the main force could clearly hear the master bomber. However the subsequent concentrated bombing, conducted amidst moderately heavy flak, caused smoke to obscure the markers and, compounded with cloud affecting bombing runs, the results of the raid were believed to be poor although one large explosion was witnessed by crews. Flying Officer R. Hart, a pilot with 44 (Rhodesia) Squadron, gives an example of one other difficulty experienced on this raid:

> We commenced our bomb run at 14.31 hours from a height of 15,200 feet. The target was visually identified and bombed with no markers seen. It was quite impossible to carry out a good bomb run as the formation on the way to and over the target was far too tight. The controller advised all aircrews to increase airspeed with the result that we bombed ninety seconds early, and I believe that the bombs fell northwest of the target. A good trip. [101]

Flying Officer Ron Biggs, a navigator with 44 (Rhodesia) Squadron, experienced one of the problems of the tight formation and recorded in his diary:

> Late on take-off and we had to belt the engines to make up time. Have difficulty in finding our concentration but finally do and we are on track and on time at Reading. Terrific concentration over target which is not visible. Great danger of being hit by bombs from chaps above us.

The experience left a lasting impression in Ron Biggs' memory, as he would later recall:

> I can remember this very well as I was up front trying to spot the target when I looked up and saw a Lanc directly above with its bomb doors open. I quickly nudged the skipper and he steered clear.

Many crews had problems with their bombing runs and in taking their bomb photographs. Three aircraft of 463 Squadron had to complete bombing interrogation reports. The reasons given by the pilots for their bombing problems were:

> *Flying Officer Noon:* . . . approx 10 secs after release of bombs forced to turn to starboard to avoid being bombed by several aircraft above (with bomb doors open).
> *Flying Officer Dack:* Too many aircraft on target at once. Speed too slow for accurate flying in slipstreams. I had to take avoiding action after releasing as bombs were falling around.
> *Flight Lieutenant Morris:* Just after dropping bombs our aircraft was hit violently by slipstream making it impossible to

keep straight and level during the taking of the photograph.[102]

The defensive flak and tight formations led to other problems for some crews:

Sergeant Fred Fossett, bomb aimer with 463 Squadron: I took part in the Trossy raid [on 3 August] . . . there were a few groans at briefing because some had already paid their respects to the area.

We started our run up a bit too early, and held straight and level a bit too long, so they predicted our course, and sent us a present, which went through the fuselage on our starboard side, just aft of the mid upper turret. It fired off the rear gunner's ammo, cut some control lines, isolated the rear turret making it in-operative, took out the main gyro that operated the compasses, and generally caused problems, but we flew back with a bit of difficulty for the pilot, and each of us wearing our parachutes just in case something dreadful happened. One of our squadron pals saw our damage, and stuck off just behind us, to the starboard side to give us protection. Aircraft was out of action for about a week having a rear fuselage fitted.

Sergeant Fred Whitfield, rear gunner with 9 Squadron: In my opinion this operation turned into a shambles. When nearing the target area, the anti-aircraft guns opened up good and proper. Apparently there were one or two crews on their first operation who after glimpsing the big black puffs of flak began weaving all over the sky, thinking they could weave out of it. The result was planes crashing into each other.

Two planes crashed alongside us, and the last I saw was pieces of aircraft floating down to earth. We stuck our noses down and got below the rest of them for safety. While the anti-aircraft fire was bursting about four thousand feet above us we were quite safe and got home.

After the operation 207 Squadron carried out a raid assessment and laid the blame on the Controller of the raid:

The execution of the plan was not at all successful, difficulties being reported, both on the way to the target, at the target itself and on the return journey. 207 Squadron was accused of getting ahead of the base leader but in point of fact the leaders themselves straggled considerably, which made it virtually impossible for them to be followed. The trouble seemed to start when the Controller gave the order over the Channel to reduce speed and close up, presumably because the force was ahead of time. This caused congestion at the target with the result that during the bombing run aircraft were so busy avoiding other aircraft and falling bombs that accurate bombing was extremely difficult and the whole operation was dangerous.[103]

In all five Lancasters were lost on this raid. Flying Officer Gilmore's 61 Squadron Lancaster did not return and the pilot and five others from his crew were killed. His navigator Flying Officer Forbes did manage to survive the ordeal and it is believed he had further fortune by coming to earth close to the Allied lines. The 166 Squadron Lancaster piloted by Flying Officer Wagner was believed to have been shot down by flak. Wagner was captured, five others from his crew were killed and his flight engineer evaded capture. There were no survivors from the crews of the 460 Squadron Lancaster flown by Flying Officer Fidock and the 619 Squadron Lancaster flown by Warrant Officer Bennett. The 625 Squadron Lancaster flown by Flying Officer Jobson also failed to return from the raid. The pilot and four of his crew were captured, the other two men losing their lives.

Only partial photographic reconnaissance was achieved of the target area, on 4 August, owing to cloud cover but interpreters were able to discern that of the two road over rail bridges on the Creil to Paris lines, the southern one had been demolished. There were many craters in the target area and it was believed that one, possibly three, of the tunnel entrances were blocked, with damage to a gantry in the quarry area alongside the main railway. Flying Officer Ron Biggs, navigator with 44 (Rhodesia) Squadron, recorded in his diary, that his crew's bombing had resulted in some success, but not on the intended target:

> Find, by yesterday's photo, that we didn't hit the target but instead we knocked out 4 heavy guns and 3 light. Very satisfying when the Intelligence Officer pulled out the marker pins.

The force attacking Bois de Cassan experienced excellent visibility over the partially cloud-covered target. The master bomber identified the aiming point, which was duly marked. However smoke soon covered the markers and bombing had to be directed at the centre of the smoke, then at a position 100 yards off the centre. The attack was believed to be successful. Bomber Command lost two aircraft on the raid. Although the 78 Squadron Halifax of Flying Officer McCarthy received considerable flak damage, the pilot was able to bring his stricken aircraft back to base. The aircraft was deemed a write-off but the crew had managed to get through the ordeal with no physical injury. Flying Officer Topham's 514 Squadron Lancaster, flying with the addition to the normal crew of seven of a mid under gunner, was shot down. The pilot and his mid under gunner managed to evade capture but the rest of the crew became POWs.

On 4 August Bomber Command once more detailed another force, comprising 5 Mosquitos and 61 Lancasters, to attack the suspected supply depot at Trossy St Maximin. The raid was believed to have been fairly successful as returning crews reported concentrated bombing and seeing one large explosion. In combination with the attacks on 2 and 3 August Bomber Command had dropped 3,059 tons of explosive on the target. Damage was assessed thus:

> As a result of the first two attacks a large rectangular building

has received severe damage and subsidences can be seen in the southern portion just north and south of the four cylindrical holes and there are 16 holes in the quarry floor. A large building in this area has been hit several times and railways are cut in many places.[104]

However the attacking crews, on 4 August, had experienced considerable ground defences whilst over the target. Sergeant Jack Watson, a flight engineer with 156 Squadron, flew on the raid:

> We were just at the end of the straight and level for the photograph when a shell exploded beneath us. We were lucky, for although the aircraft was well peppered none of us was hurt. Only quick action by the pilot in going into a steep dive probably saved us as when we looked up there were a lot of shell bursts where we had been.

Target-marking duties on the 4 August raid had been allocated to 635 Squadron, providing both the master and a deputy bomber. One of the squadron's pilots was the experienced Squadron Leader Ian Bazalgette, who had flown his first operational flight, minelaying in a Wellington with 115 Squadron, on 30 September 1942. Since then he had completed a tour, put in time instructing on an operational training unit and was now back on operations with a pathfinder squadron, using his experience to mark targets. Sergeant 'Chuck' Godfrey DFC was Squadron Leader Bazalgette's wireless operator at 635 Squadron and recalls the morning of the raid to Trossy St Maximin.

> We were due to go on leave the day after the raid, and were not on the Battle Order to start with. But one of the other pilots had taken an aircraft to York and hadn't got back because of fog. So we said, 'We'll get another one in before we go on leave.' It wasn't going to be a long hop. The target was just north of Paris. It wouldn't take long.

Ten Lancasters from 635 Squadron took off from Downham Market that morning, including that of Wing Commander D.W.S. Clark to act as master bomber on the raid. As Clark approached the target the considerable flak defence became apparent, the Lancaster receiving damage on the bomb run. Then came the deputy master bomber, Flight Lieutenant Beveridge DFC, whose Lancaster was also hit by flak; the stricken aircraft caught fire and flew into the ground. There were no survivors from the crew of eight. As Squadron Leader Bazalgette brought his aircraft in, it too was hit by flak, straight through the starboard wing taking out both engines and setting the wing on fire. There was another flak hit on the aircraft's fuselage and the bomb aimer, Flight Lieutenant Hibbert DFC, was seriously injured.

Bazalgette managed to control the Lancaster, using only his port engines, and went on to release his markers on the target. But the fire intensified and the Lancaster began to lose height rapidly. Bazalgette nevertheless was able to wrestle back control of the Lancaster. Sergeant George Turner was

Bazalgette's flight engineer: 'The starboard wing was one mass of flames with pieces flying off it. In fact it was looking more like a skeleton.'

Flying Officer Doug Cameron DFM, the rear gunner, heard a tapping on his rear turret door. He turned to see mid upper gunner Flight Sergeant Leeder RAAF. He also noticed the fuel that was leaking into the Lancaster's fuselage:

> Removing my oxygen mask I shouted to him to get down to the front and await the order from the Skipper to bale out. 'This aircraft is going in and it won't be long.' He nodded and moved away. I shut the door and turned the turret to the beam. I could not believe my eyes. The starboard wing was like a herringbone after all the flesh has been eaten off it. I could hardly believe we were still flying. I knew we were a doomed aircraft.

The situation worsened when one of the port engines failed. Sergeant George Turner turned to his pilot:

> 'You'll have to put her down Baz.' I told him that we had no chance, only to get out of the aircraft as quickly as possible. With that he gave the order to put on parachutes and jump. We were just a flying bomb. The rear fuselage was awash with fuel swishing around. It only wanted a spark from the starboard wings to make contact and we would all have been blown to bits.

Bazalgette ordered the crew to bale out. Turner, Godfrey, Cameron and the navigator, Flight Lieutenant Goddard, obeyed their captain. The seriously injured bomb aimer, Hibbert, and the mid upper gunner, Leeder, who it was believed had been overcome by smoke and fumes, remained in the aircraft. Bazalgette could have got out. He may have been unsure if Leeder was still on the aircraft (for all Bazalgette knew he may have jumped through the crew door) but he knew that Hibbert was on board and in no fit state to bale out. Bazalgette decided to attempt a landing. The Lancaster lost further height and as it neared a village it was seen to turn to avoid houses and a farm before touching down in a field. Chuck Godfrey hanging beneath his parachute saw it all: 'He did get it down in a field about two fields from where I landed, but it was well ablaze. And with all that petrol on board it just exploded.' The three men, still on board were killed instantly.

Squadron Leader Bazalgette's extraordinary bravery in attempting to save the lives of his fellow airmen would result in the award of the Victoria Cross. The four men who baled out managed to evade capture[105]. This Lancaster was actually the one piloted by Larry Melling, previously mentioned, that had been badly damaged on the raid of 9 July to L'Hey.

A large force of 5 Mosquitos, 169 Halifaxes and 51 Lancasters was despatched to Bois de Cassan, also on 4 August. Attacking crews were able to identify the target visually and concentrated bombing resulted with two very large explosions reported at the centre of the target. Three aircraft were lost on the raid. The 424 Squadron Halifax of Flying Officer Cronin RCAF (pilot and five others killed, one captured) and the 434 Squadron

Halifax of Flying Officer Lang RCAF (pilot and two others evaded capture, four men killed) failed to return. The 433 Squadron Halifax of Flying Officer Simpson RCAF was hit by flak as they left the target and eventually the crew had to abandon the stricken bomber. All the men survived, the only casualty being the bomb aimer who was injured by the flak. In combination with the attacks made on 2 and 3 August, 3,183 tons had been dropped on the suspected supply depot at Bois de Cassan and further analysis of results led to the following conclusions:

> The entire area, with the exception of the south-east corner appears saturated with craters and previously damaged buildings have received further hits. 56 storage bunkers are now destroyed, others are damaged, only 8 remaining more or less untouched. Buildings in the railway sidings have received further damage as well as a rectangular building in the wooded south-western area of the site. Railways and roads are generally impassable and 2 of the 3 flak towers have been demolished.[106]

On 5 August, in addition to the raid to Forêt de Nieppe previously covered, a very large Bomber Command force once more attacked the underground complex at St Leu d'Esserent, dropping 2,228 tons of bombs. Three launching sites were also scheduled for attack by a total of 31 Lancasters and 5 Mosquitos, but poor weather led to these raids being abandoned.

The plan of attack on St Leu d'Esserent comprised two phases, with the first phase detailed for 196 Halifaxes and 52 Lancasters of 6 Group and 5 Mosquitos and 8 Lancasters of 8 Group, and the second phase for 189 Lancasters and 1 Mosquito of 5 Group and 5 Mosquitos of 8 Group.

Over the target the first phase force experienced good visibility, with the master bomber clearly heard, and although there was some scattered early bombing a good concentration developed. The second phase force had more difficulty in carrying out their attack.

On this raid 5 Group tried a new method of attack with aircraft flying in base formation. All aircraft were to take off and then form up over their base, then to take position behind the Coningsby formation, which was leading the group. Wing Commander J.F. Grey, from 207 Squadron, led his base's formation.

Following some minor difficulties in forming up, owing to cloud cover, Wing Commander Grey approached the target, leading his formation and positioned behind the Coningsby formation, in which flew the raid Controller. Partial cloud cover over the target led to difficulties identifying the aiming point and the Controller led the formations in a sharp right-angled turn. Some confusion followed and crews had little time to conduct their bomb runs. As a result the bombing was reported as scattered.

Wing Commander Grey had just released his bombs and led his squadron over the target when a burst of heavy flak exploded under the nose of his Lancaster. The bomb aimer could claim considerable luck as flak splinters missed him ripping into his maps and the fusing switch and fuse box. Grey started having difficulty keeping speed and height, as the starboard outer and port inner engines had been damaged by the flak. Oil streamed back from the damaged engines covering the perspex of several aircraft trailing in the formation. Whilst the disabled Lancaster steadily lost height and became separated from the formation, the crew grabbed their parachutes and then made great efforts to reduce the weight of the aircraft. Most of the ammunition went out, some of the guns (the rest later), oxygen bottles and anything else that was superfluous to requirements and removable either freely or with the help of an axe.

Another Lancaster, seeing the predicament of their fellow airmen and no doubt a welcome sight to Grey's crew, gave some support and accompanied Grey's Lancaster to the French coast. The crew were further comforted, briefly, when contact was made with 11 Group and fighter support promised, but this did not show up. Over the Channel the crew witnessed the struggle of one of their fallen colleagues swimming between two dinghies. Now Grey's starboard inner engine began to play up and it appeared that a ditching would follow, but the pilot's skill brought his failing aircraft over the English coast. Hydraulic trouble than forced him to head for the airfield at Manston, Kent, where he put the Lancaster down safely.

Two aircraft were lost on the raid. The 425 Squadron Halifax of Squadron Leader Philbin RCAF fell victim to the flak, six men were killed, the pilot evaded capture and one man was captured. The 433 Squadron Halifax of Flying Officer Harrison had an engine failure as it prepared to land back at Skipton-on-Swale. The pilot and one other crew member were killed and the rest of the crew were injured in the resultant crash. A particularly tragic casualty of the crash was local boy, five-year-old Kenneth Battensby who was killed when he could not get away as the Halifax skidded to a halt in his village.[107]

Reconnaissance of the St Leu d'Esserent complex, on 7 August, revealed a substantial increase in the number of craters in the target area, with some further areas of subsidence around the southern entrances to the caves. The previously repaired rail lines to the east of the tunnels had been obliterated for a substantial length. The roads to the north and south of the entrances were also blocked.

The raid to St Leu d'Esserent on 5 August had a lasting effect on the local civilian population of the area:

> *Raymonde Carbon:* On 5 August we had the most serious raid and bombs were dropping for two hours. At the time we had little portable gas lamps to help get to the air raid shelters and the blast from the bombs was blowing them out.

The town was assessed as 85% destroyed. Electricity and water were cut off and the food supply seriously disrupted. The German forces also began to treat the local civilians more severely. Unsurprisingly many families evacuated the area. The bombing was however of benefit to some people working in the area. Russian prisoners that had been involved in the building and assembly of the caves succeeded in making their escape, many of them joining the Maquis.

Squadron Leader Herbert E. Bates[108] had been given the task, by the Air Ministry and Director of Public Relations, of writing the story of the flying bomb only a few weeks after the first flying bombs were launched against England. As part of his investigations in France he visited the area around St Leu d'Esserent once it was liberated by the Allied land forces. In the narrative of the account that he later wrote about the flying bomb campaign, he commented on the information provided by the French underground movement in directing the Allied bombing:

> How accurate it was may be judged by the man who makes the journey along the road from Creil to St Leu and on to Précy, for that road, the railway running beside it, the branch tracks, the concrete by-ways, the block-houses, the gantries and everything else had, by September 1944, been blown to hell. All that remained for miles and miles, was something like a huge river bed of mud and rocks from which a torrent had swept practically everything else away.[109]

The Gehlmaer Industrial Unit's (ITG) team of civil engineers, which had been working with the German flying bomb organisation in northern France since before the offensive had started, was also to act as an advisory body for maintenance of the sites. Early in August it compiled a report on the flying bomb supply situation:

> Since the beginning of operations, ITG has stationed engineers in the Field Ammunition Depots 'Nordpol' and 'Leopold' [Nucourt and St Leu d'Esserent] to give technical advice and to check missiles. After about 3,500 missiles had passed through the ammunition depots the technical organisation was functioning perfectly. The personnel is now completely conversant with the equipment. Repeated air raids on 'Nordpol' and Leopold' have resulted in 'Nordpol' being put out of action altogether and in 'Leopold' being used only for the repair of missiles. Storing missiles in caves has proved unsatisfactory. Therefore, following plans drawn up by GHQ LXV A.K. [Armee Korps], mobile Field Ammunition Depots were created with storage sites in forest land.[110]

The reference to 'forest land' probably refers to the depots at sites such as Bois de Cassan and Forêt de Nieppe.

CHAPTER 15

NEW THREATS AND CITY TARGETS

On 5 August the Joint Crossbow Committee met for the third time. A major point for discussion was the future of the heavy and harassing attacks on the launching sites, and whether they could be redirected for a more profitable gain. The minutes for the meeting detail that neither form of attack on the launch sites seemed to have made any impact on the rate of firing, and were unlikely to until the number of sites in use was reduced to between 10 and 20. Also noted was that the total effort required, weekly, for harassing attacks against 40 to 50 sites would be about 2,000 to 3,000 aircraft (in terms of the United States Eighth Air Force). The Committee considered that experience to date had shown that attacks on the production, supply, and transportation of the flying bombs provided the most gain, and that the number of targets in this bracket was likely to rise and therefore require all the available bombing effort. The Committee unanimously agreed, therefore, to recommend that specific targeting of the launching sites should be 'suspended forthwith'. The heavy bombers were just not best equipped to hit such small targets.

This was not all based on speculation. Further evidence was provided by a review paper prepared on 6 August concerning the schedule of targets which was issued on 29 July. An analysis of the raids against the launching sites listed on the schedule came up with the following:

	Confirmed Category A damage	Confirmed Category B damage	Confirmed no serious damage	Not yet photographed or not interpreted	Totals
Bomber Command	1	2	6	2	11
Eighth Air Force	4	1	19	7	31
Total	5	3	25	9	42[111]

A new way of categorising damage to sites was now employed in assessing attacks on modified sites:

Category A   Concentrated groups of bursts with visible damage to one or more of the following:
i)   Foundations for launching ramps or square building;
ii)   Foundations of any other building known to be connected with the operation of the site;

iii) Or visible damage to all buildings in the immediate vicinity of the square building.

Category B   Visible damage to:
i)   rails of launching ramp;
ii)   roof or walls of square building;
iii) roof or walls of other buildings known to be used in connection with the operation of the site or hits within target area near enough to cause damage to essential elements at i) to iii) above.[112]

Since 29 July Bomber Command had conducted 13 attacks on their sites and dropped 9,447 tons of bombs, just under a third of which were delayed action. The United States Eighth Air Force dropped 2,017 tons of bombs, approximately a sixth of which were delayed action, on their 31 sites. The review paper went on to conclude about the attacks that, 'this considerable expenditure of effort appeared to have had little effect on the rate of launching by the enemy, which averaged 129 daily during the period [although German records give 140, see page 177]. It can not be said, of course, that the effort would not have been greater had not attacks taken place'.[113]

From the 42 sites examined, a confirmed 1 in 5 had been damaged, and following reconnaissance and interpretation the best that could be expected was 2 in 5. The review went on to say that the attacks against the supply depots were successful but that there had not been enough time to see the effect on the flying bomb launch rates. It also commented on the apparent speed that the Germans recovered from the attacks on the supply depots, suggesting that they had plans in place to deal with supply problems resulting from expected Allied intervention. The weight of evidence supporting the suspension of attacks on the launch sites continued to grow. On 6 August 1 Lightning, 5 Mosquitos and 99 Lancasters were detailed to attack Bois de Cassan. The heavies became split up on route to the target owing to considerable cloud. Static and interference made radio communication very difficult. In 207 Squadron's post-raid assessment they firmly laid the blame on the Controller once more:

> Just before the target the force ran into thick cumulus and the force began to split although it is thought that if the Controller had acted in time the force could have been brought down below cloud. The fighter cover too, were lost sight of by our aircraft.[114]

The Lightning did not attack and a number of aircraft did not bomb. The remaining crews continued to the target, their persistence rewarded with a clear target area and they were able to drop 238 tons of high explosive. Reconnaissance on 8 August revealed numerous fresh craters around the aiming point, damage to the storage units and several new hits on rails and roads.

There had been considerable fighter activity on the raid with resultant combats. Bomber Command aircraft claimed two Me109s as destroyed and two damaged. The fighter escort claimed three German aircraft destroyed and one damaged without loss.

Flying Officer Cupit, flying the 207 Squadron Lancaster V-Vic, thought he had released all his bombs on the target, but one hung up. Immediately his bomb aimer, Sergeant Bird, acted, jettisoning the remaining bomb in the target area. Just as the bomb parted company with the bomber the Lancaster was fired on by an Me109. The rear gunner, Sergeant Elmes, was killed and his turret taken out. The mid upper gunner received serious injury from numerous gunfire wounds to both his arms and legs, and his turret perspex shattered. The flight engineer, Sergeant Mills, also sustained serious injury and died within a few seconds. At the same time as the Me109 attacked, the Lancaster also shuddered, and was further damaged, from an explosion directly underneath the aircraft, possibly from a flak burst, possibly owing to the Me109's gunfire hitting the jettisoned bomb. The Lancaster's two inner engines were damaged, the starboard one catching fire and having to be feathered, and bits of the aircraft flew off the wings. With the fear of a further attack from the German fighter the wireless operator, Sergeant Taylor, climbed into the mid upper turret. The lack of perspex made this a particularly uncomfortable experience and the bomb aimer soon replaced the wireless operator. Both men maintained a vigil until it was clear there would be no further attacks.

Cupit's flying skills were then to be tested to the full. He had lost three of his crew, of which two were killed, his Lancaster was severely battered leaking oil and fuel, and he had to cross northern France in daylight. A Spitfire approached but did not hang around too long, possibly owing to a lack of fuel. Eventually Cupit brought his men to the French coast and began crossing the Channel. The wireless operator applied his skill and got his equipment working, thereby identifying his aircraft and getting permission to land at Ford, Sussex. Cupit then had to land without any of the usual help from his flight engineer. Throttle controls proved extremely difficult and with the aircraft juddering Cupit eventually touched down and brought his damaged Lancaster to a halt with no further injury to his crew. Four aircraft were lost on the raid. The 50 Squadron Lancaster of Flying Officer Coombs failed to return, the pilot and four others killed, two men evaded capture. The 83 Squadron Lancaster of Flight Lieutenant Drinkall fell victim to fighters, the crew of eight killed. The 83 Squadron Lancaster of Flight Lieutenant Kelly was seriously damaged in an attack with an FW190. The rear gunner was wounded and a fire started. Some of the crew baled out. However Kelly managed to bring the aircraft back, crash landing at Ford airfield, but the Lancaster was written off. The 97 Squadron Lancaster of Flying Officer Bucknell RAAF fell victim to the flak, the pilot and six of the crew killed, one man evading capture.

On the same day Bomber Command also sent 51 Halifaxes, 6 Lancasters and 5 Mosquitos to attack the rail centre at Hazebrouck, a target that had been linked with the flying bombs. Part of the fourth meeting of the Joint Crossbow Committee which would take place on 13 August (and will be further detailed later) would deal with the rail transportation of the flying bombs. Intelligence had indicated that two trains a day passed through Mouscron and arrived in the Hazebrouck area (which lay just to the north of the suspected supply depot at Forêt de Nieppes). The unloading stations, confirmed by intelligence, were listed in the revised target schedules. The Committee was to recommend attacks against the trains whilst in transit and during unloading. Bomber Command's raid took place a week before this meeting. The third Joint Crossbow Committee meeting had indicated that attacking the transportation system would be profitable. Bomber Command had obviously been given target information following this third meeting.

The attacking force whilst experiencing no cloud over the target area did have the problem of considerable haze. The markers were deemed as being well placed around the aiming point and the following main force attack achieved a strong concentration of bombing with numerous sticks falling right across some of the markers. Defences were non-existent and returning crews reported several fires. Reconnaissance later supported initial post-raid analysis revealing a concentration of craters in the sorting sidings, extensive damage to rolling stocks and rail tracks and part of the repair shops obliterated. The 51 Squadron Halifax of Flight Lieutenant Brown RNZAF failed to return and was seen to ditch and sink in flames north of Dunkirk. There were no survivors.

The raid to Bois de Cassan on 6 August all but completed Bomber Command's main period of attacks on flying bomb supply depots, although there would be two further large-scale attacks, one to Forêt de Nieppe on the night of 9/10 August and one on 18 August to L'Isle Adam (Bois de Cassan). Following the decline in German flying bomb launch rates after the attacks on St Leu d'Esserent and Nucourt in early and mid July, which at one point fell to a weekly average of 80 per day, a slight recovery had been achieved. For the first week in August an average of 140 firings per day was achieved, which comes close to the launch rates in the early days of the German offensive. However from 8 August onwards the flying bomb launch rates fell drastically and on 10 August only 22 firings were achieved. As we know, Flakregiment 155(W) was facing weather conditions unfavourable to launchings at the time and they were having to redeploy owing to the Allied land army advances. Bomber Command's attacks on the flying bomb supply lines had, in all probability compounded the regiment's problems. Tedder had asked the COPC to come up with a plan with the objective of reducing the number of flying bombs seen by the defences over England to 30 a day. The Eiderdown plan had resulted and whilst not being completed in the 24-hour period required, most of the bombing had been carried out. By mid August the German flying bomb rates had fallen dramatically and while it is not clear how much of this was due to Allied bombing attacks, the objectives of Eiderdown were virtually achieved.

On 8 August Bomber Command returned to attacking the launch sites. The raid to Chappelle Notre Dame (14 Halifaxes and 5 Mosquitos) was said to be well concentrated whilst the raid to Fromental (14 Halifaxes and 5 Mosquitos) was reported as lacking in concentration, owing to markers slightly off target, which some crews bombed with the rest of the force bombing visually. Photographic reconnaissance the next day revealed that in fact both raids were a failure with no craters or damage in the target area. One aircraft was lost on the Fromental raid. A Halifax from 347 Squadron piloted by Adjutant L Millet FFAF was hit by flak as it crossed the French coast. One crew member, Adjutant Chef Meyer, got clear of the stricken aircraft but was reported as being shot as he parachuted down.[115] All the other members of the crew were killed.

The raids to Belle Croix les Bruyères and St Philibert Ferme (both 15 Halifaxes and 5 Mosquitos) were more successful. Crews reported good concentrations and a large explosion was noted at Belle Croix les Bruyères. Photographic reconnaissance on 9 August showed numerous craters in the target areas. The launching platform at Belle Croix les Bruyères appeared damaged, whilst the platform at St Philibert Ferme was destroyed, and it was noted that a new platform appeared to be in the process of being erected. One Halifax was written off just after take-off on the St Philibert Ferme raid, from 10 Squadron. Pilot Flight Sergeant Thorne had to deal with losing control owing to failed elevators. The aircraft flew into trees and despite the aircraft being subsequently written off there were fortunately no casualties.

On 9 August seven modified sites were attacked. The raids to Coqueraux (18 Halifaxes and 5 Mosquitos), Les Landes Vielles et Neuves (15 Halifaxes and 5 Mosquitos) and Prouville (2 Lancasters, 23 Halifaxes and 5 Mosquitos) were all reported as accurate. It was believed that the following raids were less successful, however: La Neuville (2 Lancasters, 23 Halifaxes and 5 Mosquitos), where the master bomber was hit by heavy flak but managed to resume control quickly; Bois de la Haie (16 Halifaxes and 5 Mosquitos), where marking was slightly to the east of the aiming point although three large explosions were seen; Les Catelliers (15 Halifaxes and 5 Mosquitos), where marking was east of the aiming point; and Coulonvillers (19 Lancasters, 4 Halifaxes and 5 Mosquitos), where crews had difficulty in interpreting the master bomber's instructions, the difficulties being compounded by errors with the forecast winds. Follow-up reconnaissance on Coulonvillers and La Neuville backed up the assessment with no obvious damage visible.

One new crew had its operational baptism on one of these raids. It was an experience that was in stark contrast to those of fresh crews a year previously who could find themselves over the Ruhr attacking a German city, or targeting Berlin or Leipzig:

> *Flying Officer Len Skipper DFC, pilot 158 Squadron:* In July 1944 I was a pilot on Halifaxes and did a Heavy Conversion course on Halifaxes at Riccall [Yorkshire]. The aircraft were Halifax IIs and were rather the worse for wear. Ground school covered the Mark III, which we would be flying on the squadrons and we would convert at the Squadron on to the Mk III. We finished the course at Riccall and were posted to 158 Squadron at Lissett, Yorks. Our conversion course consisted of

15 minutes of 'circuits & bumps' . . . and we then did one hour on our own and that was it. Our first operation was without any second pilot or other experienced crew member. Luckily it was a V1 site at Les Landes Vielles et Neuves. . . the flying time was 3 hours 30 minutes and it was in daylight. The target was on the coast and we were over enemy territory for only a few minutes as the bombing run was from the sea. I remember a small amount of radar-controlled flak which followed us as we turned for the course home. The aircraft was C for Charlie which . . . had flown over 100 operations. You can imagine the worried looks of the ground crew when they heard their beloved aircraft was to be flown by a sprog crew on their first op! They were delighted to see us back.

The trip was so easy that I asked several other pilots about the V1 raids. They were all delighted with them as they had been doing about one a day, and although they were only three points as opposed to German ops that were four points (a tour in 4 Group was 120 points at that time), this meant that a lot of crews were doing their tours in 2 months or so and with great ease.

Other crews did not find the raids on this day as easy and three aircraft were lost. Flight Sergeant Burrows' 466 Squadron Halifax was hit by flak whilst on the raid to Coqueraux. Burrows and one other member of his crew were killed, three others became POWs and two men evaded capture. Sergeant Cass's 640 Squadron Halifax was lost on the raid to Les Landes Vielles et Neuves. The pilot and four other crew members were killed, the two others captured and becoming POWs. Flight Lieutenant Wyse's 427 Squadron Halifax did not return from the raid to La Neuville and the whole crew lost their lives.

That night, in addition to the attack on Forêt de Nieppe, the modified sites at Le Breteque (2 Lancasters, 20 Halifaxes and 5 Mosquitos), Acquet (22 Lancasters and 5 Mosquitos) and Forêt du Croc (2 Lancasters, 21 Halifaxes and 5 Mosquitos) were targeted. Accurate and concentrated raids were reported, except at La Breteque where crews were unable to hear the master bomber which resulted in some of them bombing the wrong markers. However follow-up reconnaissance revealed that none of the raids was successful. Despite some craters in the target areas no damage was revealed. This particular night had seen a large number of aircraft despatched by Bomber Command. In addition to the 311 aircraft sent to flying bomb targets, 190 aircraft attacked an oil storage dump at Forêt de Châtellerault, and a further 125 aircraft on minor operations. All the targets, with the exception of Forêt de Nieppe, were attacked before midnight, in darkness prior to moonrise. German nightfighters were certainly active trying to locate the RAF's bombers. Early in the night's operations radio intercepts informed British Intelligence that a wave of single-engine fighters of JG301 were prowling over northern France. Soon after a second wave of approximately 20 aircraft took off and headed for a searchlight concentration near Amiens. Later on, as midnight approached, the forward control of 4 *Jagddivision* (fighter division) was heard directing nightfighters of I and III NJG4 from Florennes and Juvincourt. The controller was trying to vector his fighters into the bomber streams detailed to attack either Forêt du Croc or La Breteque, which had been plotted to the west of Dieppe. Despite all this activity the nightfighters located and engaged hardly any of the bombers. Only two Lancasters were lost owing to a collision over the target, on the raid to Forêt de Châtellerault, a particularly low loss rate.

The German night aircrews not only had the problem of locating their enemy's bombers, they had to contend with being hunted themselves. Mosquitos had been active over France in support of the raids on the flying bomb targets. A 100 Group 169 Squadron Mosquito piloted by Flight Lieutenant Woodman crossed the French coast at 2248 hours and began patrolling around the German nightfighter beacon *Mucke* and the Pas de Calais area. After initial disappointment whilst investigating searchlights for contacts, at 2335 hours the British nightfighter picked up a contact on the Mosquito's radar, behind at a range of about 3,000 feet. Woodman turned starboard and his contact passed from starboard to port ahead at 10,000 feet range. The Allied airmen peered out into the darkness and caught sight of their contact orbiting a vertical searchlight, no doubt awaiting instructions from a controller. Woodman closed in to 600 feet trying to silhouette the contact against the sky and hence make an identification. Despite it being very dark, it was clear that it was single-engined and on gaining height the exhausts were recognised as those of an FW190. Woodman closed to 150 yards and fired a 3-second burst into his foe, seeing three strikes. The German nightfighter stalled, turned and dived. The Mosquito pursued maintaining contact by radar and visual sighting of the exhausts. Despite full boost being used and the Mosquito tearing along at an indicated air speed of 380 to 400 mph Woodman was unable to close the range. The German nightfighter pilot then sealed his fate as he turned starboard enabling the Mosquito to close to 200 yards. Woodman opened fire, a five-second burst, and a number of strikes registered on the FW190. Despite there being no fire the Mosquito crew, still able to see the FW190's exhausts, watched as its foe dived straight down and blew up on the ground. Woodman turned back to the searchlight to see if he could make any further contacts. On the approach another searchlight was exposed near to the original one and flashed on and off, six times. At the original searchlight a red light was flashing at its base. Woodman assumed that these were either warning signals to German nightfighters to stay away, or that the Mosquito was assumed to be a friendly aircraft and they were warning it away. The Mosquitos were still proving a major problem for the German nightfighters, particularly in support of main force raids over France.

On 10 August modified sites were targeted again. The force (15 Lancasters and 5 Mosquitos) sent to Ferme du Forestal experienced considerable cloud cover. The bombers came below the cloud and two aircraft bombed the red TI believed 100 yards from the aiming point. The other bombers identified the target visually and could see the launch platform, on which some direct hits were reported. However photographic reconnaissance on 12 August suggested that the crews had been somewhat optimistic in their initial raid assessment with no change to the target area and no visible damage to any of the installations. Three other forces were sent to modified sites (45 Lancasters and 15 Mosquitos) but owing to the cloud cover no pathfinder markers could be seen and only one aircraft actually bombed (at Oeuf-en-Ternois), visually identifying the target through a small gap in the clouds. In addition to these raids Bomber Command acted on the prioritising of fuel dumps associated with the flying bomb organisation, sending 98 Lancasters and 5 Mosquitos to Dugny near Paris, where it was believed that aviation fuel was stored. Although there were early problems with the bombing, 605 tons were dropped, and returning crew reports indicated that it became concentrated.

On 11 August four small forces, each made up of ten Lancasters and five Mosquitos, were despatched to the modified sites at Ferfay, Wemaers Cappel, Chapelle Notre Dame and La Nieppe. All attacks were reported accurate, taking place in excellent weather. Again, however these reports were not backed up by reconnaissance, with no craters or damage in the target area at Ferfay, no damage at Chapelle Notre Dame, and at La Nieppe only a few craters around the target area but no damage. That night two Mosquitos were sent to harass Trossy St Maximin, one of which aborted.

The next Bomber Command attack on flying bomb targets was on the night of 12/13 August when two forces both consisting of 20 Halifaxes and 5 Mosquitos attacked the modified sites at La Neuville and La Breteque. The Mosquitos were reported to have successfully marked the target at La Neuville and it was believed that concentrated bombing followed, three fires and two explosions reported by the returning crew. Follow-up reconnaissance was hindered by the presence of shadows from the trees but new craters were visible in the target area. The marking and bombing at La Breteque was reported as not concentrated and reconnaissance would later reveal only three craters in the target area with no visible damage, although a road was cut in two places. Two Mosquitos were also sent to continue harassing Trossy St Maximin of which one aborted.

In addition to these raids a force of 191 Lancasters, 96 Halifaxes and 10 Mosquitos were despatched to target the Opel motor factory in Rüsselheim, which Allied Intelligence had associated with flying bomb production. The bomber force dropped 866 tons and damage was later assessed by post-raid reconnaissance:

> Damage from this attack is widespread but not severe. In the Opel Works two reconstructed buildings, the loading and despatch hall, about half of a complex of buildings to the east, and a store have been burnt out and a small unidentified building has been damaged. In the town area a few houses and a shop in an unidentified industrial premises have been gutted. Further [south-east] there are points of destruction in three large housing estates and scattered craters in open country on all

sides. Three miles from the target fires are still burning in a
thickly wooded area and a near by village has been partially
devastated.[116]

This night was the first that summer in which the hours of darkness allowed
a heavy bomber force to penetrate into central Germany. In addition to the
raid on Rüsselheim another heavy bomber force was sent to Brunswick.
The intention was for the two forces, just after 2300 hours, to reach the
continent simultaneously, their approach to be covered by a Mandrel screen
operating from 2130 hours. It was also hoped that the attacks on the flying
bomb targets at La Neuville and La Breteque would draw a few nightfighter
Gruppen towards Dieppe, which were bolstered in numbers by a
diversionary sweep of 150 aircraft. Small Mosquito forces sent to Kiel and
Frankfurt were also planned in an attempt to confuse the German
nightfighter controllers.

The planning did have some effect in confusing the enemy and the
Brunswick bomber force had a fairly combat free route to target. After the
target was a different matter, when the fighters arrived. Also strong winds
blew some bombers off track and into flak defended areas. Of the 27
aircraft lost on the raid Bomber Command estimated 15 losses to fighters
and 8 to flak. The Rüsselheim force was engaged from the Brussels area to
the target and back with numerous combats. Of the 20 aircraft lost Bomber
Command estimated 12 losses to fighters and 5 to flak. Returning Bomber
Command airmen also claimed success against their aerial counterparts; 10
enemy aircraft destroyed, 3 probables and 2 damaged on the Brunswick
raid; 2 enemy aircraft destroyed and 4 damaged on the Rüsselheim raid.

The poor bombing results achieved on the 12/13 August raid to
Rüsselheim led to a second Bomber Command force being sent back on
25/26 August. Bomber Command reached a new record for the war on this
night with 1,311 sorties conducted. The attack on the Opel works at
Rüsselheim involved 412 Lancasters, despatched to drop 1,451 tons.
Accurate marking led to successful bombing being reported, which was
indeed partially true. Follow-up reconnaissance revealed severe damage
throughout the plant with virtually all the major units hit. The Labour Camp
to the west of the plant had been virtually obliterated and numerous storage
buildings and railway sheds were also damaged. There was also some
damage to some of the residential properties close to the factory. Research
by Martin Middlebrook and Chris Everitt for the *Bomber Command War
Diaries* revealed that the 'Forge and the gearbox assembly departments
were put out of action for several weeks, but 90 per cent of the machine
tools in other departments escaped damage. The assembly line and part of
the pressworks were able to recommence work 2 days later and lorry
assembly was unaffected because of considerable stocks of ready-made
parts. 179 people were killed in the raid but their nationalities were not
recorded'.[117]

Since the 12/13 August attack the military situation had changed and
Bomber Command planners found it possible to route the bomber force
near Caen and south of Paris, without the enemy gaining much radar

information or ground reported plots until the bombers were about 200 miles from target. There was also the removal of fighters from airfields in east France along the route, but it was realised that this would be at the cost of strengthening the forces available in Germany. The nightfighters' success would depend on how quickly they received warning of the bombers' approach and whether they came far enough westwards to meet them. Bomber Command also sent a bomber force to Darmstadt, which was very close to Rüsselheim, with the two forces following the same route to the targets. Then 5 Group would attack Darmstadt at the close of the Rüsselheim attack.

The main bomber force was not plotted by the German controllers until it was far into eastern France and then, approximately ³/₄ hour before the bombing was scheduled to start, the nightfighters moved in, at Saarbrücken, near the Franco-German border. There were a considerable number of engagements but few losses. As the bombers reached a searchlight belt the opposition grew, German nightfighters working with the beams, and then engaging the bombers over Rüsselheim and Darmstadt almost as soon as each attack began. The German nightfighters became more aggressive as the bombers turned for home, with half the raid's losses on the leg from Wiesbaden to north of Saarbrücken. Apart from the odd isolated incident, the majority of combats occurred in a continuous period covering the bombers' time over German territory proper. One bomber crew had more than just the enemy to worry about. The 156 Squadron Lancaster of Flight Lieutenant Cuthill had just left the target area when it had some company. No. 156 Squadron's gunnery leader Squadron Leader Allen later recorded the incident:

> . . . while still silhouetted the mid upper gunner sighted a Lancaster on the port quarter above at a range of approx. 400 yards. The mid upper gunner warned the captain and the other Lancaster passed towards the starboard quarter up. When the other Lancaster was on the starboard quarter up one of its gunners, probably the rear, opened fire. The first burst went over the top of our aircraft . . . Almost immediately fire was reopened and damage to our aircraft sustained . . . All the crew of our aircraft comment on excellent visibility at the time and no excuse whatsoever for this attack. It is thought that the other Lanc may have been firing at a FW190, which attacked our aircraft at approximately the same time. If this was the case the fire was hopelessly inaccurate.[118]

Indeed Flight Lieutenant Cuthill's Lancaster had been attacked, his rear gunner sighting the FW190 coming in from 150 yards on the port quarter, just after its fire passed astern. The rear gunner maintained fire from 100 yards range right through the attack until the FW190 broke away diving steeply. The rear gunner would later claim his enemy's aircraft as damaged. The damage to the Lancaster, from the friendly fire, was two starboard panels in the rear turret shot away, one port panel smashed and the reflector sight smashed by a bullet.

Losses on the Rüsselheim raid totaled 15 Lancasters (with two more written off in crashes in England) and on the Darmstadt raid 7 Lancasters. Bomber Command put down 4 losses to flak, 13 to fighters and 5 to unknown causes. Bomber Command airmen claimed 7 enemy aircraft destroyed, 1 probable and 2 damaged.

The Joint Crossbow Committee met again for its fourth meeting on 13 August. There were a few changes in the committee personnel. Air Commodore Grierson was replaced by Air Commodore Pelly as chairman. Air Commodore J.A. Easton, Director of Intelligence (Research) also attended as an Air Staff representative as it was now felt that a representative of the Combined Operations Planning Committee need not attend as this body was only really associated with the tactical side of operations. The prioritising of flying bomb targets now became much more complex. Target schedule number 34 detailed seven priorities for attack. First priority was industrial production, second liquid oxygen plants, third supply depots (Mery-Sur-Oise and L'Isle Adam II and IIa (just south of Bois de Cassan), fourth Benito (navigational beam) stations, fifth flying bomb unloading stations, sixth launch sites and seventh secondary industrial targets. Notably Forêt de Nieppe, Nucourt, Thiverny, St Leu d'Esserent, Rilly-la-Montagne and Trossy St Maximin were all suspended from attack. There was also an obvious shift of emphasis in the targeting priorities with the V2 rocket threat starting to gain in importance in the scheme of things.

Despite the new priorities for flying bomb targets there followed a five-day pause in Bomber Command's counter-measure responsibilities against launch sites or supply depots. However there would now be a new type of flying bomb target attacked by Bomber Command. On 31 July the Air Ministry had sent a cypher to the headquarters of both the Air Defence of Great Britain and Allied Expeditionary Air Force stating that:

> Increasing numbers of flying bombs are being launched from area Ostend/Dutch islands and despite intensive efforts no sites have yet been detected in this area. Bombs appear to be launched between Knocke and Noordwal, with main concentration coming from between Nieuwe Sluis and West Schouwen.[119]

The Air Ministry went on further to ask for plots to be made, by radar, of launched flying bombs so that an extrapolation could be made to the point of launch. It was suspected that V1 flying bombs were now being air launched, and not for the first time high ranking officers were prepared to act upon the suspicions. Indeed Sir Charles Portal, Chief of the Air Staff, wrote to his Deputy Chief of the Air Staff, Air Vice-Marshal N.H. Bottomley, on 2 August, stating that it was unlikely that there were launching sites over 150 miles from London and that the probability was that the flying bombs in question were air launched.

I hope that Intelligence will not be over cautious about reaching conclusions, as this simply means a waste of time and does not in any way enhance their reputation. What we want to do now is to act quickly on probabilities, not to wait for certainties, and this applies to all things connected with anti-Crossbow work.

I should have thought that the answer to the problem would be a combination of Intruder patrols off the Dutch islands and strong bomber attacks against the airfields, which the He 111s are believed to use.[120]

This was acted upon and on 3 August a cypher arrived at Bomber Command from the Air Ministry, asking to amend the current target's schedule and adding as special targets of opportunity, the airfields at Venlo, Eindhoven and Gilze Rijen. Bomber Command was unable to attack these special targets immediately, owing to its commitment to the sustained attacks on the supply depots. At the fourth meeting of the Joint Crossbow Committee on 13 August, however, the necessity of attacking airfields associated with air launched flying bombs was highlighted:

The enemy is known to be using certain airfields in the Low Countries and France for the operation of Heinkel 111's specially fitted to launch the flying bomb. The number of flying bombs launched by this method is not large and there are at least eight suitable airfields in the Low Countries, and also one in France which intelligence indicates has been used for this purpose. These nine airfields have been shown in the attached schedule and it is recommended they be attacked if airborne launching activity resumes after the present lull.[121]

On 15 August a massive force of 1,004 aircraft was despatched to attack the nine airfields associated with the air-launched flying bombs, escorted by 480 fighter aircraft. An hour previous, 144 fighters patrolled the various targets. Approximately 1,100 American bombers attacked other airfield targets. Not only were these operations an attempt to disrupt the air-launched flying bomb programme but it also constituted a massive attack against the Luftwaffe night and day fighters. With a renewed offensive against German industry beginning to feature more prominently in the minds of the Allied Commanders, they hoped to accomplish a devastating setback for their opposing air force.

In perfect visibility all the attacking bomb aimers were able to aim their destructive loads visually. There was absolutely no airborne opposition seen by any of the bombers. Photographs taken immediately after the raids revealed successful attacks and Allied intelligence concluded the following:[122]

Target	Aircraft despatched	Runways temporarily unserviceable	Airfield heavily cratered
Volkel	110 Lancasters 4 Mosquitos	2 out of 2	Yes except south-west corner
Le Culot	110 Lancasters 6 Mosquitos	2 out of 2	Yes
St Trond	109 Lancasters	3 out of 3	Yes except north section
Eindhoven	108 Halifaxes 9 Lancasters	Not available	
Tirlemont	109 Halifaxes 9 Lancasters	No runways	Yes except south corner
Gilze Rijen	103 Lancasters 4 Mosquitos 1 Lightning	3 out of 3	Yes except north section
Deelen	94 Lancasters 5 Mosquitos	Not available	
Brussels/ Melsbroek	94 Halifaxes 16 Lancasters	2 out of 3	Yes except north-east and south-west corner
Soesterberg	83 Lancasters 30 Halifaxes	2 out of 3	Craters not heavily concentrated

The cost to Bomber Command was three Lancasters. Two of these were lost on the raid to Deelen where there had been some opposition from flak. The 97 Squadron Lancaster piloted by Flying Officer Lindsay RAAF was hit by the flak over the target and was forced to ditch in the sea. Fortunately all the men were rescued within two hours. Dutchman Flight Lieutenant Overgaauw RAFVR, pilot of a 207 Squadron Lancaster, was conducting his 34th operation on the raid to Deelen. On seeing the location of the target at briefing he remarked that his parents lived only a few miles from the airfield. Flight Lieutenant Overgaauw's 'homecoming' ended tragically when the Lancaster fell to earth near Arnhem with a total loss of life. The third aircraft lost was the 428 Squadron Lancaster piloted by Warrant Officer Jakeman RCAF, on the raid to Soesterberg, which exploded resulting in the death of five of the crew and the imprisonment of the pilot and his flight engineer.

Bomber Command would continue to harass any attempts to repair damaged airfields over the next few weeks. On 15/16, 23, 25/26, 26/27 and 28/29 August small Mosquito forces dropped their loads on Venlo. On 26/27, 28/29 and 29/30 August small Mosquito forces similarly attacked Le Culot. On 16, 25/26 and 26/27 August Mosquitos harassed Deelen. In the same period Eindhoven, Deelen and the airfield at Roye-Amy would also be targeted by American heavies.

The second week of August involved major organisational changes for Flakregiment 155(W) owing to the progress of the Allied invasion. The

Americans had advanced into Brittany and were swinging round across France taking Nantes, Angers and Le Mans. The Germans had some success counter-attacking towards Avranches but slowly the Allied armies closed in around the Falaise pocket, threatening to encircle the German forces. On 15 August Allied forces landed in the south of France. The situation was becoming more and more desperate for the German Army, which was certainly recognised in orders sent to Wachtel's unit.

On 7 August an order was issued by the German Army prohibiting the building of new 'reprisal weapon' installations south of the Somme. Repairs were permitted only if there was a chance of firing within a short period. The order also required that the launch site organisation should be extended northwards, with the flying bomb's range the limiting factor. Flakregiment 155(W) began to regroup north of the Somme, prepare for the rapid redeployment of the *III* and *IV Abteilungen*, and reconnoitre areas further north. On the evening of 9 August the firing readiness of *IV Abteilung* was cancelled. The next day *III Abteilung* followed suit, with orders to move north. At the time the weather conditions were unfavourable for firing and with this in mind, combined with serious transportation problems, a decision was made to scale back on firings. This was further compounded when the regiment was informed by the Army that the supply of missiles was likely to be disrupted between 11 and 16 August owing to troop movements. As such LXV Armee Korps ordered the regiment to use their missiles sparingly with firings conducted when the weather conditions were favourable. With *Abteilungen* redeploying and regrouping at the same time as the low supplies were expected the regiment regarded the limitations on firings as timely.

From 1 to 15 August Flakregiment 155(W) noted 62 raids against flying bomb launch sites. Serious damage was recorded at 11 sites, medium damage at 10 and slight damage at 8. They also lost 18 of their personnel killed or missing and 53 wounded. During the period their main concern, however, had been the general situation with regard to the Allied invasion.

CHAPTER 16

CLOSURE

In the middle of August the numbers of flying bombs reaching England fell sharply. Despite this, further attacks on launch sites by Allied heavy bombers were deemed necessary albeit in a very scaled-down fashion. On 18 August the modified launch sites were again attacked by the Bomber Command heavies, with eight small forces consisting of four Lancasters each sent to Wemaers Cappel, La Nieppe, Fromental, Vincly, Anderbelck, Westrove, L'Hey and Bois St Rémy. The attacking Lancasters experienced variable cloud cover and bombing was conducted through the gaps. Of those targets that later underwent reconnaissance, photographs of Fromental, Westrove, L'Hey and Bois St Rémy would reveal no damage and failed attacks. At Vincly the reconnaissance showed a few craters in the target area and a near miss to the launching platform. Two aircraft were lost on the raids: Pilot Officer Austin, piloting a 103 Squadron Lancaster and detailed to attack La Nieppe, was killed with two other members of his crew, the other four men becoming POWs; the 576 Squadron Lancaster, piloted by Flight Lieutenant Bibby and detailed to attack Wemaers Cappel, was also lost. Five of the crew were killed, the pilot and one other crew member becoming POWs.

In addition to the attacks on the launch sites Bomber Command sent a force of 158 Lancasters and 11 Mosquitos to the suspected supply depot at L'Isle Adam, close to Bois de Cassan, as identified in the Joint Crossbow Committee meeting of 13 August, dropping 770 tons in a scattered attack which cut roads and partially destroyed a small shed in the centre of the target area. There may have been further damage but the presence of trees hindered assessment of photographs.

A week would pass before there were any further attacks on flying bomb targets by Bomber Command. The minutes of the Joint Crossbow Committee meeting on 20 August clearly show that there had been a change in emphasis from counter-attacking the flying bomb threat to focusing on the details of potential rocket attacks. The working committee also interestingly noted in their minutes of 17 August the following:

> The working committee noted the expenditure of 1232 tons of bombs on launching sites in the week ending 0600 hours, 16 August, and the change in damage status of only one site of the fifteen attacked due to bombing. It noted further that in 17

attacks on 15 targets, involving 366 aircraft, only in the case of 7 targets were any hits obtained within the target area. The self immolation of Bois de la Haie and of Houpeville however was regarded as a Good Thing.[123]

Yet again the committee set up to examine the flying bomb counter-measures was highlighting the poor rate of return, with regard actual damage caused, for attacks made against the modified launch sites. The surmised value of the harassing nature of the attacks must have still held sway when selecting targets, however, for the modified launch sites still continued to be targeted. On 25 August Bomber Command attacks on Vincly (12 Lancasters), Wemaers Cappel (17 Halifaxes) and Ferfay (14 Halifaxes) were reported as good but reconnaissance photographs revealed them as failures. The raid on Chapelle Notre Dame (16 Halifaxes and 3 Mosquitos) was similarly reported as good and reconnaissance did later show a near miss and blast damage to buildings. Watten was attacked by a large force (2 Lancasters, 92 Halifaxes and 5 Mosquitos despatched) and it was reported as an accurate raid. Three aircraft were lost on the raid: the 10 Squadron Halifax of Flying Officer Walton (pilot and four others killed, two evaders); the 640 Squadron Halifax of Pilot Officer White (no survivors); and the 158 Squadron Halifax of Pilot Officer Fletcher. Fletcher's aircraft was damaged by flak, wounding him and three of his crew. Despite then losing one engine and a loss of power in two others, the Halifax was brought back to Woodbridge in Suffolk, though later written off. Two aircraft were lost on the raid to Vincly. Flight Lieutenant Haggis, piloting a 218 Squadron Lancaster, was killed with all his crew. Flying Officer Cossens RNZAF, piloting a 514 Squadron Lancaster, managed to bring his flak-damaged aircraft back to base but it was later written off.

On 27 August the large site at Mimoyecques was detailed for attack by 40 Lancasters, 176 Halifaxes and 10 Mosquitos, with two aiming points to receive the attentions of the RAF heavies. Returning crews reported a good concentration of bombs around the first aiming point but with the second aiming point scheduled for attack just after the first attack smoke and dust drifted across and made accurate identification difficult. However a good concentration was believed. Reconnaissance later revealed a reasonably successful attack with the odd direct hit.

The culmination of Bomber Command's attacks against the flying bomb installations in France took place on 28 August when 12 separate forces were sent to modified sites. This was to be the largest number of single targets, in the whole flying bomb counter-offensive, attacked by Bomber Command in a day or night operation.

Target and number of aircraft	Initial raid assessment	Photographic reconnaissance of the target area (where taken)
Fromental 12 Lancasters,	Excellent weather reported, but markers overshot and	No damage was visible.

5 Mosquitos	the crews were instructed to bomb short. Some scatter was reported.	
Wemaers Cappel 10 Lancasters	Excellent weather reported, good concentration of bombing believed with some overshooting.	No new craters and no obvious damage.
Vincly 10 Lancasters	Clear weather reported. Bombing scattered although some bursts were seen across the aiming point.	Not available.
Chapelle Notre Dame 10 Lancasters	Excellent weather and an accurate concentration of bombing reported.	No damage was visible.
L'Hey 2 Lancasters, 9 Halifaxes, 5 Mosquitos	Clear weather and accurate concentration reported on the markers.	No inclined ramp visible and no attempts made to fill in craters. Site appeared to have been abandoned.
Ferme du Grand Bois 2 Lancasters, 10 Halifaxes, 5 Mosquitos	Good weather and most of the crews were able to bomb visually. Apart from two undershoots a good concentration was reported.	Photos taken but assessment difficult due to tree shadows and poor quality of the pictures.
Fresnoy 10 Halifaxes	Nil to complete cloud cover reported by crews. The target was visually identified but results were difficult to assess although some bomb bursts were seen wide of the aiming point.	Not available.
Anderbelck 10 Halifaxes	Good visibility and a good concentration of bombing reported.	One crater on the site of one of the buildings but the site appeared abandoned.
Ferme du Forestal 10 Halifaxes	3/10ths cloud cover experienced but good visibility. Target was visually identified and checked by the attack on the adjacent target. Bursts were seen to straddle the aiming point.	Tree shadows hindered interpretation but there appeared to be no damage. Some of the craters had been filled in, apart from two lying between two buildings. There were no tracks passing these craters.
Oeuf-en-Ternois 2 Lancasters, 10 Halifaxes, 5 Mosquitos	Markers were well placed in good visibility. Some crews could not hear the master bomber and there was some undershooting.	Not available.
Bois St Rémy	In clear weather the target	Not available.

| 8 Halifaxes | was identified visually. There were some undershoots but bomb bursts were seen in the target area. | |
| *Ferfay* 10 Halifaxes | Target visually identified in clear weather and a fair concentration was reported with some undershooting. | No damage visible. |

Two aircraft were lost on the raids. The 420 Squadron Halifax of Flight Sergeant Reid RCAF was hit by flak on the raid to Anderbelck and the bomb aimer was severely wounded. Reid brought the aircraft back to England, landing at Woodbridge, still with a full bombload as the bomb doors had jammed. The 550 Squadron Lancaster of Flying Officer Beeson failed to return from the raid to Wemaers Cappel. The pilot and three of his crew were captured. Sergeants J.K. Norgate, J.A. Trayhorn and H.S. Picton were killed. This was to be the last aircraft lost, and these three young airmen the last fatalities, on raids against the flying bomb installations in northern France.

On 23 August most of the personnel of Flakregiment 155(W) had moved into new headquarters in Roubaix. The rapid Allied advance and continued disruption of German transport caused further chaos. The Allied armies had closed the Falaise pocket inflicting substantial losses of manpower and equipment on the Germans, and were now driving rapidly through France liberating Paris on 25 August. On 26 August, for the first time since the full flying bomb offensive had opened, no launchings took place. On 25 August the last transports of III and IV *Abteilungen* left the area south of the Somme. On 30 August II and IV *Abteilungen* were ordered to move to rest camps in central Holland, with the III *Abteilung* to begin preparation for a move. The I *Abteilung* was ordered to remain operational until the Allies had forced surrender and then only when all the equipment had been destroyed. On 31 August the situation had reached crisis point. II, III and IV *Abteilungen* were all withdrawing and demolition work had begun on equipment. I *Abteilung* was still conducting firings until 04.00 hours on 1 September when it too received the orders to withdraw. By then the regiment was in full retreat entailing a considerable loss of equipment and the rapid Allied advance would cut off many of the regiment's troops.

By the beginning of September 1944 the main threat against England from the flying bombs had been overcome. Despite the fact that the Allied land armies had overrun the French flying bomb launch sites the Allies still considered the air-launched flying bombs to be a threat. On 3 September Bomber Command aircraft conducted another major attack on some of the airfields associated with them. As before, this attack was ordered not only to prevent the operations of the flying bomb carrying Heinkels, but also to seriously disrupt the German nightfighter organisation. German targets were once more beginning to feature regularly in operational orders sent to Bomber Command squadrons.

The airfields had been previously attacked on 15 August but there had been sufficient repairs to warrant further attacks. Three main routes were chosen for the attacking bombers. One stream crossed the Dutch coast north of The Hague, to target Deelen and Soesterburg, A second stream crossed at Overflakee targeting Gilze Rijen and Venlo and the third stream crossed at Beveland to target Eindhoven and Volkel. At these points the bombers met 16 squadrons of Spitfires and in the case of Venlo with two squadrons of Mustangs. A further two flights of Mustangs covered the Mosquitos which were detailed to mark Venlo and Volkel and went in over Zuider Zee. Bomber Command received evidence that the Germans plotted all the bomber routes but there was no aerial resistance seen on any of the attacks, put down to the chaotic nature of the retreating land forces. Some flak was experienced at the airfields.

Target	Aircraft despatched	Narrative of Attack	Initial reconnaissance summary
Gilze Rijen	108 Lancasters	Attacking bombers experienced 5/10 cloud although visual identification was still possible. Red markers were deemed to be accurate and a concentrated attack followed. These were later obscured but the attack continued on some yellow markers. The area was reported as 'well and truly plastered'.	The bulk of the attack fell in northern half of target area, approximately 90 craters were identifiable over the 3 runways. Two runways were serviceable for approximately 1,000 yards.
Eindhoven	110 Lancasters	Attackers experienced 4/10 cloud. Marking reported as accurate and most of the bombing was seen to fall in the triangle created by the runways.	70 craters visible on the runways and all three deemed temporarily out of action.
Venlo	105 Halifaxes, 9 Lancasters, 6 Mosquitos	3/10 over target but target area clearly seen. Marking deemed as good and an accurate concentration reported.	N/A
Soesterburg	105 Halifaxes, 9 Mosquitos	Attack reported heavy on runways, through 5/10 cloud, and some buildings seen to explode.	N/A
Deelen	103 Lancasters, 3 Mosquitos	Attacking bombers orbited the airfield until a suitable gap opened in the 5 to 7/10 cloud. Marking	The target area was not fully covered but at least 60 craters were seen in

		deemed accurate and a concentrated attack was reported.	partial cover of the runways.
Volkel	105 Halifaxes, 9 Lancasters, 4 Mosquitos	The aiming point was visually identified and bombed by most of the crews. Other crews bombed markers after correction from the master bomber. The runways were reported as heavily bombed with buildings and 2 'dumps' hit.	75 craters were visible on two runways and deemed temporarily out of action

The attacking bombers experienced no fighter opposition at all. The 426 Squadron Halifax of Pilot Officer Lamb RCAF, detailed for the Volkel raid, crashed soon after take-off near Cambridge, and the pilot and three of his crew were killed. The 51 Squadron Halifax of Warrant Officer Potts was written off after returning from the raid to Venlo and force landing, fortunately with no casualties.

The 347 Squadron Halifax of Adjutant Rouillay FFAF was hit by flak on the raid to Venlo. Other crews witnessed the demise of Rouillay's aircraft and saw three parachutes leave the stricken bomber. However the pilot and four of his crew were to be killed, with the two surviving airmen caught. Squadron Leader Frank Lord DFC had been detailed to take his 77 Squadron crew to attack Venlo. His flight engineer, Pilot Officer Thomas Fox, recalls the raid:

> The bomb aimer had not yet arrived back from his refresher course so Frank had to visit the Bombing Leader to loan a bomb aimer from another crew. . . We set off that night with a new man in the crew and by all accounts he had done a super job on the bombing run. The flak was a bit rough to say the least and we received engine damage which caused us to 'limp' home and later over the North Sea we were beginning to run low in fuel and at the top of all that, we were told to land away on a designated airfield in Suffolk because of fog which had settled over the Yorkshire airfields. We crossed the English coast and after a struggle we landed at Hethel airfield which was actually the wrong one, but who cared, we got down safely. This was an American Liberator bomber base where we were treated very well indeed and had to stay there for 10 days until our aircraft was repaired and made airworthy.[124]

(Whilst at Hethel Pilot Officer Fox also had the memorable experience of meeting film star James Stewart, then a major with the Eighth Air Force.)

The fact that the attacking bombers had not had any fighter opposition on the raids to the airfields, created considerable frustration for the German airmen and soldiers witnessing the attacks. Despite ideal weather for fighter operations, lack of fuel and aircraft kept the Luftwaffe's airmen at bay.

Many watched as the Allied bombers had free reign over their airfields, seeing the bombs leave the bomb bays in clear weather, with only flak offering any defence.[125]

Even though the relevant airfields had been seriously hit, there would still be further attacks against England from air-launched flying bombs, but southern England would not experience anything like the scale of the 1944 summer offensive. RAF Bomber Command's main offensive to counter the flying bomb threat finished with the operations against the airfields on 3 September. Targeting priorities returned once more to the attack on Germany, in particular synthetic oil production and the German transportation system, although support to Allied ground troops was often called for. The Air Ministry took back direct control of the RAF's heavies, from the Supreme Headquarters AEAF. For many of the aircrew of Bomber Command, the change of emphasis passed unnoticed as they just looked ahead to the next operation and completing their tour.

From the opening of the German flying bomb offensive on the night of 12/13 June 1944 to 5th September 1944, 3,463 flying bombs were destroyed by the Allied fighter, gun and balloon defences of southern England from 6,725 observed and an estimated 9,000 launched[126] (the diary of Flakregiment 155(W), whilst not giving complete statistics, recorded over 8,500 flying bombs fired up until the end of August).

From 16 September 1944 to 14 January 1945, a further 1,200 air-launched V1 flying bombs would be directed at England, only 638 of which were observed by the defences. The fighter and the guns accounted for 403, and of the remainder 66 fell on the London Civil Defence Region, 1 on Manchester and the remainder elsewhere. During this period Bomber Command would still have a small involvement in counter-measure responsibilities, with small attacks carried out against airfields associated with air-launched flying bombs from He111s. In March 1945 the Germans were able to launch new versions of the flying bomb at England, from launch sites in Holland. In fact 275 flying bombs were launched, but the fighter and gun defences only had to deal with 125. Only 34 penetrated the defences from which 13 reached targets.[127]

In total 6,184 civilians were killed throughout the offensive, 17,981 were seriously injured, 23,000 homes were destroyed with approximately one million damaged. The summer of 1944 had seen the main German flying bomb offensive and despite considerable damage and disruption, the civilian morale in southern England had not collapsed to the extent the Germans hoped for. The main threat from the flying bomb had been seen off, but there was still no respite. On 8 September 1944 there was an explosion in a housing estate in Chiswick, west London, which killed three people. Further similar explosions followed and were initially reported as gas explosions. In fact a new menace had arrived. It would continue to cause further loss of life and serious injury until March 1945; both in Britain and on the continent (notably Antwerp). Unlike the flying bombs there would be no audible warning as these missiles approached. The V2 rocket threat had materialised.

CHAPTER 17

FINAL ANALYSIS

The Allied bombing counter-offensive had attempted to disrupt seriously the ability of the Germans to launch their flying bomb attacks. Sir Arthur Harris, writing after the war, claimed a success against the ski sites:

> In December 1943, there began a most successful attack, in which Bomber Command played some part, on 56 sites for launching flying bombs in the Pas de Calais and another eight on the Cherbourg peninsula. These objectives were naturally very small, but they were well within Oboe range and both Bomber Command and the Americans were able to bomb them so accurately that the enemy was forced to abandon the whole system which he had originally worked out for the launching of flying bombs . . . They would have been able to launch a considerably greater number of flying bombs than those which were subsequently used, but they had the great disadvantage that they were easily detected from the air and vulnerable to air attack. By forcing the enemy to abandon this first method of launching flying bombs the Allied bombers gained about six months' vital respite for Southern England, and, when the flying bombs were eventually launched, the enemy was compelled to use a much less efficient form of temporary site.[128]

When the flying bombs started appearing over southern England Harris had been reluctant to use his forces on what he considered was a diversion:

> . . . and the enormous bomber effort that had to be brought to bear on the launching sites was certainly one of the major contributory causes of the long respite which German industry had from air attack. During the second half of June, Bomber Command dropped more than 16,000 tons of bombs on targets connected with V-weapons, mostly on launching sites, and up to the beginning of September, until the allied armies occupied the Pas de Calais, a further 44,000 tons of bombs. This 60,000 tons of bombs was equivalent to one month's bombing at a time when the bomber offensive was at its height.[129]

What is quite clear from the research is that once more Harris's airmen and groundcrews took up their responsibilities with determination. Of course most men had very little choice about whether or not they could fly on a raid. But they did, despite the loss rates, particularly high during the period known as the Battle of Berlin, despite losing friends and colleagues and despite being required to conduct more operations to complete a tour of duty than they would have initially expected.

Bomber Command's performance as part of the flying bomb counter-offensive depended upon the successful use of the weaponry available; the aircraft, the bombs and the target marking methods. The aircraft had been designed for a strategic bombing offensive, attacking large targets. In response to political pressure Bomber Command had been asked to attack very small targets, the flying bomb ski sites, during December 1943 and January 1944. Harris had been reluctant to commit his force, he knew the limitations of his weaponry. One of the main problems being finding the targets. Target marking incorporating Oboe and/or visual identification was developed. Each method had its benefits and its limitations. The airmen of 8 Group still advocated the use of Oboe in precision attacks. Airmen of 5 Group airmen remained loyal to visual identification and marking. At a 627 Squadron (5 Group) briefing in May 1944 Leonard Cheshire had said 'What on earth was the use of an Oboe target marker half a mile beyond or to the side of a V1 site which was only a few yards wide and one hundred yards long?'[130]

However the raids against the ski sites were only a partial success in terms of effort required against damage caused. As we have seen, the actual damage done to the sites themselves was patchy and it is questionable as to the exact reason why the Germans changed to the modified launching system. Nevertheless they did change, and part of the reason given was because of the susceptibility of the ski sites to bombing raids and the effect the raids were having on the work force constructing the sites. All this required further resources on the Germans' part. The United States Strategic Bombing Survey (USSBS) claimed that the attacks against the ski sites had delayed the beginning of the flying bomb attacks by three to four months. However, there was another factor in providing southern England's six months vital respite claimed by Harris. Flakregiment 155(W) had actually been ready to start launching in early 1944. German industry let them down. Probably the greatest contribution made by the Allied bombers therefore, in particular Bomber Command, to delaying the opening of the flying bomb attacks had been the area bombing attacks, notably the raids on Kassel in October 1943. The USSBS claimed that:

> Although there is no evidence that bombing caused a decrease in output, failure to meet planned production schedules for V-1 is attributable partly to the direct effects of attacks on known or suspected manufacturing plants, partly to the bombing of plants whose connection was unknown at the time and partly to the gradual disintegration of German industry and transport which led to shortage of materials and delays in deliveries.[131]

The delay did of course mean the Allied land forces were able to establish a foothold on Normandy before the flying bombs had the chance of disrupting the preparations and opening phase of Western Europe's liberation. The raids carried out against the ski sites did also have some value in providing operational data for precision attacks, which could be applied when Bomber Command began committing its force to the support of Overlord, the disruption of the French and Belgian transport system.

The Allies, at the time, believed that the raids against the ski sites between December 1943 and June 1944 had been successful. The Germans were also successful in drawing the Allied bombing effort on to the ski sites, sites that had become redundant early in 1944, by using the bluff of continuing construction work. From the end of January to early June 1944, with other Allied air forces continuing the attacks on the ski sites and with the demands of operation Overlord approaching, Bomber Command, except for a very few small Mosquito raids, took no further part in the flying bomb counter-offensive.

However, when the Germans began conducting the flying bomb attack on England in earnest, mid June 1944, Bomber Command was called upon to attack the suspected supply sites. But political pressure because of mounting civilian casualties again forced the bombers to also be used in further attacks on the modified and ski launching sites. It would take a few weeks before it was realised that the ski sites were not being used. Target lists grew and certain targets only suspected of a connection with the flying bombs were placed on the list. Once a confirmed connection had been made between the three supply depots at St Leu d'Esserent, Nucourt and Rilly-la-Montagne and the modified launch sites, Bomber Command was then able to make a major contribution to disrupting the flying bomb supply lines. Bomber Command raids on all three targets, in combination with smaller attacks by the American heavy bomber forces, resulted in significant reductions in the German launch rates, lessening the chance of the defensive guns and fighters in England being swamped, and reducing the number of bombs that the English civilians in the south had to suffer. During the 23 days from 16 June to 8 July 1944, the diary of Flakregiment 155(W) records 3,463 flying bombs launched. In the next 23 days, to the end of July, the diary records 2,453 flying bombs launched. As Bomber Command dropped 95% of the bomb tonnage on the supply depots (see Appendix II), and the significant attacks took place in the first half of July, the RAF bomber squadrons and their airmen can justifiably claim to have reduced the scale of the flying bomb launchings by at least 1,000. There was also a substantial decrease in flying bombs launched after July, and although Bomber Command maintained attacks on the German flying bomb supply organisation, this reduction was mainly owing to the advance of the Allied land armies and subsequent retreat of Flakregiment 155(W).

The lowering of the German launch rates also assisted with the success of England's gun and fighter defences. The defences accounted for 41 per cent of the flying bombs observed between 30 June and 5 July. In the next week they accounted for 57 per cent. The numbers reaching London fell from 48 per cent of those observed to 34 per cent. In mid July there had been a re-deployment of the defences and, whilst not part of the Allied planning, the lower flying bomb launch rates resulting from the bombing of Nucourt and St Leu d'Esserent, gave some breathing space while the guns were moved. From then on the defences' success rate rose. In the five weeks prior to the re-deployment the success rate was 43 per cent. In the week after this rose to 50 per cent. This continued rising to 74 per cent in the third week in August, 62 per cent the next week and 83 per cent until the end of the flying bomb attacks from northern France.[132]

However although attacks on the supply depots were bearing fruit, target lists would again grow as further suspected supply sites/depots were added and more modified launch sites were identified. Suspected industrial production centres, airfields connected with the air-launched flying bombs, fuel depots and command centres were also added to the lists. If the bombers had maintained a focus on the known supply depots then quite probably Wachtel's regiment would have had to find alternative supply methods when time was running out for them as the Allied armies advanced from the Normandy beachhead into France. The large Crossbow target lists, with all possibilities covered, combined with the requirements in support of Overlord did lead to a dissipation of force and a considerable waste of effort, aircraft and airmen. Moreover, the USSBS claims that after the flying bomb attacks on England had started, the Allied bombing had little effect. The research for this book suggests that, on the contrary, the attacks on the three main supply depots did have a significant effect in reducing German firing rates.

Alas the RAF was not to receive the political recognition of its contribution to the German secret weapon counter-offensive (predominantly against the flying bomb). On 28 March 1945 Winston Churchill minuted the Secretary of State for Air, Sir Archibald Sinclair:

> You have no grounds to claim that the Royal Air Force frustrated the attacks by the V-weapons. The RAF took their part, but in my opinion their effort ranks definitely below that of the anti-aircraft artillery, and still further below the achievements of the Army in cleaning out all the establishments in the Pas de Calais, which so soon would have opened a new devastating attack upon us in spite of all the Air Force could do.
>
> As to V2, nothing has been done or can be done by the RAF. I thought it a pity to mar the glories of the Battle of Britain, by trying to claim overweening credit in this business of the V-weapons. It only leads to scoffing comments by very large bodies of people.[133]

However Lord Cherwell, Scientific Adviser to Winston Churchill, on 6 April 1945, saw the RAF's contribution to the flying bomb counter-offensive differently:

> The Germans had planned to fire from 88 ski sites beginning

about March 1. Over 80 of these were destroyed by air bombardment. The Germans thereupon planned to use 98 modified sites, which could be erected quickly and unostentatiously and which were much more difficult to pick up or injure, and the bombardment was opened up from these on June 16th – over three months late. By continuous air attack the number of sites in action was kept down to about 30, which allowed the discharge of about 100 a day during the 80 days from June 16 to September 4. Roughly one quarter of these failed for technical reasons. Averaged over the whole period the fighters claimed 24 per day, the balloons 4 per day and A.A 20 per day, though A.A claims rose to 30 per day in the later stages when proximity fuses were being used. Some of these claims, particularly in the early days, were no doubt exaggerated; but broadly 30 a day reached London.

If the German plans had not been interfered with, they would have been able to launch 300 a day – or more if they had drawn on stocks. 200 or more a day would have crossed the coast instead of 68. I do not know whether with this greater concentration we could have brought down such a large proportion; even if we had done, London would have received over three times what it actually did.

It seems fair, therefore, to say that the R.A.F cut down the scale of attack to at least one-quarter – one-third by bombing on the continent and the rest by shooting down bombs on the wing.[134]

Many of the airmen of Bomber Command had to make the ultimate sacrifice while their force countered the German secret weapon threat. Bomber Command had 137 aircraft fail to return from raids against Crossbow launch and supply targets in France during the period December 1943 to the end of August 1944. The majority of them were lost against flying bomb targets. In addition to these were a number of aircraft that either crashed in England or were written off owing to enemy damage. Just over 1,750 Bomber Command airmen were lost on Crossbow raids (which includes the attack on Peenemünde). Just short of 1,000 men were lost on the raids to the targets in France, three-quarters of these men killed. The Allies in total lost 443 aircraft and sacrificed 2,924 airmen on Crossbow operations.

Across all the Allied air forces employed in the Crossbow counter-offensive, approximately 118,000 tons had been dropped, (about 98,000 tons of bombs against targets associated with flying bombs), over half of which were dropped by Bomber Command aircraft. This was a massive use of force. The scale of attack by Bomber Command becomes clear when a few comparisons are made. The RAF's heavies dropped a greater tonnage of bombs on Crossbow targets than was dropped, throughout the whole war, on Berlin and more than was dropped on all targets in the whole of 1942.[135]

In terms of direct costs to the war effort, the loss of trained airmen and aircraft, bombs, anti-aircraft shells, balloons, the flying bomb offensive was a victory for the Germans. Also taking into account the cost of the damage resulting in England the cost of the flying bomb offensive was of the order of £70 million. The cost to Germany to conduct the offensive was approximately £14 million.[136] However these costs can not be viewed in isolation with respect to the overall outcome of the war. If the flying bomb offensive had been launched prior to the opening of the Allied invasion on the Normandy beaches, and on a much larger scale than actually happened, the strategic cost caused by the disruption, whilst materially unquantifiable, would have been substantial.

In conclusion Bomber Command had been called upon and made a major commitment to the flying bomb counter-offensive in the summer of 1944. Much of this in truth was misdirected; the raids on the small modified sites, the supply sites, and the ski sites after they became redundant – apart from the harassing nature of the attacks – had little impact on the Germans' ability to conduct their offensive. During the summer of 1944 Air Chief Marshal Sir Arthur Tedder had referred to the use of heavy bombers in the flying bomb counter-offensive as 'using a sledgehammer for a tintack'. With respect to the attacks on the launch sites his analogy is certainly appropriate. The attacks on the French and Belgian transportation system, German industry, the large site at Siracourt, which never fired a flying bomb, and the known flying bomb supply depots, did, however, make a significant impact on German supply lines and launch capabilities, and lead to a delay in the opening of the offensive and, once started, a diminishing in the scale of attack. The sledgehammers were the right tools for crushing both the machines that made the tintacks and the cans in which they were stored. It must be re-emphasised that it was Bomber Command who conducted the significant attacks on the flying bomb supply depots, reducing the number launched by at least 1,000. If these types of attacks, particularly those on the supply depots, had been prosecuted earlier and with greater force then their effect would have been greater.

APPENDIX 1

Bomber Command Losses on Crossbow Operations
17 August 1943 to 3 September 1944

Type of target	Aircraft lost	Type of target	Aircraft lost
Peenemünde	40	Supply dumps	65
Large sites	12	Forward rocket storage	5
Ski sites	4	Industrial	76
Supply sites	4	Airfields	3
Modified sites	44		
Total	**253**		

Bomber Command losses on Crossbow operations
(excluding Peenemünde) by aircraft type

Type of aircraft	Number of aircraft lost	Aircrew lost
Halifax	46	322
Lancaster	161	1127
Stirling	4	28
Mosquito	2	4
Total	**213**	**1,481**

In total, across all the Allied air forces, 443 aircraft were lost on raids to Crossbow targets and 2,924 airmen.

Source: Public Record Office AIR 14 3722.

APPENDIX 2

Summary of Bomb Tonnages Dropped by Allied Air Forces on
Crossbow Targets, before and after V1 attacks start on England.

Type of target	5 December 1943 to 11 June 1944	12 June 1944 to 3 September 1944
Ski sites	23,196	2,432
Large sites	8,130	7,399
Supply sites	293	11,951
Modified sites		25,001
Supply depots		21,901
Industrial targets		5,106
Headquarters		415
Electric Installations		588
Fuel		1,030
Forward rocket storage		2,922
Liquid oxygen		223
Airfields		6,628
Benito stations		41
Totals	**31,619**	**85,637**

Note: Bomber Command dropped 84% of the total tonnage of bombs on supply sites and 95% of the total tonnage on supply depots.

Source: Public Record Office AIR 14 3727.

APPENDIX 3

**Daily rate of flying bombs fired and weekly averages
Showing the impact of the July 1944 Bomber Command attacks on
St Leu d'Esserent and Nucourt (primary source; Diary of
Flakregiment 155(w) Imperial War Museum MI 14/1038 1-2)**

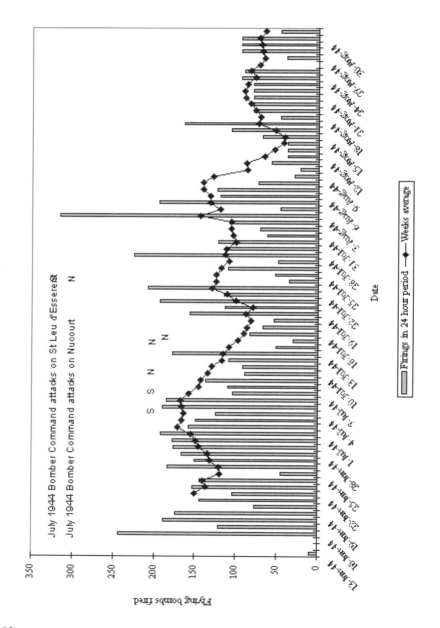

APPENDIX 4

**Ailly-le-Haut-Clocher flying bomb 'ski' site
Plot of markers and bombs dropped on Bomber Command attacks
of 16/17 and 22/23 December 1943**

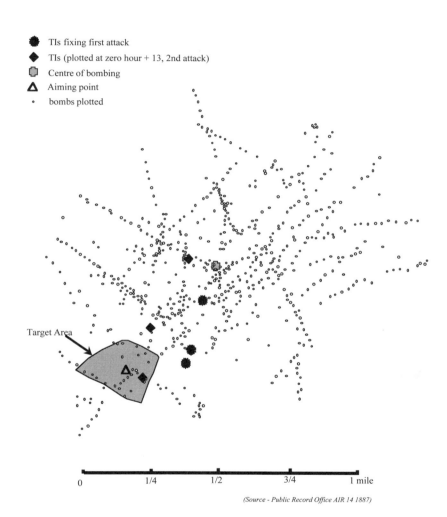

(Source - Public Record Office AIR 14 1887)

SOURCES

Primary Sources

Interviews and correspondence with Bomber Command and Photo Reconnaissance Unit veterans.

Interview with Madame Raymond Carbon, resident of St Leu d'Esserent and former mayor.

Information supplied by Monsieur Marionval, leader of a French Resistance group in the St Leu d'Esserent area (via Bob Farrell and Ron Biggs).

Correspondence with French civilians alive at the time of the Allied raids against the flying bomb targets.

Personal papers held at the Imperial War Museum.

The Medmenham Collection.

The war diary of Flakregiment 155(W), Imperial War Museum file MI 14/1038/1-2.

United States Strategic Bombing Survey, Report No. 60 V-Weapons (held at the Imperial War Museum).

Public Record Office files

AIR 8 – Air Ministry and Ministry of Defence: Department of the Chief of the Air Staff: Registered file

AIR 14 – Air Ministry: Bomber Command: Registered files

AIR 20 – Air Ministry and Ministry of Defence: Air Historical Branch: Unregistered Paper

AIR 24 – Air Ministry and Ministry of Defence: Operations Record Books, Commands

AIR 25 – Air Ministry and Ministry of Defence: Operations Record Books, Groups

AIR 27 – Air Ministry and successors: Operations Record Books, Squadrons

AIR 28 – Air Ministry and Ministry of Defence: Operations Record Books, Royal Air Force Stations

AIR 34 – Air Ministry: Central Interpretation Unit, predecessors and related bodies: Reports and Photographs

AIR 37 – Air Ministry: Allied Expeditionary Air Force, later Supreme Headquarters Allied Expeditionary Force (Air) and 2nd Tactical Air Force: Registered files and reports

AIR 40 – Air Ministry: Directorate of Intelligence and related bodies: Intelligence reports and papers

AIR 42 – Air Ministry: Combined Operational Planning Committee: Papers

CAB 121 – Cabinet Office: Special Secret Information Centre: Files

HW1 – Government Code and Cypher School: Signals Intelligence passed to the Prime Minister, Messages and Correspondence

DEFE 3 – Admiralty: Operation Intelligence Centre: Intelligence from Intercepted German, Italian and Japanese Radio Communications, WWII

BIBLIOGRAPHY AND SECONDARY SOURCES

Aders, G., *History of the German Nightfighter Force 1917–1945* (Jane's Publishing, 1979)

Babington Smith, C., *Evidence in Camera* (1957)

Bennett, Air Vice-Marshal D.C.T, CB, CBE, DSO, *Pathfinder* (Goodall Publications Limited, 1983)

Birrell, D., *Baz* (The Nanton Lancaster Society, 1996)

Boiten, T., Nachtjagd, *The Nightfighter versus Bomber War over the Third Reich 1939–45* (The Crowood Press Ltd, 1997)

Bowman, M., *RAF Bomber Stories* (Patrick Stephens Limited, 1998)

Bowyer C., Reed A. and Beamont R., *Mosquito, Typhoon, Tempest at War* (The Promotional Reprint Company Ltd 1994)

Chorley, W.R., *RAF Bomber Command Losses 1943* (Midland Publishing, 1996)

Chorley, W.R., *RAF Bomber Command Losses 1944* (Midland Publishing, 1997)

Chorley, W.R., *In Brave Company, 158 Squadron Operations* (P.A. Chorley 1990)

Collier, B., *The Defence of the United Kingdom* (London HMSO, 1957)

Collier, B., *The Battle of the V–weapons 1944–45* (The Elmfield Press, 1976)

Cooper, A., *Beyond the Dams to the Tirpitz* (Goodall Publications, 1991)

Cumming, M., *Beam Bombers. The Secret War of No. 109 Squadron* (Sutton Publishing, 1998)

Darlow, S., *Lancaster Down!* (Grub Street, 2000)

Dent, R., *Press on Regardless* (privately published)

Dufour, Norbert and Doré Christian, *L'Enfer des V1 en Seine-Maritime Durant la Seconde Guerre Mondiale* (La Memoire Normande Editions Bertout, 1993)

Farrell, Tony, *From Take-Off to Touchdown, My Fifty Years of Flying* (Cirrus Associates, 2000)

Freeman, R.A., *Mighty Eighth War Diary*, (Jane's Publishing Company Limited, 1981)

Harris, Marshal of the RAF Sir Arthur, *Bomber Offensive* (Greenhill Books, 1998)

Hastings, M., *Bomber Command* (Book Club Associates by arrangement with Michael Joseph Ltd, 1980)

Hastings, M., *Overlord: D-Day & The Battle for Normandy* (Simon & Schuster, 1985)

Henshall, P., *Hitler's Rocket Sites* (Robert Hale Ltd, 1985)

Hinchliffe, P., *The Other Battle* (Airlife Publishing Ltd, 1996)

Irving D., *The Mare's Nest* (Kimber, 1964)

Jones, R.V., *Most Secret War* (Wordsworth Editions Limited, 1998)

Lawrence, W.J., *No. 5 Bomber Group RAF* (Faber & Faber, 1951)

Marshall, K., *The Pendulum and the Scythe. A History of the Operations of No.4 Group Bomber Command between 1939 and 1945* (Air Research Publications, 1996)

Maynard, J., *Bennett and the Pathfinders* (Arms and Armour, 1996)

Middlebrook, M., and Everitt, C., *The Bomber Command War Diaries* (Midland Publishing, 1996)

Middlebrook, M., *The Peenemünde Raid*, (Bobbs–Merril Company, Inc. 1983)

Middlebrook, M., *The Berlin Raids*, (Penguin Group 1990)

Murray, W., *The Luftwaffe 1933–45 Strategy for Defeat* (Brasseys, 1996)

Musgrove, G., *Pathfinder Force. A History of 8 Group* (Crécy Books, 1992)

Overy, R., *Bomber Command 1939 – 45*, (Harper Collins Publishers 1997)

Price, Dr A., *The Luftwaffe Data Book* (Greenhill Books, 1997)

Scott, S.R,. *Mosquito Thunder, No.105 Squadron RAF at War 1942-5* (Sutton Publishing Ltd, 1999)

Tedder, Lord, *With Prejudice, The War Memoirs of Marshal of the Royal Air Force Lord Tedder G.C.B.* (Cassell and Company Ltd 1966)

Webster, Sir Charles and Frankland, Noble, *The Strategic Air Offensive against Germany 1939–1945* (London HMSO, 1961)

Whitfield, F. DFM, *We Sat Alone: Diary of a Rear Gunner*, (privately published)

NOTES

1   Public Record Office HO 192/492.

2   Translated from *L'Enfer des V1 en Seine-Maritime Durant la Seconde Guerre Mondiale*, Dufour, Norbert and Doré, Christian, La Memoire Normande Editions Bertout, 1993.

3   Initially called the Fieseler 103, the pilotless bomb was later called FZG 76, standing for *Flakzielgerät* (anti-aircraft artillery apparatus) 76; an attempt to confuse Allied intelligence efforts. Much later the bomb was to adopt the name *Vergeltungswaffe* 1 (reprisal weapon 1) leading to the familiar naming 'V1'. Within this book, and for the sake of simplicity the term flying bomb will be used for the weapon.

4   *Most Secret War*, R.V. Jones, Wordsworth Editions Limited, 1998, p351-352.

5   *Most Secret War* op. cit., p355-356.

6   Translation of the diary of Flakregiment 155(W), Imperial War Museum file MI 14/1038/1-2.

7   Translation of the diary of Flakregiment 155(W), Imperial War Museum file MI 14/1038/1-2.

8   Translation of the diary of Flakregiment 155(W), Imperial War Museum file MI 14/1038/1-2.

9   *The Strategic Air Offensive against Germany, Vol. II* Webster and Frankland, HMSO London 1961.

10   *The Strategic Air Offensive against Germany, Vol. II* op. cit.

11   *The Strategic Air Offensive against Germany, Vol. II* op cit, p 190.

12   *The Mare's Nest* by David Irving, Kimber, 1964.

13   *The Peenemünde Raid* by Martin Middlebrook, The Bobbs-Merrill Company, Inc, 1983.

14   *The Berlin Raids* by Martin Middlebrook, Penguin, 1990.

15   Arthur Darlow is the grandfather of Steve Darlow, the author. The complete story of Arthur Darlow and his crew's time in the war; operations, shooting down, evasion, capture and liberation is told in *Lancaster Down!* by Steve Darlow, Grub Street, 2000.

16   *The Bomber Command War Diaries* by Martin Middlebrook and Chris Everitt, Midland Publishing, 1996.

17   *The Mare's Nest* by David Irving, Kimber, 1964.

18   Public Record Office AIR 14 743.

19   Public Record Office AIR 14 743.

20   *The Bomber Command War Diaries* by Martin Middlebrook and Chris Everitt, op.cit. p446.

21   Public Record Office AIR 20 3424.

22   *From Take-Off to Touchdown, My Fifty Years of Flying* by Tony Farrell, DFC, AFC, Cirrus Associates 2000.

23   Cheshire had attained group captain status but when he took over at 617 Squadron he had to return to the rank of wing commander.

24   Public Record Office AIR 14 1887.

25   Public Record Office AIR 27 2128.

26   Public Record Office AIR 20 3427.

27   Translation of the diary of Flakregiment 155(W), Imperial War Museum file MI 14/1038/1-2.

28   Public Record Office AIR 14 743.

29   Public Record Office AIR 14 743.

30   Public Record Office AIR 20 3427.

31   *Author's note.* I visited the ski site at Ailly-le-Haut-Clocher in July 2001. The site is still well preserved, many of the buildings used by the farmer who owns the fields. The buildings, which still show the bomb damage, can be easily viewed from the road that goes around the field. One ski is badly damaged, half of it is rubble. One ski is broken up a third of the way down and at the entrance. The other ski is now used for storage in one of the local

gardens. All the other buildings are bomb damaged, some severely.

32   *The Strategic Air Offensive against Germany, Vol. IV* Webster and Frankland, HMSO London, 1961, Appendix 8 page 164.

33   *The Strategic Air Offensive against Germany, Vol. IV* Webster and Frankland, HMSO London 1961, Appendix 8 page 169, 17 April 1944. Directive by the Supreme Command to USSTAF. and Bomber Command for support of Overlord during the preparatory period.

34   Translation of the diary of Flakregiment 155(W), Imperial War Museum file MI 14/1038/1-2.

35   Public Record Office AIR 20 3427.

36   Public Record Office AIR 20 3427.

37   Public Record Office AIR 24 272.

38   Translation of the diary of Flakregiment 155(W), Imperial War Museum file MI 14/1038/1-2.

39   Public Record Office AIR 20 3427.

40   Public Record Office AIR 20 3427.

41   www.calvin.edu/academic/cas/gpa/goeb52.htm.

42   Translation of the diary of Flakregiment 155(W), Imperial War Museum file MI 14/1038/1-2.

43   Translation of the diary of Flakregiment 155(W), Imperial War Museum file MI 14/1038/1-2.

44   Source of statistics: *The Defence of the United Kingdom*, Basil Collier, HMSO London 1957.

45   Note: NJG 2 stands for *Nachtjagdgeschwader* 2, meaning nightfighter *Geschwader* 2. A *Geschwader* generally contained three *Gruppen*, a *Gruppe* contained three *Staffeln*. A *Staffel* was similar to a squadron but smaller, usually composed of about nine aircraft.

46   Provided by Mr J. Whiteley, 619 Squadron Association, from the Squadron Operational Record Book.

47   Reproduced by permission from *Barnet at War* by Percy Reboul and John Heathfield, Alan Sutton Publishing Limited, 1995.

48   Public Record Office AIR 20 6016.

49   Public Record Office AIR 14 2343 & 2348.

50   Source of statistics: *The Defence of the United Kingdom*, Basil Collier, HMSO London 1957.

51   Public Record Office AIR 37 784.

52   44 (Rhodesia) Squadron records supplied by Ron Biggs.

53   Investigation of the 'Heavy' Crossbow Installations in Northern France – Report by the Sanders Mission to the Chairman of the Crossbow Committee 21st February 1945, Imperial War Museum reference Misc 10 Box 2.

54   Private papers of Flight Sergeant G.H. Hobbs Imperial War Museum file 92/10/1.

55   André Rolin's account from research carried out by Jim Shortland.

56   Public Record Office AIR 20 3427.

57   Public Record Office AIR 20 3427.

58   The papers of Graham Inward held by the Department of Documents at the Imperial War Museum. Permission granted by the Trustees of the Imperial War Museum and Graham Inward.

59   Translation of the diary of Flakregiment 155(W), Imperial War Museum file MI 14/1038/1-2.

60   Author's note: These were 5 Group aircraft used for target location and marking and not to be confused with 8 Group Pathfinders.

61   Public Record Office AIR 50 200.

62   Marshall, K. T*he Pendulum and the Scythe. A History of the Operations of No.4 Group Bomber Command between 1939 and 1945*, Air Research Publications, 1996 pp 348-349.

63   From research carried out by, and reproduced with the kind permission of, Jim Sheffield.

64   From research carried out by, and reproduced with the kind permission of, Jim Sheffield.

65   Translation of the diary of Flakregiment 155(W), Imperial War Museum file MI 14/1038/1-2.
66   *Author's note:* When I visited the site in July 2001, the layout could still be clearly seen. One ski is completely demolished and one remains intact. The other is in some woods, with one large hole blown out of one side approximately half way down, and the front is demolished with two large bomb craters either side. The square building is roofless but otherwise intact. The walls to protect the launch ramp and the other buildings are all demolished.
67   Private papers of Flight Lieutenant T.W. Fox RAFVR Imperial Museum file 98/8/1.
68   Public Record Office AIR 28 531.
69   From correspondence between Leonard Cheshire and Jim Shortland.
70   Public Record Office CAB 121/213.
71   Public Record Office AIR 20 2633.
72   Translation of the diary of Flakregiment 155(W), Imperial War Museum file MI 14/1038/1-2.
73   A device called *Tinsell* was used to jam German nightfighter controller's running commentaries. *Airborne Cigar* was used to disrupt German radio telephone communication and *Corona* was used to broadcast false instructions to the German pilots.
74   Public Record Office AIR 27 1921.
75   Public Record Office AIR 28 532.
76   Public Record Office HW1 3037.
77   The term comes from *schräg* meaning slanting, a word which also could be used to describe jazz music, hence *Schräge Musik*.
78   Public Record Office AIR 8 1223.
79   *L'Enfer des V1 en Seine-Maritime Durant la Seconde Guerre Mondiale*, Norbert Dufour, and Christian Doré, La Memoire Normande Editions Bertout, 1993.
80   *Mighty Eighth War Diary*, Freeman, R.A., Jane's Publishing Company Limited, 1981.
81   *Press on Regardless*, Ron Dent, privately published, 1994.
82   Private papers of Sergeant Len Barham. Imperial War Museum file 97/23/1.
83   *The Mare's Nest*, David Irving, William Kimber 1964, p 245.
84   Pilot Officer Gradwell's evasion is detailed in Alan Cooper's *Free to Fight Again:RAF Escapes and Evasions 1940-45*, Kimber 1988.
85   Public Record Office AIR 24 291.
86   *The Other Battle*, Peter Hinchliffe, Airlife Publishing Ltd, 1996.
87   Reproduced by permission from *Barnet at War* by Percy Reboul and John Heathfield, Alan Sutton Publishing Limited, 1995.
88   Quoted in *RAF Bomber Stories*, Martin W. Bowman, Patrick Stephens Limited, 1998 pp 134-135.
89   Scott, S.R., *Mosquito Thunder No. 105 Squadron RAF at War 1942-5*, (Sutton Publishing Ltd, 1998, pp 155-156).
90   Public Record Office AIR 20 3427.
91   Public Record Office HW1 3037 .
92   Figures calculated from the translation of the diary of Flakregiment 155(W), Imperial War Museum file MI 14/1038/1-2.
93   Translation of the diary of Flakregiment 155(W), Imperial War Museum file MI 14/1038/1-2.
94   Public Record Office AIR 34 69.
95   Public Record Office AIR 34 69.
96   Private papers of Flight Lieutenant T W Fox RAFVR, Imperial War Museum file 98/8/1.
97   From eye witness information provided by the Stadsbestur Nieuwpoort, obtained by John Erricker.
98   Public Record Office AIR 42 12 and AIR 42 120.
99   Public Record Office AIR 20 3427.
100 Private papers of Group Captain C.B. Owen DSO and DFC, Imperial Museum file 85/16/1.

101 No. 44 (Rhodesia) Squadron records supplied by Ron Biggs.

102 Public Record Office AIR 27 1922.

103 Public Record Office AIR 27 1238.

104 Public Record Office AIR 20 3427.

105 First hand accounts are from *Baz* by Dave Birrell (The Nanton Lancaster Society, 1996) and are reproduced with the kind permission of Dave Birrell.

106 Public Record Office AIR 20 3427.

107 Chorley, W.R., *RAF Bomber Command Losses 1944* (Midland Publishing, 1997) p 370.

108 This is indeed the famous author H.E. Bates, who is probably best known for his novel *The Darling Buds of May*.

109 Public Record Office AIR 20 4140.

110 Translation of the diary of Flakregiment 155(W), Imperial War Museum file MI 14/1038/1-2.

111 Public Record Office AIR 34 70.

112 Public Record Office AIR 8 1222.

113 Public Record Office AIR 34 70.

114 Public Record Office AIR 27 1238.

115 Chorley, W.R., *RAF Bomber Command Losses 1944* (Midland Publishing, 1997) p 374.

116 Public Record Office AIR 24 290.

117 KTB Luftgaukommando VII, Bundesarchiv quoted in *The Bomber Command War Diaries* by Martin Middlebrook and Chris Everitt, Midland Publishing, 1996 p572.

118 Public Record Office AIR 50 221.

119 Public Record Office AIR 8 1223.

120 Public Record Office AIR 8 1223.

121 Public Record Office AIR 34 71.

122 Public Record Office AIR 24 288.

123 Public Record Office AIR 34 72.

124 Private papers of Flight Lieutenant T.W. Fox RAFVR, Imperial Museum file 98/8/1.

125 *The Other Battle*, Peter Hinchliffe, Airlife Publishing Ltd, 1996 p301.

126 Source of statistics: *The Defence of the United Kingdom*, Basil Collier, HMSO London 1957.

127 Source of statistics: *The Defence of the United Kingdom*, Basil Collier, HMSO London 1957.

128 Harris, Marshal of the RAF Sir Arthur, *Bomber Offensive* (Greenhill Books, 1998, first published 1947, Collins) p198.

129 Harris, Marshal of the RAF Sir Arthur, *Bomber Offensive* op.cit., p217-218.

130 Quote provided by Alan Webb, 627 Squadron Association.

131 United States Strategic Bombing Survey, Report No. 60, V-weapons, Imperial War Museum.

132 Source of statistics: *The Defence of the United Kingdom*, Basil Collier, HMSO London 1957, *The Strategic Air Offensive against Germany, Vol. IV* Webster and Frankland, HMSO London 1961 p384.

133 *The Mare's Nest*, David Irving, William Kimber 1964, p 330.

134 Public Record Office PREM 3/111A.

135 Source of statistics: *The Defence of the United Kingdom*, Basil Collier, HMSO London 1957, *The Strategic Air Offensive against Germany, Vol. IV* Webster and Frankland, HMSO London 1961 and Public Record Office AIR 14 3722.

136 *The Doodlebugs. The Story of the Flying-Bombs*, Norman Longmate, Hutchinson &Co. (Publishers) Ltd 1981 p474.

INDEX